Writing, Medium, Machine

Modern Technographies

Technographies

Series Editors: Steven Connor, David Trotter and James Purdon

How was it that technology and writing came to inform each other so extensively that today there is only information? Technographies seeks to answer that question by putting the emphasis on writing as an answer to the large question of 'through what?'. Writing about technographies in history, our contributors will themselves write technographically.

Writing, Medium, Machine

Modern Technographies

Sean Pryor and David Trotter

OPEN HUMANITIES PRESS

London 2016

First edition published by Open Humanities Press 2016

Copyright © 2016 Sean Pryor and David Trotter, chapters by respective authors

This is an open access book, licensed under Creative Commons By Attribution Share Alike license. Under this license, authors allow anyone to download, reuse, reprint, modify, distribute, and/or copy their work so long as the authors and source are cited and resulting derivative works are licensed under the same or similar license. No permission is required from the authors or the publisher. Statutory fair use and other rights are in no way affected by the above. Read more about the license at creativecommons.org/licenses/by-sa/4.0

Freely available onlne at: http://www.openhumanitiespress.org/books/titles/writing-medium-machine/

Cover Art, figures, and other media included with this book may be under different copyright restrictions.

Cover Illustration: Writin, Machin, Cod (2016) gouache on paper
Copyright © 2016 Navine G. Khan-Dossos, Creative Commons CC-BY-NC-ND

Print ISBN 978-1-78542-006-1
PDF ISBN 978-1-78542-018-4

OPEN HUMANITIES PRESS

Open Humanities Press is an international, scholar-led open access publishing collective whose mission is to make leading works of contemporary critical thought freely available worldwide. More at http://openhumanitiespress.org

Contents

Introduction
SEAN PRYOR AND DAVID TROTTER ... 7

1. How to Do Things with Writing Machines ... 18
   STEVEN CONNOR

2. Stereopticon ... 35
   KRISTEN TREEN

3. The Great American Novel and the Census ... 52
   KASIA BODDY

4. The *Milieu* Is the Message: Henry James and Mediation ... 67
   JOHN ATTRIDGE

5. D.W. Griffith, Victorian Poetry, and the Sound of Silent Film ... 84
   RUTH ABBOTT

6. Enigma Variations: Mallarmé, Joyce, and the Aesthetics of Encryption ... 106
   PAUL SHEEHAN

7. Teletype ... 120
   JAMES PURDON

8. Ticker Tape and the Superhuman Reader ... 137
   ROBBIE MOORE

9. Bibliographic Technography: Ezra Pound's *Cantos* as Philological Machine ... 153
   MARK BYRON

10. Modernist Measure: Poetry and Calculation ... 166
    SEAN PRYOR

11. Absolutist Slot Machines ... 178
    BECI CARVER

12. Touch Screen 191
    ESTHER LESLIE

13. Poetry in the Medium of Life: Text, Code, Organism 208
    JULIAN MURPHET

Introduction

Sean Pryor and David Trotter

'Is not the machine today', asked Enrico Prampolini in 1922, 'the new mythical deity which weaves the legends and histories of the contemporary human drama?' (Prampolini 1922: 236). Prampolini's enthusiastic futurism casts modern women and men as the playthings of mechanical gods that they themselves have made. But his proclamation of a machine age without precedent rather strikingly recalls the myth of origins recounted by the ancient god Prometheus, who, bound above a stage in Athens, announces that he has given to mortals the μηχανήματα or machines which shape their lives (Aeschylus 2009: 494). In classical Greek legend, after the gods had made human beings, animals, and other life-forms, they allocated to two brothers, Prometheus and Epimetheus, the task of distributing among these creatures the various gifts of nature (Plato 1924: 128-33). Stupid Epimetheus gave all the best ones to the animals, leaving human beings naked and defenceless. Clever Prometheus, understanding that human beings had somehow to clothe and protect themselves, stole fire from the workshop of Athena and Hephaestus, and donated it to them. Without fire, there would be no art, no craft, and no τέχνη (Aeschylus 2009: 444). To Prometheus we owe not just ships and chariots, but numbers and writing (γράμματα), that aid to the memory and mother of the muses (492). So the literary arts, from history to the theatre, have always been technological. Yet planes and tanks, Prampolini would have said, are machines of a different order from ships and chariots: machines which so massively supplement human agency as in effect to dwarf it. Literature had to get to grips with these new levels of mechanical supremacy, and it did so in part by reconceiving itself as a machine. Yet if technology is modernity's upstart god, it is also older even than the first incisions on a Bronze Age tablet. In *Technics and Time*, Bernard Stiegler draws extensively on the work of the palaeontologist André Leroi-Gourhan, Marshall McLuhan's eminent contemporary, to argue for the essential technicity of human evolution (Stiegler 1998). Stiegler's sub-title is *The Fault of Epimetheus*: by ancient and modern account alike, history is pretty much prosthesis all the way down.

This collection of essays began as a collaboration between the Literature-Technology-Media research group in the English Faculty at the University of Cambridge and the Centre for Modernism Studies in Australia at the

University of New South Wales. Its contents reflect, without being defined by, the original motive for that collaboration: a feeling that the 'question concerning technology' (Heidegger 1977) could and should be posed of modernist literature more variously and in greater detail than it has been hitherto, and in such a way as to enhance rather than to diminish the status and urgency of more familiar questions concerning 'literature' and 'modernism'. Criticism's attention to modernism's encounter with technology is by no means arbitrary. Prampolini, after all, was to hail his new mythical deity in the October 1922 issue of the little magazine *Broom*, which also featured art by Henri Matisse and writing by Blaise Cendrars, together with a drawing of Vladimir Tatlin's projected monument to the Third International.

It is not unusual for critics and theorists today to reach for a technological vocabulary when describing and analysing works of art. We happily speak of the mechanism of narrative, whether or not the novel in question attends in any depth or with any insight to particular machines. This can seem a relatively new state of affairs, the product of an interest spurred by the ubiquity of new technologies in contemporary social and economic life. There has certainly been a surge of interest in modern literature's interactions with the technologies of its historical moment, from Hugh Kenner's *The Mechanic Muse* (1987), through Tim Armstrong's *Modernism, Technology, and the Body* (1998), to a great many monographs and collections published in the last decade (Daly 2016). But though that surge shows no signs of abating, the discursive strategy – the freedom and the eagerness to speak of literature in technological terms – is not new.

As early as 1904, Charles Sears Baldwin praised Edgar Allan Poe for having simplified his 'narrative mechanism for directness of effect'. This represents 'the clue to Poe's advance in form, and his most instructive contribution to technic' (Baldwin 1904: 19). The language of machines allows Baldwin to measure Poe's aesthetic success, because a machine typically performs its work efficiently and repeatedly. The machine allows Baldwin to think of form as performing work upon content, and to relate the traditional forms which Poe inherited to the new forms which Poe bestowed on his successors. A similarly general notion of mechanism was useful to William Wordsworth, when in the 1802 version of the preface to *Lyrical Ballads* he explained why so few of his poems employ 'personifications of abstract ideas' (Wordsworth and Coleridge 2005: 295). 'I have endeavoured utterly to reject them as a mechanical device of style', he writes. Here, too, a technological discourse presents a form which can be put to work repeatedly, on a variety of materials. But for Wordsworth this automatic mechanism proves, very often, culpably indifferent to particulars: the machine means aesthetic failure. Instead, he concludes, 'I have wished to keep my Reader in the company of flesh and blood'. If Wordsworth thus invokes a common opposition between organism and mechanism, the human and the inhuman, this was and is only one of technology's possible connotations. 'The association of machines with ugliness or discomfort or pandemonium is very strong', Ezra Pound once remarked (Pound 1996: 59); and he recommended that, nevertheless, the aspirant artist 'might, in our time, more readily awaken his eye by looking at spare parts and at assembled machinery than by walking through galleries of painting or sculpture' (57). We 'find a thing beautiful in proportion to its aptitude to a function', he explained (69). And in the 1800 preface, offering an account of the development and psychology of the poet, Wordsworth writes: 'if we be originally possessed of much organic sensibility, such habits of mind will be produced that by obeying blindly and mechanically the impulses of those habits we shall describe objects and utter sentiments of such a nature [that the reader] must necessarily be in some degree enlightened, his taste exalted, and his affections ameliorated' (Wordsworth and Coleridge 2005: 292). Here the blind automatism of the machine enables flesh and blood, and this efficient mediation means aesthetic success.

Whatever their connotations, such abstractions stand at a considerable remove from the machines characteristic of the day, whether the steam engines of 1800 or the electric trams of 1904. This level of generality is common and powerful. To take a much more recent instance, consider the shrewd and historically informed reading of T.S. Eliot's quatrain poems in Vincent Sherry's *Modernism and the Reinvention of Decadence*. Sherry argues that Eliot's rhymed tetrameter quatrains present 'an extreme regularity of cadence, formalized by often strong rhymes', and that this generates 'an energy of palpably mechanical character' (Sherry 2015: 253). Sherry is careful to note that Eliot's contemporary critical writings demonstrate some interest in the mechanical aspects of literary technique, to acknowledge the influence on Eliot of Gautier's 'recognizably mechanical cadence' (253), and to link Eliot's mechanical prosody to the Great War, 'the negative apocalypse of modern technology' (254). The 'machine-made feeling of these tetrameter quatrains' thus reflects an age in which 'the machine has lost its discernibly human value or utility and stands as the sign of antihuman times' (253-4). Moreover, Sherry's readings distinguish the mechanical regularity of, say, the first stanza of 'Sweeney among the Nightingales' from the 'variable cadence' of the last stanzas of 'Burbank with a Baedeker: Bleistein with a Cigar' (259). The heavy caesuras and enjambments in the latter poem produce a much less mechanical effect: 'To climb the waterstair. Lights, lights, / She entertains Sir Ferdinand // Klein' (Eliot 1969: 41). For Sherry, writing thus confronts technology not through representation, but through the mediations of form.

There seems reasonable warrant for thinking that Eliot associated the modern machine with inhuman automatism, most famously in the 'automatic hand' of the typist in *The Waste Land*, who reaches to put a record on that symbol of mechanical reproduction, the gramophone (69). In a sense, the fact that Eliot's quatrain poems refer so rarely to new technologies necessitates Sherry's turn to prosody. Nevertheless, the 'hundred A.B.C.'s' in 'A Cooking Egg' – the tearooms of the Aerated Bread Company in which 'weeping multitudes' consume 'buttered scones and crumpets' (45) – do invoke the mechanical method of making bread invented by John Dauglish in 1862. Dauglish 'aerated' or leavened his bread, not by using yeast, but by dissolving carbon dioxide into the mix. There was thus no need for fermentation or for kneading by hand: the process could be automated, and the costs of labour were greatly reduced. But as an emblematic modern technology, aerated bread is very different from the Vickers machine gun. If both are consequences of industrial capitalism, the one suggests mass production, the other mass destruction. Other technologies appear in these poems, too, with their own histories and their own social meanings. When Sweeney 'Tests the razor on his leg' before shaving himself in 'Sweeney Erect' (43), Eliot deploys a tellingly anachronistic technology, for by 1919 the modern safety razor had displaced the traditional cut-throat razor. Much like an A.B.C. crumpet, the disposable safety razor represented mass production, and the Gillette safety razor had, in fact, become the market leader during the Great War, offering soldiers a convenient and effective means for staying clean-shaven on the front (Boddy 2015: 8). Sweeney's antiquated razor seems as good a figure for the sharp wit and repressed violence of Eliot's rhymed tetrameter quatrains as contemporary military apocalypse.

To think of a poem's prosody as reflecting the machine as such or the machine gun in particular, even before the poem is broadcast on the radio or coded as HTML, is to think of writing mediated by technology. But the converse, we want to argue, is equally important: writing mediates technology. It does so because writing is itself a τέχνη or art. Rhymed tetrameter quatrains are a form which can be put to work repeatedly, on a variety of materials. Eliot's form is what Baldwin calls a 'technic': the technology is in the technique. Though it seems reasonable to think Eliot associated the modern machine with inhuman automatism, it is not necessary to associate inhuman automatism with a poem's regular cadences. Rhymed tetrameter quatrains without heavy caesuras or enjambments could instead be considered sharp, witty, decisive, elegant, or sophisticated. Our sense of the form is formed, inevitably, by the content it in turn forms. Even quatrains whose lines divide into neat couplets with parallel syntax, and whose lines seem to establish 'an extreme regularity of cadence' –

> Apeneck Sweeney spreads his knees
> Letting his arms hang down to laugh,
> The zebra stripes along his jaw
> Swelling to maculate giraffe. (Eliot 1969: 56)

– make of those constraints the occasion for virtuosic variation: the parallel assonance in a single line of '-neck' and 'spreads', 'Sween-' and 'knees'; the twin stresses of the compound word 'Apeneck', echoed but transformed by the twin stresses of noun and verb in 'arms hang'; the unthinking passivity of

'Letting' matched and inverted by the brute activity of 'Swelling'; the relative lack of stress on the last syllable of 'maculate', giving the last syllable of 'giraffe' a weight quite unlike that of the first three lines' monosyllabic rhyme words; and so forth. Moreover, when Sherry registers the difference between one stanza's extremely regular cadence and another stanza's much more variable cadence, he recognises that the labour performed by the poem's mechanism is far from indifferent to particulars. The making of this verse is not like the production of bread or bullets; a general form and particular contents are instead brought into meaningful relation. Unwilling to reduce literature to the reflex of a particular technology or an abstract concept of technology, the essays collected here take the τέχνη of writing seriously.

Eliot is not the subject of any of those essays. However, we thought it right, given the origins of the collection, to invite contributions which examine the various technical-technological predispositions of other canonical modernist writers. Mark Byron considers the work of Eliot's friend and collaborator, Ezra Pound, exploring the ways in which *The Cantos* emulate the textual technologies of medieval manuscripts, early modern printing, and modern scholarship. In deluxe editions complete with illustrated capitals, in experiments with page space and typography, in the use of textual apparatus such as glossing and citation, and in its adventures in bibliographic history, Pound's poetry foregrounds the materiality of text as an information technology. Paul Sheehan turns in his essay to literature's encounters with another system for communicating and controlling information: encryption. Looking in particular at Stéphane Mallarmé and James Joyce, Sheehan rethinks the perennial problem of modernist difficulty by examining how these writers developed an aesthetic of the coded word. Unlike the famous Enigma machine used by the Germans in the Second World War, modernist encryption, Sheehan argues, is a machine not for securing but for multiplying meanings. The difference between literary and other modern technologies is also a theme in Sean Pryor's essay on the poetry of Pound, Wallace Stevens, W.B. Yeats, and others. Pryor's essay begins by linking the increasing prominence of measuring instruments in life and in language – from thermometers to 'business barometers' – to the efforts of late nineteenth- and early twentieth-century acoustic scientists to graph performances of poetry and so to develop a materialist metrics. Responding to the rise of empirical measurement, which seemed to many to reduce all things to mere quantity, the measures of modernist poetry asserted the necessary and mutual mediation of quantity and quality. Through analyses both of metrical verse and of free verse, Pryor shows how this poetry understands itself anew as its own form of measurement technology. In comparable fashion, Kasia Boddy's essay first details the history of electrical tabulating machines used, from the 1890s onwards, to gather census data in the United States. She then reflects upon how new technologies for measuring populations affected the aesthetic techniques and ambitions of the Great American Novel, most notably in the work of Sinclair Lewis and Gertrude Stein. Here, too, as Boddy argues, literature is put to work in mediating between quantity and quality, generating in the process new forms of aggregation and abstraction.

These essays treat a variety of devices: punch-card machines, kymographs for imaging speech, enciphering and deciphering machines used by the military, microfilms for preserving and reproducing medieval manuscripts. Many of the collection's other essays dig down into the rich array of machines, devices, tools, procedures, and other τέχναι shaping the world in which modern poems and novels went to work, which is also the world on which they worked. The English term 'device', in particular, is for our purposes a rich one: its senses range from mechanical invention through emblem, masque, or witty conceit to will, fancy, and desire. Our topic is not literature and technology, then, but writers left to their own devices. To that end, we have also encouraged contributors to focus on the sorts of technological device to which writers might have been left, from the middle of the nineteenth century onwards. Kristen Treen traces the history of the stereopticon from the 1850s and 1860s, when it was used both for entertainment and as therapy for the mentally ill. The stereopticon offered an ordering mechanism: its images brought audiences together, represented objects in spectacular detail, and gave those objects a remarkable new solidity. But as Treen shows, the fiction of the time expressed concerns that the stereopticon might show too much: that it might reveal the individual's innermost desires and thoughts. And for William James and Stephen Crane, the stereopticon's magnification, dissolves, and other effects offered metaphors for the experience of consciousness. James Purdon's essay turns from visual to textual technologies, beginning with the invention of mechanical printing telegraphs in the 1840s. These in turn led to the development of the teletype machine later in the century, a once ubiquitous technology now almost entirely forgotten. Examining advertising materials, technical descriptions, and appearances in literature and film, Purdon shows how the teletype established its own social rituals and rules. In the newsflash, moreover, the teletype helped to reconfigure twentieth-century media around the idea that an instantaneous transmission could at the same time be an historical record.

Robbie Moore approaches a similar phenomenon in his essay on the stock ticker, first introduced at the New York Stock Exchange in the 1870s. The stock ticker was both a machine and a network; it allowed instantaneous transmission, but the quick movement of its tape meant not a permanent record but a constant anticipation of the future. As Moore argues, the novels of Frank Norris, Will Payne, and others imagine the ticker-tape reader as a heroic figure who could grasp capital in its totality. And in the 1930s, Archibald MacLeish and Bob Brown look to the peculiar temporality of ticker-tape to reconfigure literary form itself. Finally, Beci Carver's essay explores the influence on twentieth-century literary form of a very different device, the slot machine. But like the stock-ticker, the slot machine represents capital: it dispenses commodities for coins, and its interior workings are inaccessible, unknowable. Canvassing works by Elizabeth Bishop, Louis MacNeice, John Rodker, John Steinbeck, H.G. Wells, and others, Carver traces the history of the slot machine as a site of mystery and arbitrariness, the object of fantasy and frustration.

It is this focus on the archaeology of specific devices which distinguishes the essays we have collected from research conducted under the rubric of 'literature and science'. Scholars have built informatively on the work of Gillian Beer (Beer 1996) to describe the circulation of concepts and models between or among scientists of one kind or another and writers of one kind or another, and to show how this circulation helped to bring about a 'vibratory modernism' (Enns and Trower 2013). Despite significant emphases to the contrary (Latour 1990), such studies have on the whole tended to subsume into the knowledge produced the instrument that led to its production. Our willingness to attribute agency to devices as well as to people squares with recent developments in the history and theory of a further cognate term: media. Over the last ten years or so, the conversation about the literature of Prampolini's modern machine age has broadened significantly to include various and inventive enquiries into the development of the major storage and transmission technologies which achieved institutional status as mass media during the first half of the twentieth century: cinema, radio, telephony, television (Trotter 2016). The main focus of research has been on media understood as inherently powerful systems for the distribution of messages and meanings. More recently, however, a different understanding of what constitutes τέχνη has begun to throw a critical light on the reification of modern technological mass media as that which literature is doomed either to resist or to embrace.

Recent media theory has undertaken a fundamental re-examination of the idea of a medium: that's to say, of what it means to be *in the middle*. It now speaks of a mediality which includes, but is not restricted to, systems for the distribution of messages and meanings. McLuhan's once-inflammatory insistence that all media are bodily 'extensions' has begun to look like confirmation of an enduring sense of the absolute centrality of the medial dimension of human life (McLuhan 2001). When John Durham Peters claims that for many philosophers there is no such thing as a 'media-free life', he has in mind Friedrich Kittler, the most influential media theorist since McLuhan, as well as Kittler's great precursor, Martin Heidegger, but also Emerson, Thoreau, and William James (Peters 2013: 45). John Guillory, by contrast, has traced the history of mediation as an intercession between alienated parties back to the mythology of the self-sacrifice of Christ the Redeemer and then forward again through Hegel and Marx. The economic, social, and political complexities consequent upon runaway industrialization gave rise to a theory of mediation in general as a way (the only way) to grasp both the scale and intensity of the relations thus newly established. It became the habit in modern

Western thought to present mediatory agencies as '*necessarily* characteristic of society' (Guillory 2010: 343). In the twentieth century, media assumed the shape of entertainment industries. Now they are once again what they always were: 'modes of being' (Peters 2015: 17), 'world-enabling infrastructures' (25). According to Peters, all complex societies have media 'inasmuch as they use materials to manage time, space, and power' (20). Media, in short, have been ontologized, pluralized, and back-dated to the dawn of civilization.

There are, of course, many different shapes and sizes to life's medial dimension, and media theorists have taken an interest in most of them. The times we live in seem nonetheless to demand increased attention to a mediality beyond the human scale. Peters's 'philosophy of elemental media' borders on anthropology, zoology, and theology. According to him, earth, water, fire, and air, while not 'media in themselves', become so 'for certain species in certain ways with certain techniques' (49). Some theorists prefer to speak of 'cultural techniques' rather than of media. A cultural technique creates the end to which it will come to be regarded as merely the means. Bernhard Siegert, the leading exponent of the theory of cultural techniques, describes these concatenations of mechanism and gesture as 'operative chains' that precede the media concepts they generate (Siegert 2015: 11). In them, as Cornelia Vismann has put it, resides the 'agency of media and things'. Their purpose is the 'execution of a particular act' in accordance with a built-in scheme or manner of proceeding. No wonder, then, that they should seem to possess an 'almost algorithmic dimension' (Vismann 2013: 83, 87). There is a connection, here, with the study of science and culture, or at least with Bruno Latour's actor-network theory. Siegert compares cultural techniques to Latour's 'immutable mobiles': sets of standardized data which can be transported intact from one site to another (Siegert 2015: 122-3, 148-9, 209).

Here is a little story culled from the theory of cultural techniques. Human beings decide to civilize themselves by building a city. They use a plough to draw a line in the ground which marks out the city limits. The line generates the distinctions between inside and outside, culture and nature, 'us' and 'them', necessary to the creation of a new order. Everyone forgets about the plough – until media theory, which is here to remind us that 'the agricultural tool determines the political act; and the operation itself produces the subject, who will then claim mastery over both the tool and the action associated with it' (Vismann 2013: 84). The theory of cultural techniques does not hesitate to put the cart before the horse. Indeed, it puts the cart before the animal that controls the animal that pulls the cart.

While none of our contributors has (yet) signed up as a theorist of cultural techniques, the tendency in media theory exemplified by the work of Siegert, Vismann, and others does find echoes here. John Attridge, for example, begins his analysis of the fiction of Henry James by drawing attention to the ways in which *What Maisie Knew* blurs the line between things we would not find it hard to describe as telecommunications media and things that at first seem to belong in a different category altogether: a wink, a roll of the eyes, a compression of the lips, a 'quick queer look', a small child. Attridge is able to demonstrate that telegraphy – the pre-eminent telecommunications medium of the time – functions in *The Ambassadors* and *The Golden Bowl* as a foil to a more expansive (more vibratory) understanding of medium as *milieu*, as life's general condition. James's thinking about technology is technical: it shapes the dialectic of plot and impression, incident and character, which in turn shapes the novel. Ruth Abbott starts, as it were, from the opposite end of the spectrum: from the emergence of cinema as a mass medium. The films D.W. Griffith made for the Biograph Company between 1908 and 1913 are usually taken to represent the subordination of devices hitherto displayed as attractions in their own right to the demands of narrative continuity. Abbott argues that the innovative patterns of their editing were in fact 'written into' them by the rhythms of the lines of poetry Griffith loved to read and recite, some of which he took the trouble to incorporate into decisive and resonant intertitles.

The need for theories of technology and media has of course been exacerbated by the establishment of the digital computer or network of computers as the ultimate universal machine. It seemed right, therefore, to include two essays which directly address the latest turns taken in the long story of prosthesis. Esther Leslie analyses the rise of the touch screen – in white goods, in the pocket, in the office – as an interface at once permeable and impermeable. The touch screen solicits our swipes, caresses, gestures, yet it remains a hard, glassy barrier. At once a history and a phenomenology, Leslie's account nonetheless returns again and again to the question of writing. The touch screen, she argues, has its own rhetoric. Julian Murphet addresses the ways in which we are all throughout our lifespan in the process of being written genetically. Beginning with the figural play of Shakespeare's *Sonnets*, Murphet goes on to explore two recent works which imagine what it would be like to write in DNA: Richard Powers's novel *Orpheo*, in which a retired composer attempts to use bacterial DNA as data storage; and Christian Bök's xenotext experiments, in which a one-line poem is subject to the processes of coding, recoding, transcoding, and decoding DNA in the living matter of a unicellular bacterium.

We are, in all of the essays collected here, in the domain of the device: the mechanism-conceit which articulates will, fancy, and desire. Each essay approaches that domain from an angle of its own. But one way to characterize the domain itself would be to adopt and develop the term which names the series of which this book is the first: technography. The domain of the device is that which consists of, and gives rise to, technography. The term attempts to recuperate some of the strangeness that has been lost in the course of the long naturalization of the idea of 'technology'. Originally a genre of writing – a treatise on a practical art or craft – 'technology' came to denote the material end product of such arts and crafts. Its eventual primary association was with industrial machinery or equipment. Today, we think that a 'technology' is a machine, a system, a piece of kit. What began as a term for a discourse or a way of thinking has ended up as a term for an object or a set of objects. By contrast, 'technography' came into use during – and possibly in reaction to – the late-nineteenth-century turn from words to things. A technography is a description of technologies and their application with primary regard to social and cultural context. Technography, itself technologically mediated, like all forms of writing, is a reflection upon the varying degrees to which all technologies have in some fashion been written into being. It examines the crucial role writing has played, not just in the description of technological objects and their functions, but in the inscription of technologies within social and cultural life. Technographies describe the history and theory of those transformative occasions on which writing confronts its own enabling opposite internally. Technographies attend equally to the rhetoric sedimented in machines, to machines behaving rhetorically, to rhetoric that behaves mechanically, and to rhetoric behaving in pointed opposition to mechanism. In the essay which opens this volume, Steven Connor takes on the role of technographer in order to argue that all literature is technographic in so far as it engineers in writing the particular kind of engine of writing it aims to be. He sets our scene, too, in proposing that modern literature is modern by virtue of its will, fancy, or desire to become ever more technographic.

Works Cited

Aeschylus. 2009. *Prometheus Bound*. In Aeschylus, *Persians. Seven Against Thebes. Suppliants. Prometheus Bound*, edited and translated by Alan H. Sommerstein, 442-563. Cambridge: Harvard University Press.

Baldwin, Charles Sears, editor. 1904. *American Short Stories*. New York: Longmans, Green, and Co.

Beer, Gillian. 1996. 'Translation or Transformation? The Relations of Literature and Science'. In *Open Fields: Science in Cultural Encounter*, 173-95. Oxford: Clarendon Press, 1996.

Boddy, Kasia. 2015. '"No Stropping, No Honing": Modernism's Safety Razors'. *Affirmations: of the modern* 2: 1-54.

Daly, Nicholas. 2016. 'The Aesthetics of Technology'. In *The Cambridge History of Modernism*, edited by Vincent Sherry, 531-549. Cambridge: Cambridge University Press.

Eliot, T.S. 1969. *The Complete Poems and Plays*. London: Faber and Faber.

Enns, Anthony, and Shelley Trower, editors. 2013. *Vibratory Modernism*. Houndmills: Palgrave Macmillan.

Guillory, John. 2010. 'Genesis of the Media Concept.' *Critical Inquiry* 36: 321-62.

Hayles, N. Katherine. 1999. *How We Became Posthuman: Virtual Bodies in Cybernetics, Literature, and Informatics*. Chicago: University of Chicago Press.

Heidegger, Martin. 1977. 'The Question concerning Technology'. In *The Question Concerning Technology and Other Essays*, edited and translated by William Lovitt, 3-35. New York: Garland.

Latour, Bruno. 1990. 'Drawing Things Together'. In *Representation in Scientific Practice*, edited by Michael Lynch and Steve Woolgar, 19-68. Cambridge: MIT Press.

McLuhan, Marshall. 2001. *Understanding Media: The Extensions of Man*. London: Routledge.

Peters, John Durham. 2015. *The Marvelous Clouds: Toward a Philosophy of Element Media*. Chicago: University of Chicago Press.

Plato. 1924. *Protagoras*. In Plato, *Laches. Protagoras. Meno. Euthydemus*, edited and translated by W.R.M. Lamb, 93-257. Cambridge: Harvard University Press.

Pound, Ezra. 1996. *Machine Art and Other Writings: The Lost Thought of the Italian Years*. Edited by Maria Luisa Ardizzone. Durham: Duke University Press.

Prampolini, Enrico. 1922. 'The Aesthetic of the Machine and Mechanical Introspection in Art.' Translated by E. S. *Broom* 3: 235-7.

Sherry, Vincent. 2015. *Modernism and the Reinvention of Decadence*. Cambridge: Cambridge University Press.

Siegert, Bernhard. 2015. *Cultural Techniques: Grids, Filters, Doors, and Other Articulations of the Real*. Translated by Geoffrey Winthrop-Young. New York: Fordham University Press.

Stiegler, Bernard. 1998. *Technics and Time, 1: The Fault of Epimetheus*. Translated by Richard Beardsworth and George Collins. Stanford: Stanford University Press.

Trotter, David. 2016. 'Literature between Media'. In *The Cambridge History of Modernism*, edited by Vincent Sherry, 509-530. Cambridge: Cambridge University Press.

Vismann, Cornelia. 2013. 'Cultural Techniques and Sovereignty'. Translated by Ilinca Iurascu. *Theory, Culture, & Society* 30: 83-93.

Wordsworth, William, and Samuel Taylor Coleridge. 2005. *Lyrical Ballads*. Edited by R.L. Brett and A.R. Jones. London: Routledge.

I

How to Do Things with Writing Machines

Steven Connor

I want here to argue that literary techniques, far from being the opposites or adversaries of calculation or mathematical procedures, are in fact typically much closer to this kind of procedure than other kinds of communication. Modern literary writing is moving ever closer to this kind of procedural operation. A technography may be defined as any writing about any technology that implicates or is attuned to the technological condition of its own writing. I will try to push through the claim that technography is not just one mode among others of literary writing; that all literary writing is in fact technographic, in the sense that it constitutes what, following George Spencer Brown, I will call an injunctive operation, the engineering in writing of the particular kind of engine of writing it aims at being. So modern literary writing is ever more technographic, not in the simple sense that it is concerned with other kinds of machinery, but in the sense that it is ever more taken up with the kind of machinery that it itself is. Oddly, this may mean that technography comes into its own against technology, that is the notion of a technology-in-general or technology-as-such. Technography is particular where technology is general; technography is immanent, exploratory, and procedural rather than declarative. Technography is not up to phrases like 'The question concerning technology'. This allows technography to operate both beneath and beyond the threshold of technology. Technography does not know yet for sure what a machine is or could be. I want to say that there is a particular kind of machine that literature has always aspired to be, which is a calculating machine (though all machines are in fact kinds of calculating machine).

The reciprocal of this claim about the technicity of text would be that there is something textual about all technology. If all writing is a kind of machinery, why might it be plausible to see every machine as a kind of writing? Because every mechanical or technical action can be seen as a procedure as well as a mere proceeding, where a procedure means a replicable operation. So a technical procedure is the styling of a process and, as such, the declarative performance of that process as iterable procedure. Every machine declares of what it does: 'this is the way this action may be performed'. A technic, or technical procedure, is a writing in that it tracks its own technique, following in its own tracks.

There is a fundamental distinction within philosophy of mathematics, between mathematics as discovery and mathematics as invention. Philosophers of the first persuasion believe that all mathematical relations exist already and that mathematics consists in their uncovering. Philosophers of the second persuasion believe that human beings engineer the mathematical relations they appear to unearth. Plato is the patron saint of the first kind of mathematician, Wittgenstein a principal exponent of the second.

If most people are inclined to credit the idea of mathematical discovery, there is one respect in which the mathematical experience of most people may actually incline them towards the idea that mathematics is a making, not a making manifest. For most people, mathematics is something that has to be done, rather than displayed. Sums are procedures, to be performed, often with difficulty. Mathematics is worked out, as exertion, often as *ordeal*, the etymology of which, from Old English *adaelan*, to divide or separate, implies the allocation or dealing out of a penalty.

As such mathematics requires mediating objects. Even Plato, demonstrating to the slave at the beginning of *Meno* that he already in some sense knew how to construct a square *b* of exactly twice the area of a given square *a*, required a stick and a patch of sand for the demonstration. The demonstration is a procedure that is articulated in stages, and cannot be shown all in one go. And this procedure requires – indeed, in some important sense, actually *is* – an apparatus. It is a technography: a writing out of an operation that consists in the work of that writing.

What is a calculation? It is an operation performed by some means, through some intermediary machinery – fingers, or toes, or the calculi of the abacus from which calculation derives its name. ('Abacus' sounds as though it might be abecedarial, but in fact may derive from Hebrew *abaq*, sand or dust, referring to the surface in which figures would be inscribed.) Calculation machines are a kind of writing, because they have, because they largely are, memory. They allow quantities to be stored, processed, and moved around – as we say, 'carried across'. One might note that there is a secondary calculation module in the mnemonic chant that may accompany these operations, subvocally or out loud.

Calculations perform work, the work of sorting. One does not need stones (*calculi*) in particular, but one does need some apparatus, something prepared or made ready, something that is hard and external, precisely in order that it can allow for manipulation. No play without a plaything: no work without workings. The soft requires the hard, variation requires the invariant.

Calculation is performed with what are called figures, arranged spatially in diagrams. These diagrams make a machinery of the page-space, or exploit its machinery for what is called 'working out'. Calculations are a sort of primary technography – the writing out of a mechanism, the mechanism that functions through a particular machinery. The earliest mathematical notations – lists of quantities and equivalences, records of amounts – all seem to have in common the manipulation of visible space. Almost all numbering systems, for example, render the first two or three digits as simple tallies of straight lines, like the I-III of Roman numerals.

The passage of mathematical notation from words across to numbers is not accomplished easily or straightforwardly, and calculations were much impeded in the Greek and Roman worlds by the lingering attraction and interference between words and numbers. But, as numbers and number functions become more autonomous, so it becomes easier to perform calculative operations upon them directly, as though they were the actual objects of the calculation, which could be moved about on the space of the slate or page.

Wittgenstein's mathematical constructivism involves the view that mathematical operations do not refer to anything in the world in such a way that they may be said to be true or false. Mathematical operations are wholly syntactic, having reference only to the procedure they apply or the game they may be said to be playing. The fact that numbers do not refer to the world means that they are wholly present in a way that signs are not: '[n]umbers are not represented by proxies; numbers *are there*' (Waismann 1979: 34n.1). Because the signs of numbers are also the numbers themselves, mathematical operations are not signified by arithmetical notations: '[a]rithmetic doesn't talk about numbers, it works with numbers' (Wittgenstein 1975: §109). This means that 'mathematics is always a machine, a calculus' and a 'calculus is an abacus, a calculator, a calculating machine; it works by means of strokes, numerals, etc.' (Waismann 1979: 106). 'In mathematics, *everything* is algorithm and *nothing* is meaning: even when it doesn't look like that because we seem to be using words to talk about mathematical things' (Wittgenstein 1974: 468). 'Let's remember that in mathematics, the signs themselves *do* mathematics, they don't describe it. The mathematical signs *are* like the beads of an abacus. And the beads are in space, and an investigation of the abacus is an investigation of space' (Wittgenstein 1975: §157). Again: 'What we find in books of mathematics is not a description of something but the thing itself. We *make* mathematics. Just as one speaks of "writing history" and "making history", mathematics can in a certain sense only be made' (Waissman 1979: 34). Wittgenstein will also declare that 'Language is a calculus. Thinking is playing the game, using the calculus. [...] Thought is the actual use of the linguistic calculus' (Wittgenstein 1980: 117). The meaning of such a statement changes over the course of Wittgenstein's writing. Having begun by believing that language could be reduced to the kind of logical calculus provided by Russell, Wittgenstein came to believe that there were many games or calculative operations at work in language.

Calculations become possible in the graphematic space of mathematics – and only there, for they do not take place so much in a space, as with space, because of the self-referentiality of the symbolic machine of mathematics. Calculating procedures are themselves kinds of spatial machinery. Sums and accounts have in common with abacuses the manipulation of space. Since space and place have numerical significance, the movement of numerals across and between spaces performs operations. The simple arrangement of numbers in particular configurations is enough to effect mathematical operations, not just to display relations. The zero is the most important mediator between sign and function. The zero signifies not just a void or gap, but an active holding open of a space, the effect of which is to change the values of the numbers adjacent to it. In effect, inserting a zero has the effect of multiplying the number to its left by ten and dividing the number to its right by ten (or whatever numerical base is being employed). The zero is both the indication of this relation and the injunction to make this shift to left or right, just as one would in an abacus. The zero materialises the space that previously would have been just that, a space left between two numbers. This spatiality is one of the most important latent affinities between sums and poems.

I want to claim that the writing we progressively come to think of as literary mimics and in recent times increasingly approaches this condition. I propose to call mathematical expressions which perform the functions they actively figure *operatives*. This is in the model of John Austin's performatives – utterances that do not represent a state of affairs but carry out a function or procedure. You read a book, but do a sum; but perhaps literature is the name for that kind of text that wants to be done as much as read.

A good example of the operative function of mathematical figuring is the Sieve of Eratosthenes, a procedure designed to find prime numbers. The numbers are arranged in rows from 1-10, 11-20, 21-30, and so on. First of all multiples of 2, which are in alternate columns from 4 onwards, are struck out. Then the same is done for multiples of the next three numbers, 3, 5, and 7 (4 and 6 having already been struck out). Once all the multiples of these numbers have been removed, the remaining numbers will be all the primes below 121. The sieve is one of the earliest forms of the number square, which has been used for many purposes.

One is able to 'run' as well as to show the sieve in an animation, because its operations have been coded. We can say that code is the mediator between sign and function, *dynamos* and *energeia*, in that a code is a set of instructions for performing an action. A sieve is, of course, literally a kind of riddle, something used to sift and sort, a suggestive coincidence given that riddles of speech can also be seen as mechanisms for sorting the right answer from mistaken ones. Sadly, the two kinds of riddle have different roots, the one deriving from *reden*, to give counsel, yielding the word *read*, the other from a root cognate with Greek *krinein*, to separate; but the latter affiliation does allow us to see *riddle* as first-cousin to *crisis* and *criticism*.

Riddles, puzzles, and poems are closely cognate; sometimes, as in *Oedipus Rex*, a riddle is seen as central to the operations of a literary text. One of the earliest and most influential collections of Greek poems, the *Greek Anthology*, mixes poems (some of them early examples of 'pattern-poetry' or poetry set out in shapes that correspond to their subjects, like eggs, swords, and wings) with epigrams, enigmas, and mathematical puzzles. Whatever poems were thought to be at this date, it seems clear that they were regarded as things to do things with, to be worked with or operated upon, more hopscotch than well-wrought urn. Fibonacci's *Liber Abaci*, or *Book of Calculation* (1202), mixes description of the Hindu-Arabic numerals and the methods of calculation (without the use of an abacus) that they allowed with practical puzzles and conundrums. Many calculative or diagrammatic procedures pass across to literary writing from magical or religious usages, such as Psalm 19, the so-called Abecedarian Psalm, in which each verse begins with a successive letter of the Hebrew alphabet.

The most literary form of calculative puzzle is the crossword, which came into being remarkably late, but is perhaps the modernist technographic form par excellence. The first crossword (or 'Word Cross' as it was intended to be called) was by Arthur Wynne and appeared in the 'Fun' section of the *New York World* on 21 December 1913 (Danesi 2002: 62-3). The techniques of the 'cryptic' crossword clue were developed during the 1920s, again in the US, though it has become a speciality of British crossword puzzles. The classic cryptic clue couples a definition with a set of instructions for constructing the solution word. It therefore requires a kind of double vision; the apparent reference suggested by reading the whole clue must be ignored in favour of what might be called the principle of modular construction, in which the elements of the required word are decomposed and then recomposed in turn, following a series of coded functions. Among the most common of these codes is that any word suggesting revision, disordering, or scrambling is likely to be an injunction to reorder the letters of one or more words, that is, to construct an anagram to reveal the solution. There is always a kind of magic implied in the anagram. Perhaps the most amazing of all crossword anagrams was that effected by the *Guardian*'s Araucaria, the pseudonym of the Rev. John Graham: 'O hark the herald angels sing the boy's descent which lifted up the world (5, 9, 7, 5, 6, 2, 5, 3, 6, 2 3, 6)' has as its solution 'While shepherds watched their flocks by night, all seated on the ground'. Literary writing has rejoined these kinds of game-like procedure in the work of Queneau, Perec, and the Oulipo group, which in its turn anticipates the developments in electronic text of recent years.

Sorting

Reading and reasoning are both conceived as a kind of sorting, which has always had an unusual status. Sorting has links with divination, through the practice of the *sors*, in which a text, usually a sacred or prestigious text such as the Bible or Virgil, would be used as the source for divinatory wisdom. This gave the action of sorting considerable prestige – sorting was not only divinatory, it was also literally regarded as the action of a divinity, as in the seventeenth-century expression, evidenced in *The Merchant of Venice* 5.1, 'God sort all' (Shakespeare 2010: 379). J.C. Maxwell puzzled mightily over the apparent paradox that a hypothetical demon guarding a trapdoor between two chambers containing a gas of a given temperature might be able to open the trapdoor selectively to let through more energetic molecules, and thereby create a thermal differential between the two chambers, which would then be capable of performing work. The apparent puzzle lay in the fact that this would have created the possibility of work (that is, reduced the entropy of the system), from nothing, or from the simple action of sorting, which would contradict the second law of thermodynamics, and indeed make it possible for there to be perpetual motion. The pseudo-problem (as it has always seemed to me) is generated by the assumption that the act of sorting does not itself do any work, or thereby introduce any energy into the system. But of course the demon has to do some kind of work in opening the valve, unless we are to assume that the mental act of distinguishing the molecules is enough to cause their physical separation. There will have to be some kind of work because there is some kind of sorting. Maxwell introduced this molecular bureaucrat in a letter to P.G. Tait of 1867, as 'a very observant and neat-fingered being' (Knott 1911: 214), and the fingers, or their equivalent, seem as important as the observant eyes. But we seem to have a strong prejudice against seeing the simple act of arranging as any kind of work, or operation in itself. Of course, I may have to perform some physical work in going through my filing cabinet and deciding which files to shred, walking over to the shredder and feeding them in, and so forth. But our tendency is to feel that the sorting is here being put to work, rather than constituting work in itself. Against this, we should probably set Michel Serres's principle that, not only is all sorting a kind of work, but in fact all work amounts to a kind of sorting (Serres 2007: 86).

Indeed, the history of one of the key terms in thermodynamics, energy, seems to enact this interchange between the informational and the physical. The word *energy* enters English through Philip Sidney's usage in his *Apology for Poetry*, as a term signifying force or vigour in language, so is rhetorical rather than mechanical. Sidney is comparing the mere assertion of love with the kind of writing which is likely actually to have some desired effect:

> But truly, many of such writings as come under the banner of unresistible love; if I were a mistress, would never persuade me they were in love; so coldly they apply fiery speeches, as men that had rather read lovers' writings (and so caught up certain swelling phrases which hang together like a man which once told me the wind was at north-west and by south, because he

would be sure to name winds enough) than that in truth they feel those passions, which easily (as I think) may be betrayed by that same forcibleness, or *energia* (as the Greeks call it) of the writer. (Sidney 2002: 113)

Sidney is here referring to the discussion in Aristotle's *Rhetoric* III.xi of the means whereby metaphors make us see things, which, for Aristotle, depends on using expressions that represent things in a state of activity. The word *energeia* that Aristotle coins for this, and which he tends to use interchangeably with his other coinage, *entelechy*, has been translated by Joe Sachs in Heideggerian fashion as 'being at work': 'the thinghood (*ousia*) of a thing is what it keeps on being in order to be at all (*to ti ēn einai*) and must be a being-at-work (*energeia*) so that it may achieve and sustain its being-at-work-staying-itself (*entelecheia*)' (Sachs 2005: 14-15).

The dynamism of such verbal operations often depends upon the conjunction of words, letters, and numerals. Ciphering (derived from the Arabic word for 'zero') often involves the numerisation of the alphabet, such that one series of letters is translated into another by some regularly-applied principle – at its simplest, something like transposing each letter into another letter a given number of letters along in the alphabet. More complex forms of transposition may involve the use of a key, to move each letter according to a different number, corresponding to the letters in the keyword. This was elaborated in the German Second World War Enigma machine by a series of gearings, which shifted letters along. The Enigma machine was indeed an actual physical device, and work on breaking its code was materially advanced by the capture of particular examples. But breaking the code depended on the puzzling through of the interaction between different kinds of components or machinic processes, some of them having to do with the structure of language. The weakest part of any code lies in the fact that it must produce an output that can be translated back reliably into language – and language is full of redundancies or machinic elements, iterable modules about which it is not necessary to think, which may then provide ways in to understanding the code. The codebreakers at Bletchley Park were able to make considerable headway with the recognition that there must be something like a zero-degree formula that was frequently exchanged, since in any human communication there is a great deal of this kind of thing: the formula 'Keine besondere Ereignisse', or 'nothing special to report', proved to be an important point of entry into the code (Smith 2007: 38-9).

The essential principle here is *alphametical*, to adopt the usual name of a kind of puzzle invented by Henry Dudeney in 1924, in which the idea is that the reader has to reverse engineer the code that allows for an operation such as the following:

SEND
+MORE=
MONEY

The operativity of this puzzle depends upon the fact that the alphabet is in fact a numerical series – an ordered sequence of reorderable because equivalent elements. Claude Shannon demonstrated the stochastic nature of word formation by applying a series of sieving operations to a randomly generated series of letters, first of all applying the probability of letters like T and H clustering together, then the probability of three letter combinations, then the probability of these letters clustering in words of typical letter-length. After only 6 such filters an output such as

XFOML RXKHRJFFJUJ ZLPWCFWKCYJ FFJEYVKCQSGHYD QPAAMKBZAACIBZLHJQD

turns into an output like

THE HEAD AND IN FRONTAL ATTACK ON AN ENGLISH WRITER THAT THE CHARACTER OF THIS POINT IS THEREFORE ANOTHER METHOD FOR THE LETTERS THAT THE TIME OF WHO EVER TOLD THE PROBLEM FOR AN UNEXPECTED. (Shannon 1948: 7)

Literary writing is commonly thought of as being at the other extreme from how-to books, instruction manuals, and other uses of writing to assist mechanical or other procedures, whether recipe books, almanacs, change-ringing manuals, musical scores, prayer-books and liturgies, horticultural guides, almanacs, or all-purpose guides such as Joseph Moxon's *Mechanick Exercises*, the second volume of which is devoted to the arts of printing, that is to say, is an operation upon itself. As Moxon remarked: '*by a* Typographer [...] *I mean such a one who, by his own Judgement, from solid reasoning with himself, can either perform, or direct others to perform from the beginning to the end, all the Handy-works and Physical Operations relating to* Typographie. *Such a Scientifick man was doubtless he who was the first Inventor of* Typographie' (Moxon 1683: 36). As the name suggests, manuals are intended to be held in the hand while other kinds of procedure (other kinds of procedure than reading, that is) are conducted. But this physical involvement in the designated action, along with the implied breaking-up of the reading process required by the action of putting the recommended actions into practice in the way recommended, blends or interleaves text and action. As with the working out of a calculation, or the keeping of a ledger of transactions, the book does not merely describe or record some state of affairs: it enters into its operation. It is not an operation described or implied by the book: it is something that one does, as we say, *by the book*. Nothing could seem further away from a literary text than a recipe-book; and yet there are respects in which literary texts can be regarded as programming the action of their reading, in something of the same way that a recipe book programmes the making of a pie. A recipe says 'make a pie like this'; the kind of text that we think of as literary seems to say 'try reading me like this'.

There is a long history of overlap between number and the kinds of performative we call 'spells'. These 'mathemagical' procedures are strong indications of the ways in which treating words as numbers makes them operatives, or treating words as operatives helps to make them seem number-like. One of the most obvious examples of the magical confluence of number and word is the counting-out rhyme, used for centuries worldwide as a way of drawing lots or casting fortunes. The counting rhyme exploits the fact that most human beings lose count very easily. In this respect counting rhymes are really a form of divination procedure. They have in common the fact that they are determinate operations designed to produce indeterminate outputs. They are literally the machinery of the divine, the *machina dei*. But divination is also akin to a kind of calculation, a procedure for revealing a solution or set of relations that is latent in a set of numbers or a statement of relations but not apparent in it. The sifting of a quadratic equation is an operation that is cognitively equivalent to the riddling of grain.

Divination procedures are designed to be magical. Perhaps all machines tend towards the magical, in that they are designed to work by themselves, that is, they work without needing to be worked. This means that we can know that they work without knowing or needing to know precisely how. This makes mechanisms useful in the devising of magical procedures. We may characterise the magical through Freud's formula of 'omnipotence of thoughts' (Freud 1955: 75-99), where the act of thought is supposed to be all-powerful but occult in its workings. Indeed, thinking may perhaps be regarded as the ultimate magical machinery, since all thinking is unconscious thinking, given that I do not know how I do it. I don't mean that nobody has any idea what is going on, for example neurologically, when I perform the action I call thinking, for we are surely much more aware than we used to be of the complex physiological correlates of thinking and are likely to become ever more so. What is magical in thinking is its particular ratio of knowledge to ignorance. I know how to think; I know just how to set myself to the work of reflecting, reverie, calculation of consequences, and so on. What I don't know is how I know how to do this. I do it by just willing it, but I do not know how that act of willing makes it happen. I have to will harder to overcome distraction, but I don't know exactly what I do when I will harder. And willing does not in fact always do the trick – sometimes I have to will myself not to concentrate so hard in order to remember an errant fact or name, and it seems even harder to know how I do that. Magical thinking is thinking that ascribes powers to mental operations – powers for example to make things happen in the world – while keeping hidden the actual operation of those powers. Magical machines often provide the mediation between the known and the known-unknown. There always seems to be some kind of black box by means of which thought makes thinking thinkable.

This is apparent in the huge and systematic confluence between technology and magical thinking. Dirk Bruere's self-published book *Technomage*, to take only one contemporary example, has a chapter entitled 'Machines'. Bruere explains that, despite drawing on quantum mechanics for his theories of magical influence, 'we do not need radio telescopes or the paraphernalia of real science, because we are essentially performing a series of symbolic actions' (Bruere 2009: 92). This unwittingly goes to the heart of the question of what a writing machine is. Is a symbolic machine really a machine, or just the symbol of one? What if the machine in question is designed to process symbols? Can we securely distinguish between a real symbol-processing machine and a symbolic one? (Is the mechanical processing of symbols itself symbolic?)

Sit

What is a machine? A machine is a material device that allows the iterable and automatic performance of a specific task in the stead of some performer, usually with some gain in efficiency. A machine performs operations without needing or being able to know how or perhaps even that it performs them. The four defining elements of a machine are iterability, automaticity, specificity, and surrogacy. Machines do specific jobs for us repeatedly. That they have a material form is usual, but not necessary for them. Most especially, machines usually involve what Ian Bogost, extrapolating from the design of video-games to game-like structures in general, calls 'unit operations' (Bogost 2008). That is, machines are assemblages of autonomous components that can be linked together in variable ways. Machines, we may say, are defined by the fact that they do not know everything about themselves – that they contain encapsulated sub-routines or black boxes. A.N. Whitehead points to the importance of what a later generation would begin to call 'object-orientation' in his 1911 introduction to mathematical thinking:

> It is a profoundly erroneous truism, repeated by all copy-books and by eminent people when they are making speeches, that we should cultivate the habit of thinking of what we are doing. The precise opposite is the case. Civilization advances by extending the number of important operations which we can perform without thinking about them. Operations of thought are like cavalry charges in a battle – they are strictly limited in number, they require fresh horses, and must only be made at decisive moments. (Whitehead 1911: 61)

If there is something machinic about codes and ciphers it is not just because they are constructed mechanically, but because they are also, as we say, 'machine-readable'. HTML code is probably the most familiar of the forms of machine-readable code. Like most codes, it involves a combination of natural language and machine-language, as signified by the pointed brackets which must enclose all the tags. The human reader who is able to distinguish and discount the HTML tags will have the whole of the text available for them, albeit unadorned by any format. The browsers for which HTML is written 'understand' only the tags which tell them how to format the otherwise unreadable text. So, like the crossword clue, the code embodies a difference between reading and processing. Literature is perhaps like HTML in that it is full of visible and invisible marks of formatting. These moments when the text becomes operative are the moments where the text is, or aspires to become, most machine-readable. Puns, for example – 'to catch with his surcease success' – are such stochastic hotspots.

When the term 'word-processing' appeared in around 1967, it was in fact applied to the IBM's 'Selectric' typewriter, which had been launched in 1961. The innovation was mechanical, in the replacement of the cradle of type bars with a golf ball, which in itself increased the speed and accuracy of typing immeasurably, by avoiding the clashing of type bars which inevitably occurred at high typing speeds. The electric typewriter made the transition to word-processing in 1964, when a magnetic tape system was added, to enable the storing of characters. A word-processor was blind to the meanings of words, which it was able to treat as mere blocks of matter, but it could only do this effectively once the words were no longer in fact hard, but soft, that is, once they were encoded, as instructions to display a particular shape in a matrix of dots. This movement from the electric to the electronic (from a machine mechanically powered by electricity to a machine using electricity to encode and decode) meant that the Selectric typewriter became the favoured interface for engineers and computer scientists to input data to computers.

If machine-readable code is to be regarded as a kind of language, in what mood or mode does that language operate? We may say that the language of operation is subjunctive, as in the Latin third-person present subjunctive of *fiat*, let it be made, or *sit*, let it be, in expressions such as 'sit Deus in nobis et nos maneamus in ipso' – may God be in us and may we remain in him. The process of running computer code or putting it into operation moves it from the optative (God rest ye merry gentlemen) to the cohortative (let us pray, or let x be y, or simply, Leibniz's hearty 'calculemus' [Leibniz 1951: 51]). This is the mode in which most mathematical reasoning occurs: that of the 'let it be that'. It also governs the logic laid out in Brown's influential *Laws of Form* (1969), which aims to provide a set of algorithmic notation-procedures, in which the notation is the procedure and the procedure is effected through the notation, for the making out of complex propositions. Indeed Brown declares that:

> the primary form of mathematical communication is not description, but injunction. In this respect it is comparable with practical art forms like cookery, in which the taste of a cake, although literally indescribable, can be conveyed to a reader in the form of a set of injunctions called a recipe. Music is a similar art form, the composer does not even attempt to describe the set of sounds he has in mind, much less the set of feelings occasioned through them, but writes down a set of commands which, if they are obeyed by the performer, can result in a reproduction, to the listener, of the composer's original experience. (Brown 1969: 77)

Like Wittgenstein, Brown sees the injunctive nature of mathematical writing as electively tied to the act of writing. That is, the writing of mathematics is an invitation to its reader to actualise the mathematical propositions in a further act of writing. Mathematics thus becomes the injunction notation of an inscription, which will itself be a notation rather than a simple image or representation:

> When we attempt to realize a piece of music composed by another person, we do so by *illustrating*, to ourselves, with a musical instrument of some kind, the composer's commands. Similarly, if we are to realize a piece of mathematics, we must find a way of illustrating, to ourselves, the commands of the mathematician. The normal way to do this is with some kind of scorer and a flat scorable surface, for example a finger and a tide-flattened stretch of sand, or a pencil and a piece of paper. (78)

The principal logical operator in Brown's scheme is what he calls the Crossing, which is a primary act of self-division whereby one entity is marked out from another. 'The theme of this book is that a universe comes into being when a space is severed or taken apart', he declares at the outset of *Laws of Form* (v); in the process of course he effects by his declaration the very action it evokes. Brown's mark makes a primary distinction between the inside and the outside of something, and may be thought of as an abbreviated bracketing. 'We take as given the idea of a distinction and the idea of an indication, and that it is not possible to make an indication without drawing a distinction. We take therefore the form of distinction for the form' (1). The making of a mark which distinguishes establishes a form in a kind of self-relation, which accounts for the success of Brown's calculus with biologists like Franciso Varela, who made it the basis for his study of organic autopoeisis in living systems, in *Principles of Biological Autonomy* (1979). The mark is not only at the heart of all form, it represents a fundamental property of the universe, which conjoins knowing and being. For Brown, this property is reflexivity:

> we cannot escape the fact that the world we know is constructed in order (and thus in such a way as to be able) to see itself.
>   This is indeed amazing. (105)

Reflexivity allows for systems not just to recognise, but also to perform work on and with themselves, this being the fundamental feature, not just of a calculation, or the difference engine that materialises it, but also of language. The power of a language, like the power of mathematics, consists not principally in its capacity to represent the world, but its capacity to signify itself to itself. This allows it to work on the world by working and reworking its own system of representation.

Brown insists that this relation of self-seeing is also an act, and an agonistic one: 'We may take it that the world undoubtedly is itself (i.e. is indistinct from itself), but, in any attempt to see itself as an object, it must, equally undoubtedly, act so as to make itself distinct from, and therefore false to, itself' – and in a cryptic footnote to the word 'act' Brown reminds his readers of the Greek *agonistes*, actor, antagonist, and invites them to 'note the identity of action with agony' (105). One of the striking features of Brown's *Laws of Form* is how easily it slips between abstract logical relations and actual engineering applications, as in his casual remark that the logical calculus he has set out exists in the form of circuits 'presently in use by British Railways' (99), for whom Brown had acted as a consulting engineer.

This active self-relation is, many have thought, a distinguishing feature of the kind of language we call 'literary'. We may say that all executable code, like all arithmetical or algebraic functions, requires something like this primary bracketing or pocketing, in which one set of conditions is first of all set out in a self-contained phrase or clause, and then some operation is performed upon it. The rucked or pocketted structure of code is signalled by the function of what has come to be known as the Enter key, which means 'put what has been proposed into operation'; 'so be it'; 'amen'. The sign for the Enter key is an abbreviation of the carriage return on a typewriter, which would signify the completion of a line. The Enter key performs the function of the 'equals' sign on a calculator keyboard, and, on early computers, was sometimes called the 'Send' or 'Execute' key. The 'entering' of the Enter function derives from the IBM 3270 made in 1971, in which the key was used to input a block of buffered code into a computer, again making the potential actual.

The hangover of all this is the 'Are you sure?' dialogue that is a familiar, wearisome but sometimes merciful routine for all computer users. Having to say 'yes' also allows one to say 'no', and to be able to undo commands. There must be bracketting, the interior delimiting of operations as bounded in extent, for an undo command to be possible – otherwise the whole linked structure could be countermanded. Programming must move by a series of encapsulated hiccups, from the proposed to the disposed, the prepared to the performed, a series of epochs in which a system is put to work to execute itself. The 'Enter' is a version of the 'yes'-function analysed in Joyce's *Ulysses* by Derrida as part of the 'gramophone effect' of an 'anamnesic machine' of utterance in the novel (Derrida 1988: 44). This primary and renewed self-relation may be regarded as a feature not just of all coded language, but also a feature of all language as such. The principle that a sentence requires a main verb to complete it is the principle of the enter or let-it-be-so. Language proceeds by the semantic rhythm of these gatherings and releasings, preparations and activations.

However, literary language is machine-like and code-like in that it depends on a greater number of processes that may be said to be 'machine-readable' than other kinds of language use, which require and are largely exhausted by the act of communication between a sender and receiver. All language depends upon this kind of implicitness, but literary language is technographic in that the work done by these pocketings of the implicit is greater and more extensive. Another way of putting it would be like this. Any piece of writing can be made available for self-scrutiny and therefore made able to act on itself by being digitised, that is, being rendered in a form that makes it machine-readable – that can, for example, count the numbers of characters or the occurrences of a particular word or even of a clause-structure. The simple sorting of the information contained in the text performs a work on it that allows it to be seen not as an event but as a structure of relations, increasing its visible redundancy. Literary texts are texts that open themselves up more and more to this possibility of machine-reading, even in advance of the existence of any actual apparatus for performing such operations. Indeed, we may say that such texts are literary to the degree that they constitute promissory machines (a promised machine and a machine for promising) for self-sorting that would anticipate the operations we call digitisation.

This is why I think that the kind of writing that tends to be called 'literary' has always in fact had a secret kinship with such technographic forms; for, in both cases, the writing is a kind of notation, which joins in the performance of what it signifies. Technography is not just a modern matter, a feature of texts that happen to arise in a world full of machinery and pay attention to that machinery in various ways. The mediation of other machines assists literature to imagine and start to become the ideal machine it is always aspiring to be. Literature is not any kind of rage against the machine: it is the name for this machinic desire, the desire of this ideal machinery. And, if I am even half-way right, writing has been a machinery of calculation from the very beginning. The particular kind of machinery that has become universal in the modern world is the computer. This machine has become universal because that is what it is, in that it is not a machine for performing one kind of operation (digging, washing up, or adding up, say) but a machine capable of operating any other kind of machine, precisely because of its powers of reflecting on itself, or taking itself as an object of calculation. We may say that the ways in which literary writing has been put to work, as a general form of programming, is a kind of computation. All literature is technographic, not in the sense that it is about some kind of machinery, but in the sense that we tend to call writing literary as it intensifies its attempt to write out, or in Brown's terms to 're-enter into the form' (Brown 1969: 69) of, the kind of machinery it itself is. Its noncoincidence with itself is the law of its form and the motive principle of its action.

Digitisation not only renders words as numerical equivalents, it activates the numerical and mathematical potential latent in literary texts (that is, the texts that tend to qualify as literary, or come to be taken as literary). All nature, we may say, is potentially on the way to number, or lies open to it. Literature is a name for what lies between language and number and moves language towards the multiple equivalences of number. The move towards the mathematical is not, as it is ritually supposed to be, a move in the direction of reduction, but of production. We must remember that the number of number is not one. Numbers are qualitatively invariant, that is, they are all exactly the same kind of thing. But it is this very fact that makes the number of games it is possible to play and functions it is possible to perform undetermined. It becomes clear that literature is a mechanical procedure and, like all mechanical procedures, a calculative machinery, at just the point at which we start to lose our certainty that we know clearly and in advance what a machine is or can be. Literature is a little like, or aspires to be like, the kind of machine a computer is, namely a universal machine – an encyclopaedia or generator of machineries.

So I have had four assertions to make here about writing machines and what they do:

1. Literature is not less but more mechanical than other forms of writing.

2. In reflecting on machinery, a text we see as literary instantiates its dream of itself as a universal, ideal machine.

3. The machinery on which literary texts electively model themselves is a calculative machinery.

4. The central principle of this machinery is that it is operative. Like code, it not only is what it indicates, it also does what it says.

Works Cited

Bogost, Ian. 2008. *Unit Operations: An Approach to Videogame Criticism*. Cambridge: MIT Press.

Brown, George Spencer. 1969. *Laws of Form*. London: George Allen and Unwin.

Bruere, Dirk. 2009. *Technomage: Technological Paradigms for the Modification of Reality in Consciousness and Magick*. Bedford: Dirk Bruere.

Danesi, Marcel. 2002. *The Puzzle Instinct: The Meaning of Puzzles in Human Life*. Bloomington: Indiana University Press.

Derrida, Jacques. 1988. '*Ulysses* Gramophone: Hear Say Yes in Joyce'. In *James Joyce: The Augmented Ninth: Proceedings of the Ninth International James Joyce Symposium, Frankfurt, 1984*, edited by Bernard Benstock, 27-74. Syracuse: Syracuse University Press.

Dudeney, Henry. 1924. 'Puzzles'. *Strand Magazine* 68: 97, 214.

Freud, Sigmund. 1955. *Totem and Taboo: Some Points of Agreement Between Savages and Neurotics*. Translated by James Strachey. *The Standard Edition of the Complete Psychological Works of Sigmund Freud*. Volume 13, 1-162. London: Hogarth Press.

Knott, Cargill Gilston. 1911. *Life and Scientific Work of Peter Guthrie Tait*. Cambridge: Cambridge University Press.

Leibniz, Gottfried Wilhelm von. 1951. *Leibniz: Selections*. Edited by Philip P. Wiener. New York: Scribner.

Moxon, Joseph. 1683. *Mechanick Exercises: Or, The Doctrine of Handy-works. Applied to the Art of Printing*. Volume 2. London: Joseph Moxon.

Sachs, Joe. 2004. *Aristotle's* Physics*: A Guided Study*. New Brunswick: Rutgers University Press.

Serres, Michel. 2007. *The Parasite*. Translated by Lawrence R. Schehr. Minneapolis: University of Minnesota Press.

Shannon, Claude E. 1948. 'A Mathematical Theory of Communication'. *Bell System Technical Journal* 27: 379–423, 623–656.

Sidney, Philip. 2002. *An Apology for Poetry (or the Defence of Poesy)*. 3rd edition. Edited by Geoffrey Shepherd and R.W. Maslen. Manchester: Manchester University Press.

Shakespeare, William. 2010. *The Merchant of Venice*. Edited by John Drakakis. London: Bloomsbury.

Smith, Michael. 2007. *Station X: The Codebreakers of Bletchley Park*. London: Pan.

Waismann, Friedrich. 1979. *Ludwig Wittgenstein and the Vienna Circle*. Edited by B.F. McGuinness. Translated by Joachim Schulte and B.F. McGuinness. Oxford: Blackwell.

Whitehead, A.N. 1911. *Introduction to Mathematics*. New York: Henry Holt.

Wittgenstein, Ludwig. 1974. *Philosophical Grammar: Part I, The Proposition, and Its Sense, Part II, On Logic and Mathematics*. Edited by Rush Rhees. Translated by Anthony Kenny. Oxford: Blackwell.

Wittgenstein, Ludwig. 1975. *Philosophical Remarks*. Edited by Rush Rhees. Translated by Raymond Hargreaves and Roger White. Oxford: Blackwell.

Wittgenstein, Ludwig. 1980. *Wittgenstein's Lectures, Cambridge 1930-1932*. From the notes of John King and Desmond Lee. Oxford: Blackwell.

2

Stereopticon

Kristen Treen

A Semblance of Sanity

In May of 1865, a member of the Philadelphia Photographic Society (PPS) spent an evening in the Pennsylvania Hospital for the Insane. Invited rather than committed, the photographer had been given permission to observe one of the stereopticon 'entertainments' with which the Hospital's superintendent, physician and reformer Thomas Story Kirkbride, was attempting to 'cure' the men and women in his care. The treatment seemed to be working, for, with one eye on the stereopticon show and one on the audience, the photographer was 'delighted by what I then saw'. 'The audience', he told his fellow enthusiasts, 'was a model audience, so quiet and so attentive':

> Dr Lee read to them from some book of travels in Rome, and as he read, the various scenes about which he was reading were thrown on the screen in a circle of light, eighteen feet in diameter. The dissolving effect was well managed, and occasionally, during pauses of the reading, and while the pictures were being shown, music was introduced to vary the entertainment. Familiar as I am with exhibitions of this class, I never passed a more agreeable evening. ('Photographic Society of Philadelphia' 1865: 120)

The man from the PPS had no problem quietly cordoning himself off from 'them' – the beneficiaries of Dr Lee's readings – and ruining, somewhat, the integrity of this 'model' audience. But he couldn't quite find his way to separating the process that wrought the patients' psychological metamorphosis from the mechanical workings of the machine itself. Ill-equipped to describe the operation with which the stereopticon was meant not simply to amuse these patients, but to restore their powers of restraint and reason, this technologically-minded observer found that a meticulous description of the stereopticon's clear focus, varied display, steady function, and 'well managed' mechanism did just as well. Photographic images of Rome and its treasures were displayed, magnified, on a clean white screen: unremarkably 'familiar' as the account might sound to the seasoned stereopticon spectator, this photographer – and, indeed, the numerous physicians implementing this novel treatment – implied that the operations of a 'model' mind might somehow correspond with exposure to the stereopticon's particular mechanisms, its visual effects. This photographer's account, in other words, let the stereopticon speak for itself.

The PPS photographer wasn't the first rhetorically to elide the stereopticon lantern's novel workings with those of a healthy mind: the stereopticon had been used to exhibit sanity for almost a decade before the PPS photographer paid his call. In fact, its incorporation into Kirkbride's Moral Treatment scheme took place shortly after the invention of its key component, the photographic slide. The stereopticon's story began with the innovations of brothers William and Frederick Langenheim, of Philadelphia, PA, whose experimentation with glass as a material upon which photographic negatives could be developed made photographic lantern slides – or 'hyalotypes', after the Greek for 'glass' – possible (Musser 1994: 30). Where previous projectors relied on hand-painted slides to entertain small audiences public and domestic, this machine brought the marvels of magnified photography to the masses, beginning officially with the Langenheims' audiences at London's Crystal Palace Exhibition of 1851 (Wells 2008: 13-15; Layne 1981: 195). Glass slides set the scene for the innovation of the magic lantern itself. By 1860, Massachusetts chemist and businessman John Fallon had coined the term 'stereopticon' in naming the large biunial lantern he imported from England and improved significantly. This lantern used powerful calcium limelight, oxy-hydrogen, or electric light to project photographic images of between twenty-five and thirty feet in diameter before music- and lecture-hall crowds (Figure 1) (Wells 2011: 5-6). Remarkable for retaining an extraordinary clarity of image, the stereopticon also delighted audiences with its innovative use of a dissolving effect between slides, which the stereopticon's double lenses, stacked one above the other, made possible. Refining the primitive effects of the older lantern's shake and slide, the stereopticon's dissolve appeared in almost every eyewitness account of the machine's entrancing scenes, including that of the PPS photographer who found himself enjoying their effect among the Hospital's curious congregation.

The Hospital had been reaping the benefits of stereopticon shows long before they became popular with the general public. A chance acquaintance with the Langenheim brothers in the early 1850s led Kirkbride to introduce the stereopticon shows into the Pennsylvania Hospital's pioneering Moral Treatment scheme as early as 1851 (Layne 1981: 196). Before long, photographic displays of European artworks, North American landmarks, and even of the Hospital's own grounds had become staple evening entertainments in a programme of therapy which replaced an asylum culture of commonplace physical restraint and punishment with '[t]he most inflexible firmness [...]

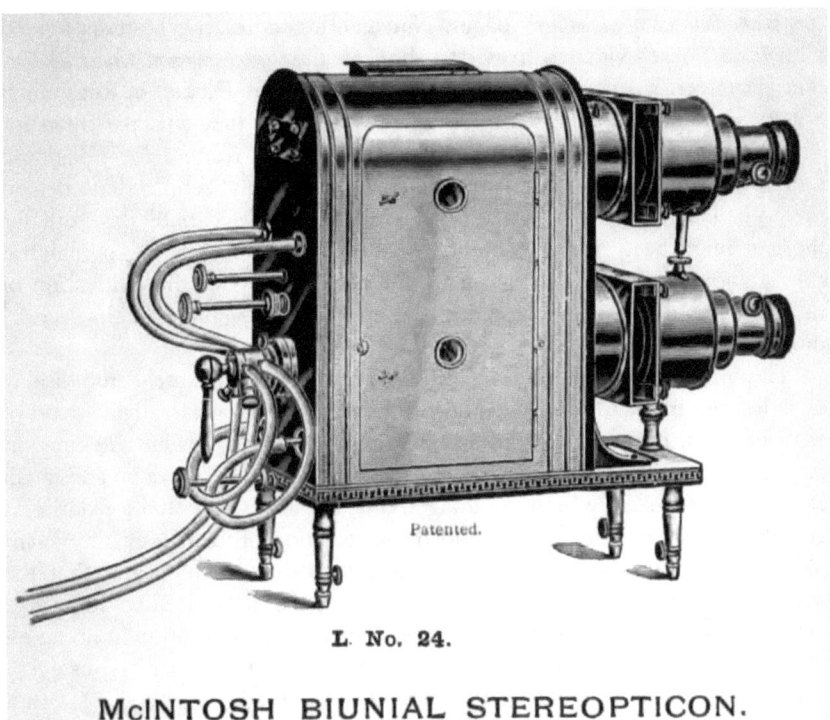

L. No. 24.

McINTOSH BIUNIAL STEREOPTICON.

Fig. 1. The McIntosh Biunial Stereopticon. 1895. *Illustrated Catalogue of Stereopticons, Sciopticons, Dissolving View Apparatus, Microscopes, Solar Microscope and Stereopticon Combination, Objectives, Photographic Transparencies, Plain and Artistically Colored Views and Microscopical Preparations*, p. 32. Chicago: McIntosh Battery & Optical Co.

combined with never-failing kindness and gentleness and sympathy' (Haller and Larsen 2005: 261; Bucknill and Tuke 1862: 546). Unlike their draconian forebears, proponents of the Moral Treatment believed that mental illness was an affliction that the patient could be helped to manage, given the right habit-forming occupations. 'The patient is to be taught habitual self-control, by habitual indulgence', wrote English psychiatrists Bucknill and Tuke, and while the physical routines of gardening and gymnastics had served Kirkbride's purposes well enough, his records of the stereopticon's successes suggest that it was clearly a habit of a different order (Godbey 2000: 36).

Regarded early on as an effective tool in wresting what one Hospital manager described as '"minds diseased" [...] from their gyrations, – their never ending rotation upon the point of fallacy', the stereopticon's gift to psychiatry was the rhetoric of its movements, the habits it might pass on to the mentally ill ('Extract of a Letter' 1852: 292).

For the language of insanity was the language of erratic shifts, abrupt transitions, obsessive gyrations, and lethargic depressions, which filled the

American Journal of Insanity's pages. Nineteenth-century psychiatrists agreed with John Locke's view, expressed in *An Essay Concerning Human Understanding*, that '*mad Men* [...] do not appear [...] to have lost the Faculty of Reasoning; but having joined together *some Ideas* very wrongly, they mistake them for Truths' (Locke 1975: 160-61). Such was their point d'appui for imagining more precisely the abnormal ruptures, conjoinings, and motions that affected the so-called 'diseased' mind. Prized for its narrative capabilities, and for the startling clarity of its content, the stereopticon struck the psychiatric eye as capable of creating the environment necessary for the cultivation of rational thought, and of projecting the emulable movement of that model thought on screen.

Halting the troubled mind's gyrations, the stereopticon's measured display of slides, fed manually through the machine, assumed a narrative thread of associations with or without an accompanying lecture to bridge the gaps. In fact, thanks to its dissolve effect, the stereopticon seemed to leave no gaps at all as it moved seamlessly between images. There was no potential for darkness and distraction, for the 'lesion[s] in the association of ideas' that physician-philosopher Louis Francisque Lélut associated with insanity, and that the Moral Treatment sought to suture (cited in Bucknill and Tuke 1862: 75). What was more, the magnification of photographic images brought about an unparalleled reality effect, that, as Kirkbride himself noted, 'give[s] us every object in a landscape, every leaf and twig, every blade of grass [...] with a degree of perfection no artist could hope to effect' (Kirkbride 1863: 57). At the same time as it impressed the social responsibilities of the 'model' audience upon its spectators, who often shared their auditorium with Hospital staff and the visiting public, the stereopticon would impress images of reality writ unavoidably large upon the wandering mind, in the hope that the purposeful progress of the life-sized, the face-to-face, the enormously real would leave its mark. The visual shaped the cognitive; the right kind of visions could set the wandering mind straight. 'If new objects of thought are not only presented to, but impressed upon the mind', wrote Bucknill and Tuke of Moral Treatment's claims to rearrange disturbed thought, 'if employment is made to replace inertia, cheerful society and recreation to replace moping dulness, new trains of ideas become the habit of the mind, and the subjects of delusion gradually fade in the perspectives of memory' (Bucknill and Tuke 1862: 555).

Kirkbride would have agreed that 'the subjects of delusion gradually fade in the perspectives of the stereopticon', for the machine seemed not only to correct habits of mind, but also to externalise the healthy movement of thought itself, from one discrete image to another. It certainly wasn't the first time that photographic or projecting technologies had been used to picture thought's daily processes, or the mind's responses to external phenomena. As Emily Godbey has shown, the asylum movement rooted its conception of the healthy mind in the Lockean doctrine of human understanding, which had famously used the *camera obscura* to delineate the relations between 'external and internal Sensation' and the *'dark Room'* of the mind (Godbey 2000: 52-3; Locke 1975: 163). Illuminating the mind's 'Closet wholly shut from light', these sensations projected 'external visible Resemblances, or *Ideas* of things without' into its darkness: 'Pictures', which 'stay there, and lie so orderly as to be found upon occasion' within memory's slide-box, as it were (Locke 1975: 163).

While Locke separated 'objects of sight and the ideas of them' into an 'orderly' system of images to be reprojected, the proponents of the Moral Treatment drew on theories of the Scottish Common Sense philosophy to make Locke's rigid set of 'pictures' a little more malleable. In its thesis that, together with Lockean sensory accrual, humans were 'born with innate propensities that could be molded by experience', the Common Sense philosophy made it possible to envisage reconditioning the thoughts that strayed from their Lockean arrangement (Godbey 2000: 52). Bringing new movement to the *camera obscura's* magnifications, the stereopticon embodied an intersection of the psychological philosophies that defined American psychiatry at mid-century.

In doing so, however, it became a means – for nineteenth-century practitioners of remedial psychiatry and for media historians alike – of reasserting the enduring conviction that the τέχνη of emerging photographic technologies could be found in their value as *ordering* mechanisms. Ordering mechanisms, moreover, with a claim to authority rooted in the apparent transparency of the photographic image. With transparency comes immediacy: when the rhetoric of the machine converges too neatly with reality's expectations, the medium itself begins to disappear, validating the rhetoric of order into which it disappears. The medium arbitrates successfully – the stereopticon cures and displays curedness – to the point of self-effacement, and the order it establishes is insidious but absolute. Indeed, until now the stereopticon has been routinely incorporated into the line-up of technologies labeled as essential mechanisms within the larger apparatus of institutional power. Kirkbride's experiment has been likened to panoptic surveillance, and his innovative use of photography in the asylum compared with the photographic categorization of mental 'diseases' undertaken by his contemporaries in European psychiatry (Haller and Larsen 2005; Godbey 2000).

Yet beyond the asylum's walls, the stereopticon's beguiling progress would challenge conceptions of consciousness and of order, just as it would leave its audiences with the strange sense that they had been caught-up in the haze of a dream. Untempered by pre-existing discourses of health and sanity, the public's stereopticon was innovator rather than conservator, a technology that gave rise to sensations of dissonance and mixed metaphor in equal measure. Telegraph, flying carpet, rolling clouds, miracle pure and simple: unable to put their fingers on the stereopticon's wondrous transportation of sight and mind, its spectators found that the machine's magnifications and dissolves dispersed and reimagined the possibilities of the real with every passing slide.

Indeed, both effects turned the spectator's attention, with a new intensity, to the unseen world around them: to the fibres of existence revealed by the stereopticon's unparalleled magnifications; to the connections that bound individual to audience and to an ever-expanding democratic nation; to the processes driving the mind between thoughts, filling the gaps in a way that the stereopticon's dissolves made suddenly conspicuous. And by the end of the century, the stereopticon had become a linguistic mechanism with which literature and Pragmatist philosophy registered their encounters with the dissonances, the chaotic relationality, of the modern American consciousness.

Magnify

At first, the stereopticon appeared to be living up to Kirkbride's rhetoric of improvement. The machine's debut tour had elicited favourable reviews where its instructive potential was concerned. When the stereopticon's inventor John Fallon partnered-up with showmen Peter Abel and Thomas Leyland to exhibit the first public stereopticon lecture shows across the Northeast, the magnifying machine he had developed with his chemist colleagues in mind quickly gained a reputation for the scientific realism it brought to popular spectacle. '*Photographic, optical,* and *chemical science* have here combined to bring the very ends of the earth near to us, in something like their natural aspect', declared one enthusiastic reviewer for the *Salem Gazette*, whose accolade appeared in a pamphlet produced by Abel and Leyland's publicity outfit. This was upmarket entertainment, the wonders and curiosities of the world unveiled with an accuracy capable, as the *Gazette*'s correspondent eagerly emphasised, of 'educating and elevating the popular taste'. 'We often lament', repined the same reviewer,

> that in a land like our own, where art is yet in its infancy, masterpieces of sculpture and painting are so rarely seen by the masses [...] But with the apparatus of which we have been speaking, a gallery of choicest sculpture may be carried to any New England village, and its matchless marbles displayed to all the people [...] We are confident that all who are interested in the education of the young, and in the cultivation of a pure taste and love of the beautiful among all classes, whether young or old, will appreciate the claims of the performance upon their approbation. (Haynes and Leyland 1863: 4-5)

As its singular clarity opened America's eyes to the Old World's treasures, so the stereopticon's vast views, accessible to unprecedentedly vast congregations of 'all classes, whether young or old', promised to transform its audiences into an apparatus fit to refine the sensibilities of its individual components, in a way Kirkbride would no doubt have endorsed. Yet Kirkbride had hoped that each individual in the asylum would internalise the restrained behaviours they learned in the shadows cast by the stereopticon's glare. The displays of lecture and music hall were understood, by comparison, to be gregarious in the extreme, generating a vivid sense of a *shared* visual experience. Advertisements boasted of improbably large audiences held spellbound by an impossible lantern of immense proportions, while the *New York Journal of Commerce* compared the stereopticon to its more famous cousin, the handheld stereoscope, noting that the 'delight which one person has when looking through the stereoscope a thousand persons can have at once – so that there is sympathetic and social pleasure' (Wells 2011: 5-6; Haynes and Leyland 1863: 12). The stereoscope induced the observer to peer into its eyepiece to partake privately of its seemingly solid photographic views, 'look[ing] selfishly at the show with your personal eyes', as the *Salem Gazette* admonished. The stereopticon, by contrast, equipped viewers with public eyes: lifting hundreds of faces in unison, it brought into being for the first time a 'sympathetic' collective connected by photographic realism writ large for public inspection.

If the stereopticon was a democratiser, then the democracy was in the detail. The stereopticon's examples of superior realism intensified the spectator's relation to those sitting around them, but they also altered the spectator's relation to the life unexpectedly exposed on screen in all its particulars. To the spectator accustomed to the magic lantern's hand-painted scenes, or what the *Rochester Express* called the panorama's 'eye-trying daub', the photographic feats of the stereopticon laid its subjects bare with a clarity that seemed to make visible the connective tissues of the world around them (Haynes and Leyland 1863: 14). To an extent, this had to do with the spate of overtly scientific shows that fascinated audiences by projecting slides containing microscopic organisms, including fleas, ticks, and even, at one display in Philadelphia, the contents of a small aquarium: fish, water, and all (Godbey 2000: 59, 63; Musser 1994: 32). The sudden disclosure of the unseen physical world was admittedly wondrous and grotesque by turns, but rather than induce audiences to regard what they saw as the stuff of curiosity and freak show, the scientific element prompted uncanny moments of self-examination.

One short story by an anonymous writer for the *Milwaukee Daily Journal* evoked the scientific stereopticon's 'great fiery eye' to imagine the infinitesimal lives and adventures of 'two charming little animalculas' named Ra and Ro. 'An Infusional Romance' began by registering the sense of 'horror' attendant on the revelation 'that, in the indiscreet glare of the magic lantern, the finest maiden's tress resembled the primeval giant of the forest, that the most delicate lace was made of rough cables, and that that romantic storied personage, Mr de Fly, Jr, was a blood-thirsty monster as large as an elephant' ('An Infusional Romance' 1887: 3). In offering a view of the trials suffered by Ra and Ro in their attempts to join (literally) in holy matrimony – at the end of the story the limelight threatens to evaporate their watery world altogether – the story

Fig. 2. 'And next, the Brownies gathered round / A stereopticon machine / That cast its rays upon a screen. / A thousand times it magnified, / Till, stretching out on every side, / An object large and larger spread, / And filled the gazing group with dread.' Palmer Cox. 1890. *Another Brownie Book*, pp. 9-10. New York: Century.

envisioned the infinite expansion of the known world, even as it broached the possibility that the stereopticon was capable of revealing more about life's intimacies than one might care to know. It was a feeling that Canadian cartoonist Palmer Cox captured in an 1890 cartoon for his popular series *The Brownies* (Figure 2). During the Brownies' visit to the Academy (which precedes their visit to Niagara Falls, their trips by locomotive and tugboat, and their excursion up a canal), microscopic becomes uncannily macroscopic: grouped in inattentive chaos beneath a screen that dwarfs them to the size of insects, Cox's brownies wriggle and squirm, larval beneath the stereopticon's glare. The audience is as much of an entomological specimen as the bright beetle, bee, and locust on screen, all of which turn their ocelliform gaze upon the peculiar figures below.

The feeling of being scrutinised beneath a microscope wasn't limited to scientific shows, either, and its insidious influence was connected to the strange optical illusion for which the stereopticon had become famous. Since the stereopticon's first shows, audience members had reported a perceived solidity to the sights they were shown that simply didn't exist. In part, this illusion of solidity (the 'stereo' part of 'stereopticon') had to do with the machine's hybridity where kit was concerned: stereopticon operators often fed one half of the stereoscope's double view before the limelight, and the three-dimensional effect enjoyed by stereoscope viewers was transferred visually just as 'stereo' was transferred verbally. The projection of small details, and of art and statuary against black backgrounds, also seemed to throw the photographic subject into relief. Reviews of statuary shows commonly waxed lyrical about the 'roundness' of the ancient marbles on screen. Eager to grasp the stereopticon's miraculous revelations, a reporter for the *Norwich Bulletin* put his finger on the curious quality of the stereopticon's absorbing detail as he reviewed Fallon's display of European art and architecture:

> The scenes were various – now a public edifice, minutely perfect, even to the stains and finger marks upon its walls; now a ruin, upon which you could almost trace the depredations of the last visitor; now an interior view of a palace or cathedral, with its beautiful play of light and shade; now a landscape or a waterfall bursting in mist from the canvas; now a statue, more perfect if possible than the original, art glorified by science as it were, dead marble brought to life; [...] What pleasure is derived from looking at Stereoscopic pictures is increased a hundred fold in viewing the same pictures as presented in magnified proportions by the Stereopticon. (Haynes and Leyland 1863: 9)

In opening up expanses and interstices, and with them the potential for personal exploration, the stereopticon seemed to match the 'pleasure derived from looking at Stereoscopic pictures'. Or, rather, it bettered it by presenting life-sized spaces into which spectators might project themselves. Offering individuals the opportunity to reassess their grasp of the world before them, the stereopticon's haptic allure became a tool in the manufacture of democratic expansion. Views of southern California drew the gaze of East Coast audiences in 1874 'for the purpose of inducing emigration thither': absorbing manifestations of agriculture and landscape, like those of 'dead marble brought to life', became substitutes for tentative travel, their brilliant progress across the screen guaranteeing Manifest Destiny's advance across the country ('Amusements' 1874: 8).

Yet lurking at the edges of awe and marvel was a disquieting awareness that the stereopticon might show too much, might be *too* democratic in the details it conjured for hundreds of curious eyes. This unsettling hyper-democratic insight marked the report of the *Norwich Bulletin*, whose descriptions of 'stains and finger marks' blemishing the walls of magnificent edifices, and 'the depredations of the last visitor' upon ancient ruins, left the seamy impression that the Old World's treasures had suffered over-exposure to an eager spectatorship. Saving graces there surely were: of beauty to counter the 'stains and finger marks' of gawking hordes, of 'art glorified by science' to shine where the whimsical plundering of relic-hunting individuals advertised the damage that consumers could so easily do. But even these brought the desires, the impulses of the individual mind into the equation: the desire to grasp, to touch, to claim an embodied relationship to the objects on the screen that not only offered themselves, but overwhelmed the field of vision to the extent that reality itself seemed temporarily removed. Recalling a stereopticon display at master showman P.T. Barnum's Museum, one observer found himself taken in by images of statuary 'so exact that the spectator forgets that he is looking upon canvass [sic], and feels half-inclined to step upon the stage to get a back view of the images' ('Barnum's Museum' 1863: 2). To be lured onto P.T. Barnum's stage – home of 'freak' and grotesquerie – let alone on to any other, was to have one's curiosity turned curio, one's desires unveiled before eager eyes. Therein lay the difference between the haptic allure of the stereoscope's miniature views and those offered by the stereopticon: where, as Jonathan Crary has argued, the parlour stereoscope's intimate play with haptic illusion 'quickly turned into a mass form of ocular possession', the stereopticon's engrossing visions seemed quite capable of possessing the viewer and putting them on display (Crary 1990: 127).

In the hands of author Charles Barnard, whose serialised novel *Applied Science* appeared in Maine's *Bangor Daily Whig and Courier* early in 1888, it was the stereopticon, more than any other modern technology, that had the power to reveal one's innermost thoughts and desires. Here, the stereopticon plays chief foil to the secret desires of the story's protagonist, one Elmer Franklin. Elmer is a dentist-cum-gadgeteer with a penchant for adapting the latest in nineteenth-century technology for his personal use, a quirk that comes into its own as he plots to save his beloved Alma from the prospects of a marriage of convenience to a swindling rogue, Mr Belford. Throughout the narrative Elmer's 'science [is] brought to bear upon rascality' as he uses his various gadgets to gather damning evidence against his rival in love (Barnard 1888a: 4). A camera is quickly produced and put to use as ether-happy Elmer uses the cover of his dentistry day job to swipe a glance at an incriminating letter that Belford is foolish enough to carry around, while Elmer is quick to provide his lady love with a miniature telegraphy kit when she confides to him her fears of meeting with her fiancée alone. Noble as our hero's intentions are, he too has his secrets: namely, a photographic slide bearing an image of Alma, surreptitiously taken as she sleeps. Of course, Elmer owns his own stereopticon machine, and it is this prized possession that ultimately gives him away during a conference with the troubled Alma:

> Suddenly she flushed a rosy red, and a strange light shone in her eyes. The sun had sunk behind the hills, and it had grown dark. As the shadows gathered in the room a strange, mystic light fell on the ground before her. A picture – dim, ghostly, gigantic and surpassingly beautiful – met her astonished gaze. She gazed at it with a beating heart, awed into silence by its mystery and its unearthly aspect. What was it? What did it mean? By what magic art had he conjured up this vision? (Barnard 1888b: 4)

Face to face with her magnified and otherworldly self, Alma faints, giving Elmer the chance to smash the incriminating slide upon the hearth, but not before he passionately presses the glass miniature to his lips. With the shattering of the slide the 'clear headed son of science seem[s] to [lose] his self control' and begins 'to turn over his books and papers in a nervous manner, as if trying to win back control of his tumultuous thoughts'. Private thoughts once contained by Elmer's private stereopticon are thrown into chaos when they are exposed before the eyes of another. Overwhelming its subject into unconsciousness, the slide magnifies Elmer's conscious desires beyond all imagined proportion, leaving him in a state of shifted perspective and mental disarray. As it spills its piercing glare beyond the screen to illuminate its audience, the stereopticon lays bare the tangles of feeling, the disordered thoughts, by which even the most 'rational' of minds connect themselves with reality.

Dissolve

Responses to stereoptic dissolves speculated still more on the dissonances of the mind's activities. The dissolve effect with which the stereopticon caught modernity's eye had led a primitive existence in the years preceding the magic lantern's sudden development. Like many of the magic lantern's early effects – from the slip-slide through the long panoramic panning movement – the dissolve was usually achieved manually rather than mechanically. With the stereopticon, though, mechanical technique was perfected by way of a dissolving tap, which as Kentwood Wells explains, 'allowed smooth simultaneous dimming and brightening of lights in the two halves of a [biunial] dissolving lantern' (Wells 2011: 6). By adjusting the supply of hydrogen in each of the lantern's compartments, the tap allowed its operator to maintain and gradually to dim the illuminations as the oxygen used to fuel the light's glare was turned off (6). Immersed as we are in a visual culture which has seen the dissolving haze become a staple of cinematic montage, not to mention an effect we might use to check the monotony of a PowerPoint presentation, it is not easy to imagine encountering it for the first time, or encountering it as main attraction rather than ornamental embellishment.

By all accounts, the dissolve's drift of gases – its 'soft, white clouds gathering and rolling themselves about like smoke' – was enrapturing, and not simply in the way it delighted its audiences (Haynes and Leyland 1863: 8). It was enrapturing in the sense that it transported its viewers, carrying them not only from one image to another, but seeming, too, to convey them to another plane of consciousness altogether. For Ralph Waldo Emerson, who attended his first stereopticon exhibition at the Concord Lyceum in 1860, 'the lovely manner in which one picture was changed for another beat the faculty of dreaming' (Emerson 1914: 287). Meanwhile, Oliver Wendell Holmes, Sr's first encounter with the stereopticon's hazy scatterings prompted an expression of astonishment in a letter to the showman George Reed Cromwell:

> To sit in darkness and have these visions of strange cities, of stately edifices, of lovely scenery, of noble statues, steal out upon the consciousness, and melt away one with other, is like dreaming a long and beautiful dream with eyes wide open. A journey with you, is the Grand Tour, *minus* the passport and the bills of exchange. (Cromwell 1870: 26-7)

Dissolving views did away with the faltering business of crossing borders and the messy back-and-forth necessitated by bills of exchange, presenting their audiences with a mode of transportation – a mediating mist – that transcended the restrictions of time and space to bring otherwise disparate images together before the eyes. It was like watching one's own imagination at work, and the literary establishment was quick to adopt the effect as a rhetorical figure for the movements of the mind, not all of which were as carefree and listless as the dreams of Emerson and Holmes, or as reasoned as Kirkbride would have had them. One poet, who may have been responding to the early dissolves of the magic lantern, saw in these unremitting shifts and turns the transience and unpredictable mutability of affective existence. 'Life's Dissolving Views', published in the *Boston Investigator* on 31 March 1858, began by evoking life's natural course: 'Life is but an April day, / Sunned by smiles and blent with showers, / Hope's bright lamp that leads the way, / But lights the thorns amid the flowers' ('Life's Dissolving Views' 1858: 4). Drawing the year's natural cycle and those of 'Hope's bright lamp' together, the first stanza promised to unite natural rhythm and technological mechanism, and in doing so to deliver an ultimate image of order and equilibrium: 'smiles [...] blent with showers', and 'thorns amid the flowers'. By the poem's end, with 'Proud ambition [...]

Fig. 3. From 'Sketches in New York During the Recent Presidential Election'. 1872. *Graphic*, November 30: 505.

Fade[d] to disappointment's canker', and 'Pleasure [...] Changing soon to care and sorrow', the constant dissipations of the inner life have displaced the natural order altogether, leaving the dubious figure of 'Fate' in its place: 'But still although the blisses spread, / Too soon dissolve into each other, / Scarce is one remembrance fled, / Ere Fate's replaced it with another.'

Fate: the hand that feeds the lantern's slide; the force that drives one thought, dissolving it irresistibly into another. Under journalism's purview 'fate' became the inscrutable chop and change of capricious politicians even as stereopticon shows broadcast election returns, and the tide of fickle public opinion, onto the walls of buildings across the nation's cities (Figure 3). 'We know not what may have influenced the President in the selection of officers', wrote the *Christian Recorder* of Abraham Lincoln's ongoing shuffle of military leadership during the Civil War, 'whether guided by the party or by the discovery of their incapacity. [...] He has been busy [...] creating and disposing of them as a manager would a series of dissolving views' ('Our Failures and Their Causes' 1864: 1). The same was true of public taste, and while Lincoln was chastised for his precarious play with the fate of the country, one columnist for *Frank Leslie's Weekly* confessed surprise that the joys of Christmas hadn't yet fallen prey to the foibles of a fashion-conscious public: 'But in the very teeth of this condition of dissolving views and general tendency of all things old to go out and all things new to come in, Christmas has held its own. Whether we be skeptic or believer, transcendentalist or materialist, we all believe in the creed of a yearly merry-making' ('The Reign of Santa Claus' 1879: 294).

The strange motivation of the dissolve effect became a way of addressing the unfathomable charge that drove the country through civil war and into the marketplace; that drew its citizens together into a newly collective public consciousness, propelled forward by the fashions and fads of a booming postwar consumer culture; that marked, too, individuals' perceptions of their place within a modern nation which drew their gaze with marvels at every turn. To one correspondent for the *Taunton Gazette*, this dissolving state of affairs, as represented by the stereopticon's persistent passage, verged on disorder, on dissonance, on chaos. 'But very queer and bewildering it grows at last', they wrote of Fallon's sensational machine,

> this chassezing and winding of scenes through the brain. Perhaps you gaze intently at some historical horse. There is a slight criss-crossing of bars, and a huge steeple blots out the horse, and finally arrives a whole city of steeples. A strange miz-maze, wherein sea views subside into Vatican or Alhambra, and lonely ruins change hands with the palace walls of the Doges. (Haynes and Leyland 1863: 8)

Dissolves ended in solutions: the loosening of rhyme and reason to the extent that the visions moving before the observer's eyes became a chaos of impressions, 'chassezing and winding' in a nightmarish 'miz-maze' of shapes and forms. Yet this dissonance, this chaos, was exactly the solution Professor William James had been searching for as he strove to access the mechanisms of conscious thought that, to his eye, had always been restricted by philosophies of mind which oriented themselves in relation to Lockean doctrine. James turned to the dissolve effect to articulate the notion of consciousness as an ongoing rearrangement of possible relations, a continuous 'flow' of what he called the 'stream of thought'. By 'stream of thought', James referred not only to the 'substantive parts' of the conscious mind – that is, the sensorial images or thoughts that Locke had imagined projected onto the mind's screen – but to the 'transitive parts' as well, with which he denoted 'a passage, a relation, a transition *from* it [the substantive part], or *between* it and something else' (he also called them 'feelings') (James 1890: 1.243). As he attempted to discern the nature of these transitive parts, in all their feelings and relations, James was forced to admit the impossibility of a task which he compared to 'seizing a spinning top to catch its motion' (1.244). The problem with trying to describe the stream of thought, he realised, was fundamentally linguistic. For centuries, the philosophy of consciousness had set its gaze upon seemingly separate and conceptually solid substantive thoughts in a way that had shaped, and been shaped by, the workings of language: 'so inveterate has our habit become of recognising the existence of the substantive parts alone, that language almost refuses to lend itself to any other use' (1.246). The closest our substantively-biased language could come to speaking of these 'feelings of relation' – constantly in a state of change, of rearrangement, of an ongoing disruption that seemed chaotic because of its namelessness – was in conjunctions, prepositions, adverbial phrases, the play of syntax. 'We ought to say a feeling of *and*, and a feeling of *if*, he wrote, 'a feeling of *but*, and a feeling of *by*, quite as readily as we say a feeling of *blue* or a feeling of *cold*' (1.245-6).

One solution to the problem of description came to mind. 'As the brain-changes are continuous, so do all these consciousnesses melt into each other', he wrote, 'like dissolving views' (1.247). It was an assertion he made again in his description of the 'time-parts' of which continuous thought was comprised: while different moments in continuous thought 'melt into each other like dissolving views' to create a 'unitary and undivided' perception, 'no two of [these moments] feel the object just alike' (1.279). Not only does James's hypothesis rely on technological metaphor to find its focus on the *in-between*, the relational constitution of consciousness, it relies too on what the stereopticon's ongoing dissolves make visible to the eye: the ungraspable indivisibility of our ongoing thoughts, a merging which must be understood as pure process, as the dynamic shifting of numberless relations, those '[d]umb or anonymous psychic states' towards which words don't seem to work. Indeed, the stereopticon provides James with a figure for the analogue movement so integral to his model of the mind: the flowing stream. Its function within his text may therefore have less to do with the symbolic workings of metaphor – the token exchange of one thing for another – and more to do with the very movement of that exchange or semantic relation: the 'carrying' that metaphor does. Calling on the stereopticon's mechanisms, the *effects* it brings to mind, James applies the stereopticon's dissolve to denote the grammar of consciousness, in all its shades of conjunction, preposition, and plays of syntax.

James's metaphor also reshapes the relationships between mind, machine, and order that previous philosophies of mind had sought to preserve. On one hand, the machine metaphor transforms chaos of consciousness into a productive mechanism, an implement with which we might act rather than an abyss into which we might jump. On the other, it locates chaos within the machine in a way that not only prompts a reappraisal of the rhetorical insistence on technological order, but which invites us to re-read the workings of chaos in the same way that James's treatise invites us to re-read the workings of metaphor. So it is that in Stephen Crane's short story 'Five White Mice', the evocation of the stereopticon's dissolve brings us closer to understanding the stream of thoughts engendered by the modern metropolis not as a kind of madness, but as a heightened sense of one's own consciousness. Crane describes the runaway thoughts of a 'New York Kid' who finds himself in a stand-off with a group of shadowy Mexicans on one of the city's dingy streets. As the danger of the other mingles with the milieu of the city's rat-race, the Kid's visions suddenly become frantic, 'perfectly stereopticon, flashing in and away from his thought with an inconceivable rapidity, until, after all, they were simply one quick, dismal impression' (Crane 1898: 328). Crane's adjectival turn recalls James's grammatical one, emphasising sheer effect and with it the Kid's immersion in a moment of pure relationality. It is only a moment: the Kid's mind doesn't disintegrate into fear or madness. Instead it teeters on the edges of chaos and disorder to bring the reader a glimpse of modernity in all the rush of connections, alliances, enmities, and struggles that the city brings, magnified, to the mind. Just as it creates that glimpse, the stereopticon contains it: a snatch of consciousness in all the complexity of its relations, briefly illuminated on a New York street before the slide changes, and the scene dissolves.

Acknowledgements

The author would like to express her gratitude to the Wolfson Foundation for supporting the research which made this essay possible.

Works Cited

'Amusements'. 1874. *Inter Ocean*, September 28: 8.

'An Infusional Romance'. 1887. *Milwaukee Daily Journal*, March 17: 3.

Barnard, Charles. 1888a. 'Applied Science'. *Bangor Daily Whig and Courier*, March 1: 4.

Barnard, Charles. 1888b. 'Applied Science'. *Bangor Daily Whig and Courier*, March 6: 4.

'Barnum's Museum'. 1863. *National Anti-Slavery Standard*, May 9: 2.

Bucknill, John Charles, and Daniel Hack Tuke. 1862. *A Manual of Psychological Medicine: Containing the History, Nosology, Description, Statistics, Diagnosis, Pathology, and Treatment of Insanity With an Appendix of Cases*. 2nd edition. London: John Churchill.

Cox, Palmer. 1890. *Another Brownie Book*. New York: Century.

Crane, Stephen. 1898. *The Open Boat and Other Tales of Adventure*. New York: Doubleday and McClure.

Crary, Jonathan. 1992. *Techniques of the Observer: On Vision and Modernity in the Nineteenth Century*. Cambridge: MIT Press.

Cromwell, George Reed. 1870. *Descriptive Catalogue of Antique and Modern Sculpture, Represented at Professor Cromwell's Art Entertainments, with Biographical Sketch by A. C. Wheeler*. New York: Evening Post Steam Presses.

Emerson, Ralph Waldo. 1914. *Journals of Ralph Waldo Emerson 1820-1876*. Volume 9. London: Constable & Co.

'Extract of a Letter'. 1852. *American Journal of Insanity*, January: 292-3.

Godbey, Emily. 2000. 'Picture Me Sane: Photography and the Magic Lantern in a Nineteenth-Century Asylum'. *American Studies* 41: 31-69.

Haller, Beth, and Robin Larsen. 2005. 'Persuading Sanity: Magic Lantern Images and the Nineteenth-Century Moral Treatment in America'. *Journal of American Culture* 28: 259-72.

Haynes, Tilly, and Thomas Leyland. 1863. *Six Tours Through Foreign Lands. A Guide to Fallon's Great Work of Art. The World Illustrated. A Complete Mirror of the Universe, from the Earliest Times down to the Present Day.* Springfield.

James, William. 1890. *The Principles of Psychology.* 2 volumes. New York: Holt.

Kirkbride, Thomas Story. 1863. *Reports of the Pennsylvania Hospital for the Insane.* Philadelphia: The Pennsylvania Hospital for the Insane.

Layne, George S. 1981. 'Kirkbride-Langenheim Collaboration: Early Use of Photography in Psychiatric Treatment in Philadelphia'. *Pennsylvania Magazine of History and Biography* 105: 182-202.

'Life's Dissolving Views'. 1858. *Boston Investigator*, March 31: 4.

Locke, John. 1975. *An Essay Concerning Human Understanding.* Edited by Peter H. Nidditch. Oxford: Clarendon Press.

Musser, Charles. 1994. *The Emergence of Cinema: The American Screen to 1907.* Berkeley: University of California Press.

'Our Failures and Their Causes'. 1864. *Christian Recorder*, February 27: 1.

'Photographic Society of Philadelphia: Minutes of Regular Stated Meeting, Wednesday Evening, June 7 1865'. 1865. *Philadelphia Photographer* 1: 119-20.

'Sketches in New York During the Recent Presidential Election'. 1872. *Graphic*, November 30: 505.

'The Reign of Santa Claus'. 1879. *Frank Leslie's Weekly*, January 4: 294.

Wells, Kentwood D. 2008. 'What's in a Name? The Magic Lantern and the Stereopticon in American Periodicals 1860-1900'. *Magic Lantern Gazette* 20: 3-19.

Wells, Kentwood D. 2011. 'The Stereopticon Men: On the Road with John Fallon's Stereopticon, 1860-1870'. *Magic Lantern Gazette* 23: 3-34.

3

The Great American Novel and the Census

KASIA BODDY

> I would sing in my copious song your census returns
> of The States,
> The tables of population and products –
>
> Walt Whitman, 'Year of Meteors (1859-1860)'

In 1868, a novelist and former Union army officer called John W. De Forest issued a rallying cry for a new kind of 'copious' novel that would create, even as it reflected, the true scope and integrity of the nation (De Forest 1868). Whether such a 'Great American Novel' was actually possible was another matter.

De Forest was writing three years after the end of the American Civil War, a war which he – like many others – believed had made 'countrymen' out of 'people whom we did not know, and only counted in the census' (Emerson 2010b: 316). The end of that war also set the United States on a path of rapid industrialisation and population growth. In other words, De Forest called for a 'single tale' – one that would be recognised by 'every American' as a 'likeness of something which he knows' – at time when the prospect of that recognition was both less likely, due to the speed at which America was changing (De Forest 1868: 28), and more likely, due to the establishment of what John Durham Peters calls 'hard' and 'soft' connective infrastructures – such as a national railway system distributing national newspapers (Peters 2015: 32). But what kind of novel would be 'consonant' with an age which communicated by means of 'the railroad, electric-telegraph, printing-press' (De Forest 2000: 49)?

An answer might be found in thinking about the 'fundamentally logistical' work that infrastructure does (Peters 2015: 37). Peters's examples of 'logistical media' range from 'calendars, clocks and towers' to 'names, indexes, addresses, maps, lists (like this one), tax rolls, logs, accounts, archives, and the census' (37). Focusing on the former group, he does not elaborate on the work of the census or the map, but Benedict Anderson does. In the revised edition of *Imagined Communities*, Anderson considers the map and the census, along with the museum, as 'institutions' of 'nation-building', shaping the ways in which a state 'imagined its dominion – the nature of the human beings it ruled, the geography of its domain, and the legitimacy of its ancestry' (Anderson 1991: 163-4). The Great American Novel might be thought of as a comparable institution or infrastructure; indeed one that has learnt a great deal from these other forms of logistical imagining.

The literary critic Thomas Sergeant Perry certainly understood the Great American Novel in this way, and he didn't approve. In 1872, Perry complained of a trend towards the kind of novel (written by the likes of De Forest) that informed readers of the length of the Connecticut River and the fact that 'Vermont has thirty-five inhabitants to the square mile'. For all that they were 'accurate to date' with regard to 'the geology, the botany, the ethnography' of the territories constituting the United States, such novels, he argued, were of only 'temporary interest', and would 'lose value at every census'. The 'real novelist', on the other hand, would 'look at life, not as the statistician, not as the census-taker, nor yet as the newspaper reporter, but with the eye that sees, through temporary disguises, the animating principles [...] that direct human existence [....] All truth does not lie in facts' (Perry 1872: 367).

That Perry thought it necessary to issue such a defence of fiction's universality and fictionality is itself an indication of the way in which the American novel had come to be understood, and valued, as a logistical medium, and in particular one that measured national progress in quantitative terms. But if 'the American obsession with size' reached an apotheosis in the late nineteenth century (Clarke 2007: 1), population had been 'integral to how America envisioned itself' from the earliest days of the republic (Prewitt 2013: 35). Each decennial census from 1790 to 1860 saw the population rise by thirty to thirty-five per cent, with notable, and changing, variations between north and south, east and west: in the 1840 census, for example, 'the growth rates in the western states frequently amounted to 100 per cent' while the 1850 and 1860 censuses resulted in the loss of southern representatives in Congress (Anderson 1988: 26, 62). Such radical 'demographic dynamism' meant that the 'imagining' of the nation was as 'inherently unstable' as its political system (62). The only constant was change.

Ralph Waldo Emerson was among those who expressed scepticism about growth as a measure of 'success': 'Our American people cannot be taxed with slowness in their performance or in praising their performance', he noted ironically. 'The world is shaken by our energies. We are feeling our youth and nerve and bone [...] We count our census, we read our valuations, we survey our map which becomes old in a year or two.' These remarks first appeared in a lecture that Emerson gave in the 1850s and repeated, with added warnings about 'brag' and 'advertisement', when he published it in 1870 (Emerson 2007: 143, 147). In the intervening years Americans had continued to count their census and to praise their performance. Fewer immigrants and fewer births, as well as an increase in deaths, meant that growth slowed for the four years of the Civil War, but the years that followed more than made up the shortfall. Immigration was a major factor but 'the single most important new development' was a decline in mortality rates (Klein 2004: 143). In 1889, Francis Walker, the Superintendent of the 1870 and 1880 censuses, and a Union Army veteran himself, was able to refer to the War as simply a four-year 'pause' in the 'course of construction and expansion' (Walker, 1899: 41, 206).

Alert to the 'sneer at "mere bigness"' that enthusiastic talk of 'the growth of the nation' was likely to engender, Walker in turn attacked the 'sententious wisdom' of (unnamed) 'moralists' and the devotion of (unnamed) novelists to 'gauzy, almost immaterial' heroines and 'slender' young men with 'a pale, interesting countenance' (193-4). Who wouldn't prefer to read 'the story of our national growth' (207), the 'big' story told by (resolutely masculine) census-takers and novelists alike? Such stories were not only necessary to do justice to 'the length of our rivers, the height of our mountains, the breadth of our lakes and inland seas, our fast-swelling numbers, our wealth springing aloft, almost in a night' (194), they would also, Walker insisted, reflect the fact that 'quantity has for us determined quality' and so 'helped to make our national character what it is' (209).

'An Interesting Alliance of the Abstract and the Concrete'

During the 1840s, the 'infant statistical community' began to lobby for a 'more professional national statistical system', one that could ask and answer more detailed questions about the population (Anderson 1988: 33). This entailed a shift in the unit of analysis from the household to the individual, and the centralisation of the bureaucracies of information-gathering in Washington. Debated in the context of increasing hostility between free and slave states, these proposals generated more than administrative interest. The 1840 census was widely recognised to have been a 'complete fiasco', the product of 'errors, frauds and political machinations' by pro-slavery campaigners determined to prove that blacks could not cope with freedom (Cohen 1982: 177-8). In *A Key to Uncle Tom's Cabin*, her compendium of the evidence her novel had drawn upon, Harriet Beecher Stowe devoted an appendix to the 1840 census which she entitled 'Facts vs Figures'. If, in the past, figures did not lie, she noted ironically, 'this arose from no native innocence of disposition, but simply from want of occasion or opportunity' (Stowe 1853: 17). The changes to the 1850 census represented an attempt to restore legitimacy to the process, but they also initiated a broader shift in perspective from households (and heads of households) to a dual focus on the individual and the aggregate. 'Pushing toward a new level of social knowledge, the census forged a direct relationship with named individuals, including women and children' – and, in 1850 and 1860, slaves (Wilson 2008: 7). The changes also led to a massive expansion in data collection, one that as the population grew became increasingly difficult to administer. The 1880 census took eight years of hand-counting to

Fig. 1. 'Electrical Counting Machines'. 1890. *Scientific American*, August 30: detail from the cover.

tabulate, and it became clear that something had to be done if the count was to keep up and Congress was to retain legitimacy (Anderson 1988: 45, 84). An 'interest in demographical data' was also intensifying in many other quarters, from industry to the nascent social sciences (Herbst 1993: 18). Gradually the 'purpose of the census' was changing (Anderson 1988: 85).

The dual needs of a full and fast population count and more complex analysis were both answered by the introduction in 1890 of a mechanised system. After experimenting with a machine using perforated tape, a Census Office clerk called Herman Hollerith adapted a technology that had been used by French weavers since the early part of the century: punch cards fed into an electrical tabulating machine. Enumerators gathered data from around the country as usual, then clerks (mainly women) transferred information about each individual onto a single card which was fed into the tabulating machine (manually until 1900). The tabulator used as 'spring-actuated needles' (one for each hole) over a plate of cups partially filled with mercury: wherever there was a hole in the card the needle dipped down into the mercury closing a circuit (Hollerith 1894: 679). The number of circuits were counted and the data then cross-tabulated. *Scientific American* marvelled that the Census Office had been transformed from a 'great counting house' into a 'vast machine shop' ('Mechanical Work' 1902: 275).

Today we're used to having details about ourselves translated into code, but at the end of the nineteenth century the process seemed miraculous. *Scientific American* wondered at the fact that 'by the special location of a hole within the limits of certain boundary lines on the card it means one thing, and in another position it means another thing'. 'Until its values are explained and understood', the card was simply 'a very insignificant and blind piece of pasteboard' (275). The surface of each card – '3 ¼ inches by 6 ⅝ inches' – 'was divided into 288 imaginary spaces ¼ inch square' (Hollerith 1894: 679). As Hollerith later explained:

> To each of these spaces some particular value or meaning is assigned; a hole in one place meaning a white person, in another a black. Here a hole means a certain age-group, there it gives the exact year in that group. A combination of two holes in another part of the card indicates the occupation of the particular individual. (679)

The introduction of the punch card added a further layer of mediation between individuals and the state, its arrangement of holes functioning as 'intermediary instrumentalities' between the 'enumerator's return sheet' (the product of face-to-face interaction until 1970) and the 'tabulating machine' ('Mechanical Work' 1902: 275). But if punch cards pioneered the digital understanding of identity through a 'mere "on" or "off", "yes or "not-yes" response' (Gaddis 2002: 17), it wasn't until they became 'ubiquitous' in the 1940s and 1950s (MacBride 1967: 24) that this process – the translation of 'personality' into a 'combination of holes and nicks' on a 'classification card' (Vonnegut 2012: 72, 70, 206) – came to be seen as sinister. In 1964, protesting students at Berkeley adopted the warning that IBM typically printed on punch cards: 'I am a U.C. student! Please don't fold, spindle or mutilate me!' (Lubar 1992: 44-8).

In 1890, however, the punch-card census was welcomed as a 'manifestation of American efficiency and technological ingenuity' (Heide 2009:15), an 'interesting alliance of the abstract and concrete' ('Census' 1890: 132). The Census Office reported the total population – nearly sixty-three million – after just six weeks, and thirty-two volumes of data appeared within the year (Anderson 1988: 85). But the Hollerith machine did not only revolutionize the speed of the process. It changed the nature of the inquiry itself. By the end of century, although the census remained what it had been since 1790 – a 'political apportionment mechanism' – it had also become what it remains today, an invaluable resource for inquiry into the 'overall state of American society' (85). The census had always been an 'organized counting', motivated by specific anxieties and ambitions (Prewitt 2013: 4), but it was the punch-card revolution that made the decennial count an effective 'instrument for social investigation' and social change (Du Bois 1978: 66).

The census was also an instrument for, or rather a provocation to, narrative, as commentators rushed to suggest what 'wonderful story' lurked within its columns of figures (Wellman 1900: 470). Novelists also joined in. In *Equality*, Edward Bellamy's 1897 sequel to *Looking Backward*, 'hard, cold statistics' initiate the tale of 'the subversion of the American Republic by the plutocracy'. At one point, the protagonist is shown a set of tables 'prepared in 1893 by a census official from the returns of the United States census' in order to demonstrate that 'out of sixty-two billions of wealth in the country a group of millionaires and multimillionaires, representing three one-hundredths of one percent of the population, owned twelve billions, or one fifth'. Add in the 'rich and well-to-do', and the remaining 91% of the population can be 'classed as the poor' (Bellamy 1897: 320-1).

Not every novelist used statistics for quite such direct educational purposes. Sinclair Lewis evokes the census for largely satirical purposes. In 1920 Lewis had published *Main Street*, a novel set in Gopher Prairie, Minnesota, a 'town of a few thousand', so small that you can walk around it in thirty-two minutes. 'This is America', Lewis declared (Lewis 1920: n.p.). Only it wasn't. One of the notable landmarks recorded by the 1920 census was the fact that a small majority of Americans – 51.2% – now lived in cities (Boehm and Corey 2015: 184). Before the year was out, Lewis set to work on *Babbitt*, another self-conscious attempt at the Great American Novel, but one that caught up with the data. 'I want the novel to be the G.A.N.', he wrote to a friend, 'in so far as it crystallizes and makes real the Average Capable American' (Lewis 1952: 59). His eponymous hero was a real-estate salesman obsessed with the position of his medium-sized city in the national rankings.

> It is true that even with our 361,000, or practically 362,000, population, there are, by the last census, almost a score of larger cities in the United States. [...] if by the next census we do not stand at least tenth, then I'll be the first to request any knocker to remove my shirt and to eat the same, with the compliments of G.F. Babbitt, Esquire! (Lewis 2002: 181)

In these examples, census data is offered as a particular kind of logistical medium that the capacious form of the novel can absorb and employ for its own (utopian or satirical) purposes. But although Lewis originally planned to confine the action of *Babbitt* to a single (census?) day, neither he nor Bellamy suggests that the novel itself should be thought of as counting the nation. Other aspirants to the Great American Novel, however, approached the challenge of national coverage from a different perspective.

'All the Accumulated Details'

In 1892, an editorial in the *Nation* argued that novelists had more or less given up on the idea of the Great American Novel, the 'single work' whose arrival had been promised for twenty five years and which would 'embody, while it unified, all the diverse elements of our national character'. Instead of struggling to produce the G.A.N., the *Nation* said, might American writers not be better employed producing a 'series of regional novels – or rather, so far has the dividing and minimizing process gone [...] local tales, neighbourhood sketches, short stories confined to the author's back-yard'? 'Is it not necessary', the magazine asked, 'to make a minute study of each local detail of character before we undertake a novel?' And to employ a team of writers, rather than expect 'one brain' to 'grasp all the accumulated details' and 'blend them into a harmonious whole'? The *Nation* noted 'possibilities in collaboration', and suggested that novelists of the future might perhaps take advantage of the 'calculators and tabulators in the Census Office which work by electricity': 'it would be peculiarly American', it joked, 'to bring labour-saving devices into the service and creation of the great American novel' ('Great American Novel' 1892: 224). While the article begins by suggesting that the labour of American literature be shared by 'dividing and minimizing' the task into 'local tales' produced by many hands, it ends by arguing that these individual efforts might after all cumulatively result, through the new 'techniques of aggregation', in a single story (Herbst 1993: 85).

The question of how particular stories might add up to a national whole was frequently rehearsed. In 1892, for example, introducing a new edition of his 1871 novel *The Hoosier School-Master*, Edward Eggleston praised the 'provincial movement in our literature' for having made 'our literature really national by the only process possible':

> The Federal nation has at length manifested a consciousness of the continental diversity of its forms of life. The 'great American novel', for which prophetic critics yearned so fondly twenty years ago, is appearing in sections. (Eggleston 1892: 7)

Eggleston's novel offered just one 'section' – a backyard in backwoods Indiana. For Americans to recognise the complete 'soul of the people', Mark Twain argued, they would need to read 'a thousand able novels', a great American library (Twain, 1892: 52). In the spirit of 'labour-saving', others felt that a short story anthology could do a similar job (Boddy 2015).

William Dean Howells made much the same point in 1891: on the one hand, he was pleased to observe that 'American life is getting represented with unexampled fullness'; on the other, 'no one writer, no one book, represents it, for this is not possible' (Howells 1959: 68). Reviewing H.H. Boyesen's *The Mammon of Unrighteousness* as the latest attempt at the G.A.N., he repeated the point: 'Of course [Boyesen] has not got America all in'. What readers required for American fullness was, if not the logistical infrastructure of the census itself, then the political structure that the census was designed to produce. Howells called for 'a force of novelists apportioned upon the basis of our Congressional representation, and working under one editorial direction' (Howells 1891: 317).

But how might representation – in the sense of 'an artistic likeness or image' – relate to representation – in the sense of 'the action or fact of one person standing for another so as to have the rights and obligations of the person represented'? As the Merriam-Webster Dictionary explains, 'the rationale of representative government is that [...] the people cannot all assemble [...] If the public is to participate in government, citizens must select a small number from among themselves to act for them.' But if the people cannot all assemble, the nature of representative government does require that the people all be counted so that the correct number of representatives per head can be allocated. In these terms, what constituency, what 'section', might each novelist or short story writer adequately represent? The lives of a hundred Americans? Ten? Or would one or two do? If Boyesen fails to get it 'all in', Howells believes that he nonetheless manages to represent more than a narrow 'section'. Indeed, using the traditional allegorical device of warring brothers, Boyesen succeeds in being 'just to both sides of the national character [...] the beauty of the idea and the ugliness of the material' (317). Howells – the great champion of realism's democratic extensiveness – sees no problem here in its concession, or capitulation, to allegorical abstraction.

The *fin-de-siècle* debate about representation through aggregation or allegory also informs Gertrude Stein's 900-page novel, *The Making of Americans, Being the Story of a Family's Progress* (1925). The title, and sheer size, of the book suggest an unswerving commitment to a story that will 'get it all in'; the subtitle something more circumspect or, in its allusion to Bunyan, allegorical. Stein began working on the novel in 1903 but abandoned it after a few months, only returning to the project in 1906, after completing *Three Lives*. Around that time she wrote to a friend: 'I am afraid that I can never write the Great American novel. I dn't [sic] know how to sell on a margin or to do anything with shorts and longs, so I have to content myself with niggers and servant girls and the foreign population generally' (Wald 1995: 239-40). The suggestion here is that 'niggers and servant girls and the foreign population generally' somehow belong to the short story, to the 'sections' of local colour, rather than to the national epic of the 'monotonous middle class' (Stein 1995: 34). The collection's title is modest – offering a limited number of increments towards the national census – and Stein's letter suggests that she, as a woman, a Jew, a lesbian, perhaps also belonged to the modest margins of representation (Wald 1995: 242). But *Three Lives* was not modest. Stein took the short story's fascination with typology and subjected it to a complete overall. Particularly daring is the book's final story, 'Melanctha', which she later described as 'the first definite step away from the nineteenth century and into the twentieth century in literature' (Stein 1966: 61).

In *The Making of Americans*, Stein relocates her attention to the transformation of the 'foreign population' into the 'ordinary middle class' (Stein 1995: 34) over the relatively short period of 'scarcely sixty years': 'We need only realise our parents, remember our grandparents and know ourselves and our history is complete' (3). The joke lies in the 'only'. More than nine hundred pages follow in which the complexities of realisation, remembering, knowing, and completion itself are teased out.

For Stein, aggregation and abstraction were not distinct methodologies: an individual, or family, class, or nation, could only be understood in terms of 'the kind of being that makes him' (136). And yet she acknowledges that a 'completer' understanding of that 'kind' developed 'gradually', cumulatively (330). So, for example, the second-generation American David Hersland is introduced as 'big and abundant and full of new ways of thinking' (42) – qualities that 'immediately identify him as a typical American' (Haselstein 2010: 231). In the pages that follow, those epithets are repeated but they are also joined by others: 'abundant and forceful and joyous and determined and always powerful in starting', and so on (Stein 1995: 43). Some qualities are 'always' present; others appear 'sometimes' (46), but Stein's ambition, as she later put it, was to present 'a continuous succession of the statement of what that person was until I had not many things but one thing' (176-7).

To consider what Stein meant in coming to define 'what that person was', it is perhaps necessary to consider traditional ways in which storytellers positions themselves in relation to the census. Since at least the eighteenth century, census-takers had appeared in stories, poems, and novels as foils for some other, better, kind of storyteller. In the humorous sketches of the 1840s Southwest, for example, the enumerator is just one example of an outside interrogator who falls victim to the native guile of characters who remain deeply suspicious of 'misrepresentation' by 'Washington city' (Hooper 1845: 153). The 'tension between the local and the national' (Pratt 2010: 152) that such tales exemplify also features in the mid-twentieth-century work of Langston Hughes. In one story, Jesse B. Simple – the recurrent protagonist of Hughes's popular *Chicago Defender* tales – offers a census-taker excessive 'data' about his 'corns and bunions' (Hughes 2002: 153), while a poem entitled 'Madam and the Census-Taker' presents Alberta K Johnson's argument with an enumerator about the letter 'K' – he won't accept that it's not an initial but her middle name (Hughes 2001: 174). These pieces are humorous, but they make serious points – in Simple's case, about the lack of attention paid to the reality of 'underfed, underpaid, undernourished' and largely under-represented black life; in the case of Madam Johnson, about who controls identity. These were hardly new concerns. For the first eighty years of the republic, in accordance with the Constitution, each slave had been counted as 'three fifths' of a 'free Person' (Article 1, Section 2). Knowing this, who could have faith in the realism of the census?

Fortunately, what 'the census did not say' provided opportunities for storytellers (Jones 2003: 21). William Faulkner's 'Go Down Moses' begins with a detailed description of a man: his 'black, smooth, impenetrable' face, his pleated trousers, his half-lying posture, his voice which, we're told, 'was anything under the sun but a southern voice or even a negro voice' (Faulkner 1982: 277). Readers might be intrigued by this combination of details, but the 'spectacled white man sitting with a broad census-taker's portfolio' opposite is not. The enumerator asks a few questions, largely ignores the answers, and then departs, leaving Faulkner to tell us properly about Samuel Worsham Beauchamp, as he awaits execution in an Illinois jail.

Tales like this suggest that the job of the census-taker is not compatible with that of the storyteller. 'To assign numbers to observed particulars', says the cultural historian Mary Poovey, 'is to make them amenable to the kind of knowledge system that privileges quantity over quality and equivalence over difference' (Poovey 1998: 4). While the enumerator, in search of quantity, believes the individual deserves attention because he or she is 'essentially a duplicate of every other individual in the aggregate' (Adams 2011: 108), the storyteller insists on qualitative difference – every one is unlike every other one else, and the more idiosyncratic the better.

One way of understanding the Great American Novel envisaged by De Forest, Howells and so many others, is as a logistical medium designed to reconcile quality and quantity, difference and equivalence. In the tradition of Balzac's *Comédie Humaine*, the G.A.N. was a narrative that relied on 'types [that] are also characters, [in the sense of] living men' (Howells 1891: 317). The sign that they were indeed 'living men' (or women) was the incompleteness of their representative status, their deviation from type. This was something that Howells's friend Henry James repeatedly insisted upon, relying on typology while demonstrating that it was 'treacherous as well as useful' (Bell 1991: 48). In *The Bostonians* (1885-1886), for example, Olive Chancellor has a 'theory' that her 'wonderful young friend' Verena Tennant is not merely, as she styles herself, 'a simple American girl' but rather 'a flower of the great Democracy' (James 2000: 50, 86). But if we are encouraged to identify this epithet as an unconvincing piece of marketing, equally unsatisfying is the notion, proposed by Mr Tennant, that his daughter is 'quite unique' (78). That claims to singularity are merely another form of type-casting, or brand-shaping, becomes clear when Verena's suitor Basil Ransom repeats that she is 'unique, extraordinary [...] a category by [her]self' (262). Categories are inevitable, no matter how many members they contain.

When Stein insisted that every 'one thing' is 'a completely different one from any other one' (902), she was not issuing an injunction to consider the individuating detail that 'animates' character; rather, this proposition led her to consider how 'real singularity' might itself be a 'habit' associated with 'us'

Americans (Stein 1995: 34). Stein was not making the point that Emerson rehearsed again and again: that 'genius' (a quality associated with inner 'growth of mind') 'belongs to all' and should be valued in so far as it takes us 'out of relation to mass and number: the census is insignificant; territory is dwarfed' (Emerson 2010a: 201-2). For Stein, the inner life has no such power, the census is never insignificant, and the qualities that make individuals 'eccentric' or 'queer' are themselves products of some process analogous to 'the type-writing which is our only way of thinking [...] always the same way' (Stein 1995: 47). Furthermore, as Barbara Will suggests, if 'the "singular" American is the "typical" American', then 'to write about "types" or to write about Americans – which may be the same thing – is to become in some sense a type-writer' (Will 2000: 112-13). Henry James had also punned on 'type' in *The Ambassadors* (1903), describing Maria Gostrey as someone who 'pigeon-holed her fellow mortals with a hand as free as a compositor scattering type' (James 1998: 7).

Type-writing is not simply writing mechanically or 'monotonously', however, nor even, as some have suggested, as a woman (Cecire 2015); it is writing 'continuously'. And this has implications for the novel's sense of what being a 'complete thing' or rather a 'completed thing', might mean (Stein 1995: 860).

In his Introduction to *The Making of Americans*, Steven Meyer notes the tension between two kinds of completion in the novel: eternal and historical (xxxv). Outside of history we encounter the totality of 'a thing not beginning and not ending' (701); that is, the kind of completion characteristic of novels of unchanging truths favoured by the likes of T.S. Perry. The challenge of eternal completion produces anxieties for Stein, as she wonders whether her novel might merely be 'right about a very great many' (574) or only 'almost completely expressing' (903). But, thinking in terms of historical completion, Stein recognises both that classification evolves – 'categories that once to some one had real meaning can later to that same one be empty' (440) – and that 'complete description' is not in fact 'such a very extensive thing [...] finally it can be done' (Stein 1957: 153). Moreover, historical classification and completion is not just 'done', it is 'done by some one. The one that did that thing began it and went on with it and finished it' (Stein 1995: 860). T.S. Perry had dismissed this kind of completion as akin to that achieved by the census and therefore not properly literary. But for Stein, 'counting everything by one and one and one' was simply what the 'making' of novels, as well as Americans, entailed (560). She compared both to the 'metallic clicking' of type-writing (47) and the 'put[ting] together' of a Ford from its 'pieces' (Stein 1966: 252).

All three of these common early-twentieth-century metaphors – typing, assembly lines, and, as I've suggested, the census – also highlight the temporary nature of completion. As soon as one car is built, the parts for the next appear on the conveyer belt, as soon as one count is finished, the Census

Office starts devising new questions for the next, and as soon as the Great American Novel is typed out, it needs to be typed out again:

> relatively few people spend all their time describing anything and they stop and so in the meantime as everything goes on somebody else can always commence and go on. And so description is really unending. (Stein 1957: 156)

Epics have often thematised their own incompletion – think of Ishmael's declaration in *Moby-Dick* that 'this whole book is but a draught – nay, but the draught of a draught' (Melville 1988: 147) – but what is new here is the unapologetic acknowledgement of built-in conceptual as well as logistical obsolescence. After all, as John Updike would note of his almost-decennial Rabbit novels (1960-1990), the 'state of the nation' requires a 'running report' (Updike 2006: 425).

Works Cited

Adams, Maeve E. 2011. 'Numbers and Narratives: Epistemologies of Aggregation in British Statistics and Social Realism, c.1790-1880'. In *Statistics and the Public Sphere: Numbers and the People in Modern Britain, c. 1800-2000*, edited by Tom Crook and Glen O'Hara, 103-120. New York: Routledge.

Anderson, Benedict. 1991. *Imagined Communities*. Revised edition. London: Verso.

Anderson, Margo. J. 1988. *The American Census: A Social History*. New Haven: Yale University Press.

Bell, Millicent. 1991. *Meaning in Henry James*. Cambridge: Harvard University Press.

Bellamy, Edward. 1897. *Equality*. Toronto: George N. Morang.

Boehm, Lisa Kissoff, and Steven Hunt Corey. 2015. *America's Urban History*. New York: Routledge.

Boddy, Kasia. 2015. '"Variety in Unity, Unity in Variety": The Liminal Space of the American Short Story Anthology'. In *Liminality and the Short Story: Boundary Crossings in American, Canadian, and British Writing*, edited by Jochem Achilles and Ina Bergmann, 145-56. New York: Routledge.

'The Census of the United States'. 1890. *Scientific American*, August 30: 132.

Cicere, Natalia. 2015. 'Ways of Not Reading Gertrude Stein'. *ELH* 82: 281-312.

Clarke, Michael Tavel. 2007. *These Days of Large Things: The Culture of Size in America, 1865-1930*. Ann Arbor: University of Michigan Press.

Cohen, Patrica Cline. 1982. *A Calculating People: The Spread of Numeracy in Early America*. Chicago: University of Chicago Press.

De Forest, John W. 1868. 'The Great American Novel'. *Nation*, January 9: 27-9.

De Forest, John W. 2000. *Miss Ravenel's Conversion from Secession to Loyalty*. London: Penguin.

Du Bois, W.E.B. 1978. *On Sociology and the Black Community*. Edited by Dan S. Green and Edwin D. Driver. Chicago: University of Chicago Press.

Eggleston, Edward. 1892. *The Hoosier School-Master*. New York: Appleton and Company.

Emerson, Ralph Waldo. 2007. 'Success'. In *The Collected Works of Ralph Waldo Emerson*, volume 7, edited by Ronald A. Bosco and Douglas Emory Wilson, 143-58. Cambridge: Harvard University Press.

Emerson, Ralph Waldo. 2010a. 'Genius and Temperament, 9 April 1861'. In *The Later Lectures of Ralph Waldo Emerson 1843-1871*, volume 2, edited by Ronald A. Bosco and Joel Myerson, 200-210. Athens: University of Georgia Press.

Emerson, Ralph Waldo. 2010b. 'The Scholar'. In *The Later Lectures of Ralph Waldo Emerson 1843-1871*, volume 2, edited by Ronald A. Bosco and Joel Myerson, 302-318. Athens: University of Georgia Press.

Faulkner, William. 1982. *Go Down, Moses and Other Stories*. Harmondsworth: Penguin.

Gaddis, William. 2002. 'Treatment for a Motion Picture on "Software" (early 1960s)'. In *The Rush for Second Place: Essays and Occasional Writings*, edited by Joseph Tabbi, 16-25. London: Penguin.

'The Great American Novel'. 1892. *Nation*, March 24: 224.

Haselstein, Ulla. 2010. 'Gertrude Stein and Seriality'. In *A Companion to Twentieth-Century United States Fiction*, edited by David Seed, 229-39. Oxford: Wiley-Blackwell.

Heide, Lars. 2009. *Punched-Card Systems and the Early Information Explosion, 1880-1945*. Baltimore: Johns Hopkins University Press.

Herbst, Susan. 1993. *Numbered Voices: How Opinion Polling Has Shaped American Politics*. Chicago: University of Chicago Press.

Hollerith, Herman. 1894. 'The Electrical Tabulating Machine'. *Journal of the Royal Statistical Society* 57: 678-89.

[Hooper, Johnson Jones]. 1845. *Some Adventures of Captain Simon Suggs, Late of the Tallapoosa Volunteers; Together with 'Taking the Census' and Other Alabama Sketches. By a Country Editor*. Philadelphia: Carey and Hart.

Howells, William Dean. 1891. 'Editor's Study'. *Harper's New Monthly Magazine*, July: 314-18.

Howells, William Dean. 1959. *Criticism and Fiction and Other Essays*. Edited by Clara Marburg Kirk and Rudolf Kirk. New York: New York University Press.

Hughes, Langston. 2001. *The Collected Works of Langston Hughes*. Volume 2. Edited by Arnold Rampersad. Columbus: University of Missouri Press.

Hughes, Langston. 2002. *The Collected Works of Langston Hughes*. Volume 8. Edited by Donna Akiba Sullivan Harper. Columbus: University of Missouri Press.

James, Henry. 1998. *The Ambassadors*. Oxford: Oxford University Press.

James, Henry. 2000. *The Bostonians*. London: Penguin.

Jones, Edward P. 2003. *The Known World*. London: HarperPerennial.

Klein, Herbert S. 2004. *A Population History of the United States*. Cambridge: Cambridge University Press.

Lewis, Sinclair. 1920. *Main Street*. New York: P.F. Collier.

Lewis, Sinclair. 1952. *From Main Street to Stockholm: Letters of Sinclair Lewis*. Edited by Harrison Smith. New York: Harcourt, Brace.

Lewis, Sinclair. 2002. *Babbitt*. New York: Modern Library.

Lubar, Steven. 1992. '"Do Not Fold, Spindle or Mutilate": A Cultural History of the Punch Card'. *Journal of American Culture* 15: 43-55.

MacBride, Robert. 1967. *The Automated State: Computer Systems as a New Force in Society*. Philadelphia: Chilton.

'The Mechanical Work of the Twelfth Census'. 1902. *Scientific American*, April 19: 275.

Melville, Herman. 1988. *Moby-Dick*. Oxford: Oxford University Press.

Perry, T.S. 1872. 'American Novels'. *North American Review* 115: 366-9.

Peters, John Durham. 2015. *The Marvelous Clouds*. Chicago: University of Chicago Press.

Poovey, Mary. 1998. *A History of the Modern Fact*. Chicago: University of Chicago Press.

Pratt, Lloyd. 2010. *Archives of Time: Literature and Modernity in the Nineteenth Century*. Philadelphia: University of Pennsylvania Press.

Prewitt, Kenneth. 2013. *What is Your Race? The Census and Our Flawed Efforts to Classify Americans*. Princeton: Princeton University Press.

Stein, Gertrude. 1957. *Lectures in America*. Boston: Beacon Press.

Stein, Gertrude. 1966. *The Autobiography of Alice B. Toklas*. Harmondsworth: Penguin.

Stein, Gertrude. 1995. *The Making of Americans*. Normal: Dalkey Archive.

Twain, Mark. 1895. 'What Paul Bourget Thinks of Us'. *New American Review*, January: 48-62.

Updike, John. 2006. 'Afterword by the Author'. In *Rabbit is Rich*, 426-40. London: Penguin.

Vonnegut, Kurt. 2012. *Novels and Stories 1950-1962*. New York: Library of America.

Wald, Patricia. 1995. *Constituting Americans: Cultural Anxiety and Narrative Form*. Durham: Duke University Press.

Walker, Francis A. 1899. *Discussions in Economics and Statistics*. Volume 2. New York: Henry Holt.

Will, Barbara, 2000. *Gertrude Stein, Modernism and the Problem of 'Genius'*. Edinburgh: Edinburgh University Press.

Wilson, Mark. E. 2008. 'Law and the American State, From the Revolution to the Civil War: Institutional Growth and Structural Change'. In *The Cambridge History of Law in America*, volume 2, edited by Michael Grossberg and Christopher Tomlins, 1-35. Cambridge: Cambridge University Press.

4

The *Milieu* Is the Message: Henry James and Mediation

JOHN ATTRIDGE

Let us begin with a text and a moral. My text is *What Maisie Knew* (1897), the fruit of an idea that James first jotted down in 1892, but which he only began to develop three years later, after his unhappy experiment with the theatre had run its course (James 1981: 126-7). And as moral, I propose the following: to grow up in Henry James is to become aware of mediation. *What Maisie Knew* is, famously, a virtuoso attempt to chart the development of a child's 'small expanding consciousness' from the child's own point of view, so that James's narrative records, not only the farcical erotic *pas de quatre* that ensues after Maisie's parents divorce, but also the progressive enlargement of her capacity to make sense of these unedifying phenomena. One of the most striking set-pieces in this latter project is James's description, in the novel's second chapter, of how Maisie becomes aware of being used by her parents as an unwitting courier of verbal abuse. Prior to this realisation, her participation in Beale and Ida Farange's remote exchange of insults had been ingenuous and unconscious, as James underlines by figuring her, not as a sentient message-bearer, but in the guise of a series of objects and tools. Maisie is the 'shuttlecock' in a game of emotional badminton, the 'receptacle' into which her parents pour their vitriol, and, ultimately, the apparatus of the postal service: her memory receives 'objurgation[s]' with the mechanical efficiency of a 'pillar-box', and they are later retrieved from this 'well-stuffed post-bag' and 'delivered [...] at the right address' (James 1996a: 22). As this last image makes explicit, Maisie has been used as a medium of communication, a fact that, when it dawns upon her, brings about 'a moral revolution' in 'the depths of her nature' (22). The nature of this revolution is, doubtless, overdetermined, and surely encompasses a developmental psychology of secrecy and interiority, but the precise circumstances under which Maisie acquires the ability to keep secrets and simulate ignorance also seem to invite a more particular interpretation. It is important to this interpretation that Maisie's discovery of her 'inner self' coincides precisely with her 'complete vision' of 'the strange office she filled' – with, that is, her realization that she has been enlisted as a medium (22-3).

When James tells us that, prior to this discovery, Maisie existed in 'that lively sense of the immediate which is the very air of a child's mind', in which the 'actual was the absolute, the present alone was vivid', he is not only, I suggest, citing a commonplace of juvenile time perception, but also saying something particular about the mediation of experience. Maisie passes from a state of consciousness in which everything is 'immediate' to one in which experience and knowledge can be mediated (22).

During the course of the same episode, Maisie makes another, related discovery about the ways in which information can be mediated. Quizzing her governess, Miss Overmore, about the meaning of one of her mother's insults, Maisie is enlightened, 'not by anything she said', but by 'a mere roll of those fine eyes' – a nonverbal signal which allows Miss Overmore to preserve a discreet reticence while conveying a wealth of unspoken meaning (23). Using the device of subjunctive dialogue that occurs with increasing frequency in the late novels, James translates the 'unmistakeable language of a pair of eyes of deep dark grey' into its remarkably subtle verbal equivalent (24). It is this act of communication that sows the 'seeds of secrecy' in Maisie's nature: interpreting Miss Overmore's eloquent eye-roll teaches her that she, too, might employ a strategy of discretion – practice the 'pacific art of stupidity' – in order to jam the exchange of insults between her parents (23, 63).

The ability to decipher the 'language' of looks will prove to be a valuable acquisition. It is, indeed, not too much to say that Miss Overmore's eye-roll initiates Maisie into the possibilities of encrypted communication and concealed meaning that will preoccupy her for the remainder of the novel. Reading nonverbal cues is one important way in which she exercises her 'sharpened sense for latent meanings': her capacity to infer 'the unuttered and the unknown' from the statements and behaviour of her elders (189, 135). When her father, for instance, attempts to draw a veil of noble self-sacrifice across the ugly fact of abandoning his daughter, Maisie 'understood as well as if he had spoken it that what he wanted, hang it, was that she should let him off with all the honours', receiving loud and clear the face-saving instructions he 'communicated in a series of tremendous pats on the back' (148). Sir Claude, similarly, is able to explain Mrs Beale's jealousy of Mrs Wix in a 'wink' (162). Earlier, an intercepted 'quick queer look' between him and Mrs Wix speaks volumes to Maisie about their complicity, and Maisie is herself able to exchange tolerably precise communications with Mrs Wix in Sir Claude's presence by means of 'compressed lips and enlarged eyes' (78, 83). That the air of *What Maisie Knew* is thick with such gestural and physiognomic messages is not in itself surprising: nonverbal communication is one of the standard props of nineteenth-century realism. Nonetheless, we should be attentive to the importance James assigns to something as banal as a roll of the eyes in the narrative of Maisie's psychological development, as well as to the ostentatious gap he inserts between the innocuous gesture and its highly sophisticated meaning. It might be unidiomatic to describe

Miss Overmore's face as a medium of communication at this moment, but it would perhaps be less unnatural to say that part of what James wants us to notice about this epiphany is Maisie's dawning awareness of mediation itself. Miss Overmore's eye-roll teaches her that information can be stored without being transmitted (these are the 'seeds of secrecy'), but also that this is how information circulates: it is mediated, fungible, translatable from one code (looks) into another (words). In short, Maisie leaves the 'immediate' world of childhood, becomes aware that she herself has been used as a medium, and learns a lesson about the way the information she craves is mediated, all at the same time.

By beginning with this episode, I want to draw attention to the way that mediums and mediation in James can turn up in unexpected places. As Mark Goble has compellingly shown, the paradoxes of modern connectedness are distributed pervasively throughout James's later novels, traceable not only in their figuration of new media technologies, but also in the very '"indirectness"' of Jamesian style (Goble 2010: 20). The novels of the so-called 'major phase' are shaped 'as much by the sheer "romance" of connection as by the material conditions of media technology', and explore the ways that communication at a distance 'distend[s] and disfigure[s] the idea of proximity itself' (62, 79). In what follows, I too want to explore the ways in which technical mediums of communication in James's novels form part of a larger process of reflection on mediation. Whereas, however, Goble's argument about 'the "romance" of connection' focuses primarily on the displaced 'pleasures' and ambient 'erotic noise' that James was able to locate in experiences of intimate distantiation (72-3), the structure of feeling that I wish to trace below is not specifically related to eros or desire. One aim of this essay is simply to show that James's representation of media and communication blurs the line between things that we are accustomed to refer to as communication media and other things – a small child, a glance – that do not at first seem to belong to this category. More particularly, I will try to trace, within James's reluctance to equate mediation with any particular medium of communication, a fleeting image in his late novels of a different kind of medium, irreducible to any concrete object or process or event. At these moments, James seems to contemplate the medium as a kind of general condition, above or behind or beyond the world of media as conventionally conceived.

I don't want to overstate the distinctiveness of this way of thinking about media: to see mediation or mediatedness as a condition that transcends any given medium is scarcely an unorthodox position in the history and theory of media and communications. As its subtitle suggests, Marshall McLuhan's *Understanding Media: The Extensions of Man* (1964) itself positioned media studies as an aggressively expansionist branch of anthropology, rather than the humble investigation of communication technologies. McLuhan's definition of a 'medium' as 'any extension of ourselves' was abstract enough to group obvious media like print, television, and radio together with an eclectic range of phenomena not normally considered under this rubric – money, clothing, electric light – while his never-clearly-defined concept of 'sense ratios' implies that media must be studied as part of an integrated cultural system (McLuhan 1967: 15, 27, 55). Reflecting on McLuhan's legacy in *Understanding Media: A Popular Philosophy*, Dominic Boyer suggests that at least part of McLuhan's usefulness for contemporary media theorists is historical, as a witness to 'a rising sense, across the nineteenth and twentieth centuries, of the presence of what I will term the "medial" dimension of human life' (Boyer 2007: 25). What Boyer retains from McLuhan's project is thus its defamiliarizing strategy of abstraction, which refuses to reduce mediation, or the 'medial', to the empirical existence of media technologies.

Thus, while it might seem unnatural to see a facial expression and a telegram, say, as part of the same inquiry into the nature of mediation, the principle that the meaning of media extends beyond the history of technology is a familiar media studies doctrine, of which other examples could be given. As a further inducement to place Miss Overmore's eye-roll in the context of a modern media ecology, we might also recall that, as David Trotter has pointed out, one of the senses of the word 'telegraphy' refers to just this kind of nonverbal communication (Trotter 2014). This meaning is recorded in the *OED* ('To make signs; signal [*to* a person]'), which dates its first printed appearance to 1818, but more opportune in the context of a discussion of Henry James is the entry for 'telegraph, v.' in the *Century Dictionary*, first published from 1889 to 1891, and reissued in a revised edition ten years later. The *Century* illustrates the sense in which to telegraph is simply '[t]o signal; communicate by signs' with two recent examples, one from Samuel White Baker's memoir *In the Heart of Africa* (1884) and the other from Henry James's 1888 story 'The Liar' (Whitney 1889-1891). This latter example of the usage – 'Besides, I hate smirking and telegraphing' – is uttered by Mrs Capadose, now married to the 'liar' of James's title but recipient, some years before, of a marriage proposal from the story's central character, the artist Oliver Lyon (James 1999: 332). It is the unexpected renewal of this association at a country-house party that occasions Lyon's unsuccessful attempt to attract her attention across the table at dinner, and later her profession of distaste for such non-verbal signals.

The implication of this example from 'The Liar' is that 'telegraphing', within the highly differentiated spectrum of Jamesian social relations, means not only to 'communicate by signs', but more particularly to do so in a gauche or obvious manner. This more specialized sense is also evident in *What Maisie Knew*, where 'telegraphy' describes the habit of silent communication established between Maisie and her governess, Mrs Wix. When Mrs Beale (formerly Miss Overmore) joins this duo unexpectedly at their hotel in Boulogne, she temporarily interrupts their habitual exchange of signals by monopolising Mrs Wix's attention:

It struck Maisie even a little that there was a rope or two Mrs Wix might have thrown out if she would, a rocket or two she might have sent up. They had at any rate never been so long together without communion or telegraphy, and their companion kept them apart by simply keeping them with her. (James 1996a: 231)

Richard Menke suggests that this passage expresses 'Maisie's desire for shared, silent contact', and that for 'Maisie as well as for the telegraph's enthusiasts, the phenomenon of telegraphy suggests the fantasy of telepathy' (Menke 2008: 206). The conventional sense of 'telegraph' recorded in the *Century*, however, as well as James's use of the verb in 'The Liar', *What Maisie Knew*, and elsewhere, suggest that 'telepathy' may imply a somewhat more exalted picture of interpersonal communication than the one James intended to convey. By contrast with immediate thought transference – certainly, as Menke shows, one of the dreams of Victorian media culture – social 'telegraphy' is insistently, even clumsily mediated by physical bodies. That 'telegraphing' is a vulgar or ridiculous mode of communication is also the implication of James's use of the term in *The Tragic Muse* (1890), where it is the tacky Mrs Rooth who signals ineffectually to Peter Sheringham through the window of the Rooths' rented house (James 1989: 1200). If, then, like Menke, I do wish to discern in James's use of 'telegraphy' here some residual association with the Victorian electric telegraph, the connotation I want to insist upon is simply that of mediation itself. Far from allowing immediate thought transference, social signalling depends upon 'smirking' and other more or less clunky mediations, just as sending a telegram required the intervention of a sophisticated technical process.

Sending a telegram, at least, in the manner permitted by the telecommunication technologies of 1897. At precisely the same moment that *What Maisie Knew* began appearing in serial form, in January of that year, the imagination of the transatlantic public was seized by a new form of telegraphic transmission, promising even more suggestive affinities with direct inter-mental communication than its predecessor. The possibility of electrical telegraphy without the mediation of conducting wires had been investigated by a variety of scientists and experimenters before Guglielmo Marconi submitted his patent for wireless electromagnetic transmission in June 1896. As early as 1838, the German C.A. Steinheil had successfully transmitted electrical impulses through the earth across a distance of fifty feet, and in 1842 Samuel Morse used the Washington City Canal to complete a telegraphic circuit connecting the opposing banks (Fahie 1901: 3, 10-11). The crucial scientific breakthrough in wireless communication, however, was the discovery by Hermann von Helmholtz in 1887-1888 of a method for generating high-oscillation, electromagnetic waves – an innovation which ultimately formed the basis for Marconi's 1896 patent (Hong 2001: 2-9, 17-23). Marconi's invention, enthusiastically presented to the public in a lecture by

Fig. 1. Edward Tennyson Reed. 1899. 'Wireless Telegraphy'. *Punch*, April 26: 204.

the P.O.'s engineer-in-chief, W.H. Preece, on 11 December 1896, precipitated a torrent of popular and journalistic discussion in the early months of 1897. As the engineer and historian J.J. Fahie observed two years later, 1897 opened with a 'great flutter in the dove-cotes of telegraphy', accompanied by a slew of '[m]ysterious paragraphs about the New, Wireless, or Space Telegraphy' (Fahie 1899: xi).

The possibility of communication by means of waves traveling through the ether seemed to provide an even more auspicious analogue for direct telepathic communication than the transmission of signals via electrical 'fluid'. To take only one example from a voluminous and well-documented discourse, an 1899 *Punch* cartoon by Edward Tennyson Reed depicts the Leader of the Opposition, Sir Henry Campbell-Bannerman, 'silently catechizing' the Conservative Prime Minister Arthur Balfour across the dispatch box, with the aid of antennae protruding from his skull (Figure 1). A caption explains that question time will, 'of course', be transformed by the 'discoveries of Signor Marconi'. Further elaboration of the cartoon's premise is considered redundant: any contemporary reader could be expected to make the short conceptual leap from Marconi's ethereal signalling masts to personal antennae, transmitting not coded messages but thought itself.

To 'telegraph' is to 'communicate by signs': not to engage in immediate thought-transference. The availability of 'telegraphy' to describe both a new communication technology and a mundane feature of face-to-face interaction is significant, in *What Maisie Knew*, because it invites us to think about this latter source of information as a medium, too. But while Maisie's social encounters never approach the immediate communion depicted in the *Punch* cartoon, there is one scene in the novel in which James seems to dwell upon the possibility of immaterial communication that Marconi's invention heralded. Left alone by Sir Claude in their sumptuous seaside hotel at Boulogne, and returning earlier than expected from a day of sightseeing, Maisie and Mrs Wix decide, at the suggestion of their coachman, to fill in the time before dinner with a promenade on the beach. Constantly in the background of this touristic interlude is a prolonged, episodic discussion of Maisie's 'moral sense', and it is in the context of this highly-strung conversation that Maisie imagines the logical endpoint of her growing store of knowledge (214-15):

> She judged that if her whole history, for Mrs Wix, had been the successive stages of her knowledge, so the very climax of the concatenation would, in the same view, be the stage at which the knowledge should overflow. As she was condemned to know more and more, how could it logically stop before she should know Most? It came to her in fact as they sat there on the sands that she was distinctly on the road to know Everything. She had not had governesses for nothing: what in the world had she ever done but learn and learn and learn? She looked at the pink sky with a placid foreboding that she soon should have learnt All. They lingered in the flushed air till at last it turned to grey and she seemed fairly to receive new information from every brush of the breeze. (James 1996a: 216)

This passage offers a kind of abstract mise-en-abyme of Maisie's whole trajectory in the novel, reducing James's story to its simplest and most essential schema. If other 'quickening[s]' of her 'perceptions' have been occasioned by the reception or interception of particular messages, here Maisie's journey from innocence to experience is figured in its ideal form, as nothing other than the reception of 'information' (85).

We need not, perhaps, think of wireless telegraphy when James describes Maisie receiving 'new information from every brush of the breeze'. But it is reasonable to suppose that at least some of the novel's first readers would have been struck by this thought, amidst the flurry of articles and interviews that began to appear in 1897. Marconi's patent had, after all, described a method of conveying electrical impulses through the 'air', and the term 'aerography' was one of the ultimately unsuccessful neologisms proposed to describe the new invention (Fahie 1899: 296; McGrath 1902: 469). The physical location of this episode might also have led readers to detect an allusion to Marconi's new discovery. One of the most excitedly contemplated potentialities of wireless telegraphy was the ability to communicate across bodies of water without the expedient of submarine cables, and plans were soon underway to test the capacity of Marconi's new system to transmit signals across the Channel. When Marconi succeeded in sending a radio transmission from France to

England on March 27, 1899, the receiving and transmitting stations were situated respectively at the South Foreland Lighthouse, near Dover, and the town of Wimereux, about five kilometres north of Boulogne (Hong 2001: 56). The first experiments in cross-channel wireless telegraphy might, of course, have been conducted between any number of appropriately coordinated locations, but the coincidence of Marconi's choosing a satellite town of Boulogne neatly underlines one available connotation of James's image – the image, that is, of air-borne 'information' received by a character sitting on a French beach and looking towards England.

In this brief visionary moment, Maisie imagines tuning her senses to a higher pitch, and gathering knowledge, not only from what she sees and hears, but from the invisible air itself. If the 'telegraphy' in which Maisie engages with Mrs Wix is crudely dependent on the body and face, and if even the subtler signals conveyed by winks and eye-rolls likewise require physical mediation, here, for once, is 'information' detached from any discernible medium. It is significant, then, that this fanciful passage, in which Maisie seems briefly to transcend the means of communication ordinarily open to her, also marks a precarious juncture in the technical construction of the narrative itself. This scene turns on Maisie's arriving at a perception of Mrs Wix's mental state, a remarkably subtle process of sympathetic intuition that lies, James himself admits, at the limit of credibility. 'I so despair', he confesses, 'of courting her noiseless mental footsteps here that I must crudely give you my word for its being from this time forward a picture literally present to her' (James 1996a: 216). The mirroring of mental states being proposed in this scene strains to breaking point the novel's system of focalization: if this vision of Mrs Wix's thoughts is still putatively relayed to us via Maisie's consciousness, the 'mental footsteps' that lead Maisie to so clairvoyant an insight are too subtle to be adduced. At the same moment, then, that we are offered a different model of information transfer than the various forms of mediated communication that Maisie has become accustomed to, James comes perilously close to violating one of the novel's own rules of information management. The possibility that the air itself might act as a medium, conveying information with 'every breath of breeze', threatens to exceed the representational parameters of the narrative.

Admit that Maisie has a premonition of wireless telegraphy on the beach at Boulogne. What would this mean for the novel's representation of mediums and mediation? It would, for one thing, introduce a limit-case into the series of signs and signals that she learns to interpret in the course of her experiences. Maisie's departure from the 'immediate' sensorium of childhood is accompanied by her discovery that looks and expressions are a rich source of information. From the point of view of a child seeking access to 'the unuttered and the unknown', it makes sense to think of looks and glances as a medium for the transmission of information, as James reminds us by referring to Maisie's exchange of pantomime messages with Mrs Wix as 'telegraphy'

– a conventional expression that nonetheless resonates suggestively with the Victorian media-sphere. If James uses 'telegraphing' to designate a particularly crude form of mediation, then Maisie's vision of wireless transmission on the beach at Boulogne represents, appropriately enough, mediation's apotheosis. Accustomed to finding messages and information all around her, mediated not only by speech but also by behaviour, Maisie momentarily glimpses a still more diffuse flow of information, liberated from any particular medium. At the same moment, we encounter a wobble in the novel's system of representation, as if to indicate that a world in which the air itself is a medium of information would require a different kind of narrative than the one we have been reading.

A little more than a year after this passage appeared in serial form in the *Chap-Book*, in July 1897, James published what has become his best-known treatment of Victorian communication technology, the long short story *In the Cage*. I do not propose to discuss this story at any length here – critics such as N. Katherine Hayles, Richard Menke, Nicola Nixon, and Jennifer Wicke have ably unpacked its portrayal of communication technology and information workers – but I would like to note in passing a basic tension within its originating conceit. The telegraphist in *In the Cage*, endowed with an irrepressible 'imaginative life' and addicted to gathering 'impressions' (James 1996b: 838), bears some of the traits that James habitually associated with artists and writers. If the telegraphist's vicarious adventure in the story depends on privileged access to a medium of confidential communication, however, James's own inspiration for this story stems, he insists in the preface, from a less intrusive perception and a less recondite source. The *donnée* at the root of *In the Cage* was, he deprecatingly confides, only 'the commonest and most taken-for-granted of London impressions', one which 'must again and again have flowered (granted the grain of observation) in generous minds' (James 1984b: 1168). Because James's imaginative process is the precise inverse of the one he attributes to the telegraphist-*cum*-romance-novelist (she speculates about the lives of her clientele, while James, a client, speculates about her), *his* imagination is triggered, not by accessing the hidden contents of the telegraphic medium, but by the 'impressions' he and everyone else receive during visits to the telegraph office, that 'commonest' and most public of spaces. In this way, James's creative process seems to be defined here in opposition to the operations of the telegraphic medium. If the sensitive telegraphist cannot resist the fascination of covert erotic messages, James's imagination is excited by something both less clandestine and more diffuse: not the space-annihilating signals of the telegraph service but the 'London impressions' to be gleaned from the 'small local office of one's immediate neighbourhood'. Like the 'information' that Maisie imagines receiving on the beach at Boulogne, the 'breeze of the human comedy' that James detects in such places is transmitted without the mediation of wires (James 1984b: 1168).

That James was at least as interested in the atmosphere of telegraph offices as he was in the transmission of telegrams is also the implication of Lambert Strether's visit to the Postes et Télégraphes in Book Twelfth of *The Ambassadors* (1903). Suffusing 'the air of these establishments', Strether detects

> the vibration of the vast strange life of the town, the influence of the types, the performers concocting their messages; the little prompt Paris women, arranging, pretexting goodness knew what, driving the dreadful needle-pointed public pen at the dreadful sand-strewn public table: implements that symbolised for Strether's too interpretative innocence something more acute in manners, more sinister in morals, more fierce in the national life. After he had put in his paper he had ranged himself, he was really amused to think, on the side of the fierce, the sinister, the acute. He was carrying on a correspondence, across the great city, quite in the key of the *Postes et Télégraphes* in general; and it was fairly as if the acceptance of that fact had come from something in his state that sorted with the occupation of his neighbours. He was mixed up with the typical tale of Paris, and so were they, poor things – how could they all together help being? (James 2010: 391)

For all its local flavour, this passage dramatizes the same paradox that James associates with London telegraph offices in the preface to *In the Cage*: at the very moment that the novel depicts a scene of mediation, and an instance of the famous nineteenth-century 'annihilation of space and time', James's gaze seems to focus not on the abstract background of the discourse network of 1900, but rather on the concrete foreground of the 'Postes et Télégraphes'. Rather than electric messages whizzing along the wires (or canisters whooshing along pneumatic tubes), Strether is arrested by the exotic 'air' of his immediate environment, its 'vibrations', its 'sand-strewn' and 'needle-pointed' textures, its possibilities for romance and melodrama. James recognized, in the preface to *In the Cage,* that the question he couldn't resist pondering as a client of the British telegraph service – 'the question of what it might "mean"' – was a 'form of waste', one to which he had long been 'prone' (James 1984b: 1168). Musing over the narrative possibilities intrinsic to the occupation of telegraphist is ironic because what the medium of telegraphy may or may not 'mean' is not only irrelevant but detrimental to its avowed purpose of ever more efficient communication. With respect to the efficient transmission of information, such meanings are indeed 'waste' – or, to use a term introduced to the vocabulary of cybernetics by Norbert Wiener in 1948, 'background noise' (Wiener 1961: 10). Strether falls prey to a similarly wasteful excess of meaning as he sends his message to Madame de Vionnet, overwhelmed, as is his wont, by romantic 'vibrations' supererogatory to his practical purpose.

Like James, he sees a 'tale' where a less waste-prone observer would see only a means of communication.

It is worth noting that Strether's reverie in the Postes et Télégraphes mirrors an earlier instance of telegraphic communication in the novel. This is the fateful cable that Strether receives from Mrs Newsome in the courtyard of his hotel, announcing the impending arrival of Sarah, Jim, and Maisie Pocock. In this earlier episode, Strether's meditation on the distinctive atmosphere of the city is interrupted, rather than occasioned, by the image of telegraphy, but the scene does similarly juxtapose telegraphic communication with a striking description of Strether's impressions of Paris. The long lyrical sentence in which these impressions are conveyed, recording a heterogeneous mixture of 'sounds and suggestions, vibrations of the air, human and dramatic', is recognisably continuous with Strether's later reverie, which also figures his sensitivity to 'vibrations' (James 2010: 227). In the hotel courtyard, no less than in the Postes et Télégraphes, an image of mediated communication is counterpointed by a welter of sensory impressions.

If we are seeking a general term for the kind of distinctive cultural atmosphere James evokes in these passages, one is suggested to us by a closely analogous scene in *The Golden Bowl* (1904), also set in the courtyard of a Parisian hotel and also revolving around the delivery of a momentous telegram. At no moment in James's fiction does the technology of rapid international communication obtrude more dramatically on the destiny of his characters than in this crucial chapter, in which Charlotte Stant's conditional acceptance of Adam Verver's marriage proposal is made definitive by a pair of telegrams from Adam's daughter, Maggie, and Maggie's husband Amerigo, the Prince. The scene seems to play self-consciously on the tension between the efficiency of modern telecommunication and the cumulative moral complexity of James's own narrative, which is, by the time Maggie dispatches her bright telegram, already formidably dense. As James's telegraphist discovers in *In the Cage*, even the most seemingly functional of coded messages can become freighted with 'allusions', which are, in their turn, 'all swimming in a sea of other allusions still, tangled in a complexity of questions' (James 1996b: 844). What appears initially to be a transparent message of congratulation – 'We start to-night to bring you all our love and joy and sympathy' – is soon tangled up in the snarl of ambiguous interests and secret agendas that James has set in place: can the telegram be trusted, Charlotte scruples, to express Amerigo's intentions as well, and is its intended addressee Adam alone or he and Charlotte both (James 2010: 612)? As for Amerigo's subsequent telegram, the content of which is revealed to the reader only several chapters later, it is, as Goble points out, a blatant affront to the kind of efficient communication that telegraphy is supposed to facilitate, a decidedly un-telegraphic 'tribute to the allure of inscrutability' (Goble 2010: 79). What is most notable about this scene for my purpose here, however, is the way that these ineffably ramifying 'allusions' are shown to be 'swimming', not only in the thick soup of unspoken desires and tacit understandings in which Adam, Maggie, Amerigo, and Charlotte are all afloat, but also in the larger surrounding element of Paris itself. The setting for this scene in *The Golden Bowl* is a more sumptuous counterpart to the 'little court' in which Strether receives his transatlantic cable in *The Ambassadors*, and Adam Verver, too, is keenly conscious as it unfolds of the fabled city lying beyond the hotel's 'porte-cochère', with its 'voices and warnings', 'bristling traps', and 'strange appearances in the air' (James 2010: 227, 610-11). The courtyard itself, 'muffled' and 'guarded', appears to him as a 'waiting-room [...] for gathered barbarians', 'suspended, as with wings folded or feebly fluttering, in the superior, the supreme, the inexorably enveloping Parisian medium' (613-14). The intoxicating mixture of sounds, smells and vibrations that both Strether and Adam Verver sense beyond their hotel gates is, of course, a medium.

It would be unwarranted to conflate two distinct senses of this word: to suggest that the urban environment evoked in these three passages is being directly assimilated to the medium of communication that features so prominently in each. The *OED* distinguishes clearly between uses of 'medium' that refer to 'the substance in which an organism lives' (in evidence as early as 1664) and, by extension, 'one's environment, conditions of life, or usual social setting', and uses of the word to designate an 'intermediate agency, instrument, or channel' (first recorded usage 1585). When a city or place is described as a 'medium', it is evidently the former of these definitions that lies nearest to hand. James's use of 'medium' to denote a set of social and cultural conditions, moreover, belonged to a well-established nineteenth-century vocabulary, associated, above all, with the work of the literary critic Hippolyte Taine. In the preface to *Histoire de la littérature anglaise* (1864), Taine had expounded an aggressively modern approach to the history of literature, which could be reduced, he argued, to the interaction of three causal factors: 'race', 'moment', and 'milieu'. If 'race' supplies a set of innate tendencies, and 'moment' refers to historical epoch, 'milieu' denotes 'all the external powers that fashion the human material, and through which the outside acts on the interior' (Taine 1863: xxviii). One of the towering figures of French intellectual life in the latter half of the nineteenth century, Taine was also widely read and discussed in the Anglosphere, where his tripartite theory of cultural causation became well known.

Although it has a slightly different etymology, combining the Old French *liu*, or place, with a prefix derived from the Latin *medium*, or middle, 'milieu' can be translated into English as 'medium' in many contexts – including the preface to Taine's *Histoire*. Nineteenth-century French dictionaries make this equivalence clear. In Emile Littré's *Dictionnaire de la langue française* (1872-1877), for instance, 'milieu' covers much the same semantic territory as 'medium', including a general spatial usage ('The material space in which a body is placed'), a sense pertaining to communication ('Anything which serves to establish a communication'), and the biological or sociological sense employed by Taine: 'The complex whole represented by the objects that surround organized bodies'. 'By extension', the entry goes on, one speaks of a 'social milieu', although no examples of this latter usage are given. 'Medium', then, would have been an accurate English translation of Taine's keyword. When, however, Henri van Laun produced an English translation of *Histoire* in 1872, he opted for idiomatic naturalness over fidelity, rendering 'milieu' as 'surroundings'.

James knew Taine's work well. He reviewed five of Taine's books between 1868 and 1876 and also reported in the *Nation* on the letter that Taine published in the *Journal des débats politiques et littéraires* after George Sand's death in 1876, during the year that James was resident in Paris. He read *Histoire* in the French original, commenting in 1868 that Taine 'is the author of a really valuable history of English literature' (James 1984b: 826), and he duly reviewed Van Laun's translation for the *Atlantic* in April of 1872. In the review, James comments on Taine's celebrity, noting that 'his three main factors' have 'lately been reiterated to satiety' (James 1984b: 843). When it came to naming two of these three 'factors', James snubbed the translation under review, substituting his own English equivalents for those offered by Van Laun. In place of 'epoch', James rendered Taine's 'moment' simply as 'time', and, in the case of 'milieu', he opted for the most literal translation available: 'surroundings' becomes 'medium' (James 1984b: 843).

'Medium' doubtless suggested itself to James as the most natural and least intrusive rendering of 'milieu', but the imagery he uses to elaborate this concept implies that he recognized some of the words' more specialized connotations. In particular, James seems given to imagine Taine's 'milieu' as a fluid substance. Summarizing Taine's deterministic model of literary creation, James notes that any intelligent observer is 'himself conscious of the attrition of infinite waves of circumstance', and goes on to figure the relationship between literature and circumambient historical forces in terms of a 'deposit' in a 'more general current' (843). Later, in the course of an unfavourable comparison between Taine and Sainte-Beuve, James figures the former battering away at historical 'truth' with 'lively hammer-blows', while the latter's 'only method was fairly to dissolve his attention in the sea of circumstance surrounding the object of his study' (844). As with the 'waves of circumstance' and the 'current' earlier, James seems drawn to imagine the contextual data of literary history as a fluid element. For someone inclined to figure socio-cultural context in this way, 'medium', and not 'surroundings', is indeed the *mot juste*.

The prefaces to James's New York Edition contain a number of well-known conceptual binaries, ranging from the opposed techniques of 'Scene' and 'Picture' to the more fluid continuum separating 'feeling' from 'doing' or 'the real' from 'the romantic' (James 1984b: 1298, 1091, 1062-3). The terms 'impression' and 'relation' are never presented as a pair in this way – whether as mutually exclusive alternatives or mutually attractive poles – but they are keywords every bit as important in James's aesthetics as scene and picture, and they would seem to be related to one another by a similar dyadic logic. A novel, James insisted in 'The Art of Fiction', is worthless if it does not proceed from a 'direct impression or perception of life', and James's receptive 'bucket of impressions' is a recurrent theme in the prefaces (James 1984a: 50, 53; 1984b: 1101). But if James repeatedly extols the value of 'direct impression[s]' to the aspiring novelist, no less axiomatic and pervasive is his belief that, as he put it in the preface to the Edition's first volume, *Roderick Hudson*, '[r]eally, universally, relations stop nowhere, and the exquisite problem of the artist is eternally but to draw, by a geometry of his own, the circle within which they shall happily *appear* to do so' (James 1984b: 1041). The same idea recurs in the preface to *The Princess Casamassima*, where James defines '[e]xperience', at least as far as the novelist is concerned, as 'our apprehension and our measure of what happens to us as social creatures': 'the picture of the entangled state is what is required' (1091). Experience, for the novelist, *is* entanglement. The normal inference to draw from James's lament that relations stop nowhere is that there is no outer limit to their ramifications. But it takes only a slight reorientation of this remark to draw from it the equally necessary inverse conclusion that really, universally, relations don't *start* anywhere, either. For James, that is, the relations are always already there, in the impressions. Whatever a 'direct impression or perception' may have been for James, it almost certainly was not an 'immediate' impression, since this implies an impression bereft of relations.

Bereft too, perhaps, to risk a synonymy with one of James's other keywords, of vibrations. Good vibrations – 'vibrations of the air' – are what Strether picks up in his hotel courtyard, immediately before he is comprehensively bummed out by Mrs Newsome's telegram, and it is, as we have seen, the 'vibration of the vast strange life of the town' that he thinks he perceives later, at the Postes et Télégraphes. For James, it seems clear, such 'impressions' of the Parisian 'medium' are no more 'immediate' than the messages conveyed by the telegraph, if by 'immediate' we mean an experience that does not carry or communicate 'relations' from afar. The scenes from *The Golden Bowl* and *The Ambassadors* I have discussed thus seem to establish, not so much a contrast, as a synecdoche between the medium of the telegraph and the surrounding Parisian atmosphere, itself an unsurpassably conductive medium of 'vibrations'. It would not be inaccurate to describe the fragments of thick ethnographic description that James inserts into these three episodes as impressions of *milieu*. James's allusion to the life of the city as a 'medium' in *The Golden Bowl* confirms this inference, and we know that 'medium' for James was a literal translation of 'milieu'. But it is also, I hope, becoming evident that 'milieu' itself, as a common borrow-word denoting social environment without any further connotative resonance, would have been no more adequate to James's purpose than the translation that he declined, 'surroundings'. 'Circumstance', he wrote in the review of Taine's *History*, makes itself felt as 'waves': when James thought about *milieu*, he thought about a conductive medium, just as when he thought about a medium of communication (telegraphy), he seems to have thought about *milieu*. Can we not conclude from this that there was, for James, no clear distinction in place between a medium in the sense of an 'intermediary' and a medium in the sense of an 'environment'? For a Henry James or a Lambert Strether – incorrigibly imaginative souls for whom the 'air' itself invariably pulsed with 'vibrations' – the distinction might well have seemed superfluous.

All of which returns us to Maisie on the beach at Boulogne. I have suggested that Maisie's impossible vision of air-borne information coincides with a breakdown in the representational machinery of James's novel. The same is true, in a less dramatic way, of the brief interludes that James introduces into his scenes of Parisian telegraphy. The telegrams that James chooses to throw into relief in these scenes all play the role of 'cardinal functions', to use Roland Barthes's terminology, logic switches that shunt the narrative off in one of two or more possible directions (Barthes 2002: 840). The lyrical evocations of Paris, on the other hand, serve to suspend rather than advance the development of the plot. In Barthes's terms, they are not 'functions' at all, but 'indices', dollops of local colour that amplify the discourse without bringing the story any closer to its conclusion (839). We know that James was exasperated by calls for more 'incident' and less 'character' in the English novel, and that his acute awareness of 'relations' made it hard for him to strike a balance between story and discourse (James 1984a: 54). If we suppose, for a moment, that the images of the Paris 'medium' that James evokes are, precisely, images of relations, relations detached from any particular narrative 'circle', then there must have been something seductive, for him, in introducing such an image at such a moment: in interrupting a crisis in this rigorously contained set of relations, this particular story, to contemplate the tantalizing prospect of relationality itself. Telegraphy in these scenes from *The Ambassadors* and *The Golden Bowl* would then appear to function as a foil to this more expansive sense of immersion in a signifying medium. To the discrete messages transmitted by telegraph, which keep the story moving on its linear track, would be opposed this dangerous background of unlocalised mediation, the fringe of 'meaning' always tugging at the corner of James's eye.

Couldn't we describe Maisie's fleeting epiphany on the beach in the same terms, as a Pisgah vision of relationality itself? The image evokes, after all, not only the 'breeze of the human comedy' from the preface to *In the Cage*, but also the figuration of 'experience' in 'The Art of Fiction' as a 'spider-web' that captures 'every air-borne particle' and 'converts the very pulses of the air into revelations' (James 1984b: 1168; 1984a: 52). Insofar as the narrative of *What Maisie Knew* takes the form of a quest for knowledge, its structure is determined by a linear series of revelations and discoveries. As I have suggested, James invites us to think about these stages in Maisie's education in terms of mediation: in particular, he emphasizes the way that gestures, expressions, and other behavioural signals operate in the novel as an important medium of communication. Maisie's vision at Boulogne, however, momentarily figures an alternative to the linear logic of this quest narrative. If 'telegraphy' in the novel is merely another medium, Maisie's fleeting glimpse of air-borne information is something different, approximating the raw 'relations' and 'revelations' that James found it so excruciatingly difficult to decant into the slim vessel of narrative form. If this is indeed a futuristic image of radio transmission, then it might have seemed to James in 1897 that media technology was at last catching up with his own media imagination, promising to transform the enveloping air itself into a medium of communication.

Works Cited

Barthes, Roland. 2002. 'Introduction à l'analyse structurale des récits'. In *Oeuvres completes II 1962-1967*, edited by Eric Marty, 828-65. Paris: Editions du Seuil.

Boyer, Dominic. 2007. *Understanding Media: A Popular Philosophy*. Chicago: Prickly Paradigm.

Fahie, J.J. 1899. *A History of Wireless Telegraphy*. Edinburgh: Blackwood.

Goble, Mark. 2010. *Beautiful Circuits: Modernism and the Mediated Life*. New York: Columbia University Press.

Hayles, N. Katherine. 2005. *My Mother Was a Computer: Digital Subjects and Literary Texts*. Chicago: University of Chicago Press.

Hong, Sungook. 2001. *Wireless: From Marconi's Black Box to the Audion*. Cambridge: MIT Press.

James, Henry. 1981. *The Notebooks of Henry James*. Edited by F.O. Matthiessen and Kenneth B. Murdock. Chicago: University of Chicago Press.

James, Henry. 1984a. *Literary Criticism: Essays on Literature, American Writers, English Writers*. New York: Library of America.

James, Henry. 1984b. *Literary Criticism: French Writers, Other European Writers, The Prefaces to the New York Edition*. New York: Library of America.

James, Henry. 1989. *Novels 1886-1890*. New York: Library of America.

James, Henry. 1994. *The American Scene*. Harmondsworth: Penguin Books.

James, Henry. 1996a. *What Maisie Knew*. Oxford: Oxford University Press.

James, Henry. 1996b. *Complete Stories 1892-1898*. New York: Library of America.

James, Henry. 1999. *Complete Stories 1884-1891*. New York: Library of America.

James, Henry. 2010. *Novels 1903-1911*. New York: Library of America.

Littré, Emil, editor. 1872-1877. *Dictionnaire de la langue française*. Paris: Hachette.

McGrath, P. 1902. 'Marconi's Ambition'. *Pall Mall Magazine* 27: 468-74.

McLuhan, Marshall. 1967. *Understanding Media: The Extensions of Man*. London: Sphere Books.

Menke, Richard. 2008. *Telegraphic Realism: Victorian Fiction and Other Information Systems*. Stanford: Stanford University Press.

Nixon, Nicola. 1999. 'The Reading Gaol of Henry James's *In the Cage*'. *ELH* 66: 179-201.

Taine, Hippolyte. 1863. *Histoire de la littérature anglaise*. Volume 1. Paris: Librairie de L. Hachette et Cie.

Trotter, David. 2014. 'Signalling Madly: Sex, Lies, and Data-Transfer in Nineteenth-Century Fiction'. Lecture presented at the University of New South Wales, Sydney, December 10.

Whitney, William Dwight, editor. 1889-1891. *The Century Dictionary: An Encyclopedic Lexicon of the English Language*. New York: The Century Co.

Wicke, Jennifer. 1989. 'Henry James's Second Wave'. *The Henry James Review* 10: 146-51.

Wiener, Norbert. 1961. *Cybernetics: or Control and Communication in the Animal and the Machine*. Cambridge: MIT Press.

5

D.W. Griffith, Victorian Poetry, and the Sound of Silent Film

RUTH ABBOTT

After Many Years, an early D.W. Griffith film released by Biograph in 1908, 'proved to write more history than any picture ever filmed' (Arvidson 1925: 66). So claimed Linda Arvidson, Griffith's ex-wife. In Arvidson's account, the history was technical: it was 'the first movie without a chase', 'the first picture to have a *dramatic* close-up', and 'the first picture to have a cut-back'. This is inaccurate, as Tom Gunning has shown; Griffith actually 'introduced no new techniques to filmmaking'. But he did transform 'how films told stories'. '[E]arly cinema did not see its main task as the presentation of narratives', Gunning explains: 'The transformation that occurs in films around 1908 derives from reorienting film style to a clear focus on the task of storytelling and characterization' (Gunning 1991: 6). For this, Griffith does deserve credit: 'Under Griffith, the devices of cinema that were generally displayed for their own sake as attractions in the work of earlier filmmakers became channelled toward the expression of characterization and story' (42-3). *After Many Years* is exemplary in this respect. Cutting between shots of Florence Lawrence, waiting faithfully at home, and Charles Inslee, her shipwrecked husband, the film abandons spatial continuity for the sake of temporal continuity, intercutting consecutive events from disparate locations to tell the tale of the couple's separation and longing for each other. *After Many Years* wrote history, Arvidson claimed, and in one sense Gunning would agree: history, in the sense of chronological record or consecutive narration of incidents, is exactly what this film so innovatively inscribes.

It is not, however, all that it inscribes, and in this chapter I would like to dwell on some of what escapes the narratives of Griffith and Gunning alike. As David Trotter has suggested, 'We need to take full account of the gradual and uneven development of a cinema of attractions into a cinema designed above all to tell stories', and what follows is an attempt to respond to that call (Trotter 2007: 8). 'Unmotivated events, rhythmic montage, highlighted parallelism, overlong spectacles – these are the excesses in the classical narrative system that alert us to the existence of a competing logic', writes

Rick Altman (Altman 1992: 34). That competing logic interests me too, and although I find Arvidson's account tempting and Gunning's as persuasive as they come, I want to dwell on the things written into Griffith's Biograph films that neither history nor narrative integration wholly encompass.

Doing so means looking beyond Arvidson's most influential claim, her account of Griffith's excuse for the experiments of *After Many Years*:

> When Mr Griffith suggested a scene showing Annie Lee waiting for her husband's return to be followed by a scene of Enoch cast away on a desert island, it was altogether too distracting. 'How can you tell a story jumping about like that? The people won't know what it's about.'
> 'Well', said Mr Griffith, 'doesn't Dickens write that way?'
> 'Yes, but that's Dickens; that's novel writing; that's different'.
> 'Oh, not so much, these are picture stories: not so different'.
> (Arvidson 1925: 66)

To identify Dickens as inspiration for the narrative techniques that made Arvidson describe *After Many Years* as 'the first "continuity"' is to emphasise the story in the picture stories (65). It is an emphasis perpetuated by Sergei Eisenstein, who proposed that Griffith 'was led to the idea of parallel action by – Dickens!', from whom 'stem the first shoots of American film aesthetic' (Eisenstein 1949: 205, 195). This genealogy has not gone unchallenged: Altman, for example, complains that Eisenstein's followers 'blithely postulate a direct connection between a film and the novel from which it is ostensibly drawn, when even minimal research clearly identifies a dramatic adaptation as an important direct source' (Altman 1992: 11-12). But as Trotter points out, 'Acknowledgement of the historical significance of theatrical adaptation should not preclude enquiry into what Griffith might have learned (montage aside) by reading the novels and poems subsequently made into plays' (Trotter 2007: 63). In this chapter, it is the poems in which I am interested, and it is just as easy to demonstrate that Griffith read and recited these poems as it is to demonstrate that they had a theatrical life.

For *After Many Years* is not based on a Dickens novel, and although Altman is obviously right to say that it was influenced by theatrical adaptations such as Arthur Mathison's – the *Biograph Bulletin* advertised it as 'more intensely heart-stirring than the original play' – there is a poem at its heart: Alfred Tennyson's *Enoch Arden*, first published in 1864 (Altman 1992: 10; Usai 1996-2006: 1.143). Griffith's well-documented, lifelong interest in poetry makes it inconceivable that he did not have Tennyson's verse as well as Mathison's melodrama (and possibly Dickens's narrative techniques) in mind. Mikhail Iampolski complains that 'Cinema has evolved along a path dictated by narrative genres, to the point of being popularly perceived as analogous to the novel', so that 'Dickens has taken the place of Tennyson' in accounts of Griffith's career (Iampolski

1998: 85). Yet in the 1930s, when James Hart asked Griffith why he 'gave public credit to Dickens for his film techniques', he 'sniffed', and 'began talking about Walt Whitman. As a highly impressionable lad, Griffith said, he had been led to tempo and parallel action in Whitman's *Leaves of Grass* by the roundtable of Flexner's bookstore' (Hart 1972: 161). The poetry that Griffith overheard in this Louisville stationary shop, where Ben Flexner held literary discussions and employed Griffith when he was a boy, remained important to him throughout his career.

This is evident in the sheer number of Griffith's films that are based on poems, for even when theatrical sources can be traced too, the many lines of verse in the intertitles indicate that he consulted or recalled the originals as well. In 1916, what he remembered most fondly of his time directing for Biograph was using poets: Browning, Tennyson, Shakespeare. 'One of my early pictures I did like was *When Pippa Passes*', he told Henry Stephen Gordon. 'Then came *Enoch Arden, The Blot on the 'Scutcheon, Taming of the Shrew*' (Geduld 1971: 38). When he left Biograph, Griffith explained to Hart, he was freer to use such material: 'We even had poetry in the screen titles' (Hart 1972: 88). As Karl Brown put it, remembering his days as assistant to Billy Bitzer, Griffith's cameraman, 'Griffith had always been obsessed by poetry', and 'Now that he had his own studio and nobody to boss him, he was dead set on bringing poetry to the screen' (Brown 1988: 44).

There was more to this than a desire for respectability. Yes, 'film aspired to the cultural prestige of poetry' during its precarious early years, as Julian Murphet suggests (Murphet 2009: 109), but Griffith was as interested in what verse sounded like as in what values it could represent. In 1923, he attributed 'Whatever of truth and beauty is discernible by a generous public in my eager output' to 'hearing Keats and Tennyson and Shakespeare read at home' (Geduld 1971: 61). Recitation was a hobby he never relinquished, and he frequently practiced it on set. Brown recalled that, preparing to shoot *The Mother and the Law* (the Mae Marsh/Bobby Harron story from *Intolerance*, released separately in 1919), Griffith 'would declaim to the skies, over the noise of the construction crews, "For who can tell to what red hell his sightless soul may stray!"', dismissing Lillian Gish to go 'about his business, which was the recitation of as much more of *The Ballad of Reading Gaol* as he could remember' (Brown 1988: 121). While building set for *The Avenging Conscience* (1914), which draws on several of Edgar Allan Poe's poems as well as his story 'The Tell-Tale Heart' (1843), Brown remembered Griffith reciting 'The Bells' (1849), 'competing with the noise of hammers and saws to declaim, with expressive gestures and with a voice pitched to a low and ominous monotone, "They are neither beast nor human, / they are neither man nor woman... / they are *ghouls*..."' (46). The metres Griffith loved even modulated his own speech. 'Sometimes, when he was under the influence of whatever poet he had been reading, he would speak metrically, falling into an easy, natural, and most certainly unplanned blank verse', Brown recalled (30). During filming for *The Avenging Conscience*, 'Griffith came by, paused, and without looking at me intoned, "Get me a peacock strutting on the green / and spreading all his glory to the sun"'. 'I didn't mind being instructed in verse', Brown admitted. 'I was used to it': Griffith 'couldn't help speaking in iambic pentameters of a sort, thanks to his love of Shakespeare and his hope of being a poet himself someday' (36-7).

Even Griffith's works of social protest once had more poetry in them than they now seem to. Take his second film based on a poem: *The Song of the Shirt* (1908), which Gunning associates with 'Genette's category of voice, expressing the filmic narrator's judgments about characters or actions through contrast edits' (Gunning 1991: 134). The voice that Griffith associated with this single reeler would have been audible rather than ideological. Its original intertitles are lost, but the *Biograph Bulletin* gives a fair clue as to what they included:

> BEAUTIFUL PORTRAYAL OF THOMAS HOOD'S FAMOUS POEM.
> Oh! men with sisters dear! Oh, men with mothers and wives!
> It is not the linen you're wearing out, but human creatures' lives! (Usai 1996-2006: 1.150)

The single paragraph advertisement quotes a full nine lines from Hood's poem, first published as 'The Song of the Shirt' in *Punch* in 1843. As Steven Higgins suggests, 'it is more than likely that Griffith used actual lines' in the intertitles too (1.151). This is not unusual – Griffith often used verse in his intertitles, as we will see – but it does confirm that the poem was important to him, as a poem and not just as the source of a scenario, and it would have made the film feel different too.

Its repeated shots of Florence Lawrence mouthing to herself, for example – over Linda Arvidson ill in bed, or over her sewing machine as she pedals – would have had a different resonance when punctuated by quotations from the poem, which is as much about a woman singing a song as it is about a woman stitching a shirt. Hood introduces her:

> With fingers weary and worn,
>   With eyelids heavy and red,
> A Woman sat, in unwomanly rags,
>   Plying her needle and thread –
>   Stitch! stitch! stitch!
> In poverty, hunger, and dirt,
>   And still with a voice of dolorous pitch
> She sang the 'Song of the Shirt!' (Hood 1843: 260)

The next nine stanzas comprise the song itself, in speech marks, before the narrator concludes by reprising the opening plus an extra line that was picked out in the *Biograph Bulletin* too:

> And still with a voice of dolorous pitch,
> Would that its tone could reach the Rich!
> She sang this 'Song of the Shirt!'

So the poem centres on and mostly comprises a song, and laments that song's inaudibility in certain quarters; it also proffers itself *as* a song, through its title and its variable lines of accentual trimeter and tetrameter, and as such it stands as something like the answer to its own wish (the 'song of the shirt' finally *will* reach the ears of the wealthy now that *The Song of the Shirt* is printed in *Punch*). I believe that Griffith was attracted to its interest in how protest can be made audible, and embedded that interest in his film by alternating Hood's descriptions of a woman singing with Bitzer's images of Lawrence mouthing laments.

Similar preoccupations characterise the next of Griffith's films inspired by a poem: *Edgar Allen Poe* (1909), which depicts Poe's composition of 'The Raven' (1845). Again the original intertitles are missing, but it is not hard to guess what they included. Arvidson is dying in bed again; Herbert Yost, playing Poe, laments over her this time. A raven appears; Yost looks inspired and starts writing. Every four lines, he shows Arvidson his manuscript; the second time he does this, she mouths and nods her head to what is unmistakeably the beat of the poem's distinctive trochaic octameter:

> ONCE upon a midnight dreary, while I pondered, weak and weary,
> Over many a quaint and curious volume of forgotten lore,
> While I nodded, nearly napping, suddenly there came a tapping,
> As of some one gently rapping, rapping at my chamber door.
>   (Poe 1845: 1)

Yost takes the poem to various publishers, most of whom hate it, but all of whom respond visibly to its metre. Charles Perley, in the first publishing house, mouths as he reads it and taps his pen to its beat as he explains its faults. Anita Hendrie, in the second publishing house, mockingly sways her head and hand from side to side as she visibly mouths 'Once upon a midnight dreary'. David Miles, her colleague, more approvingly mouths much of the first stanza before offering payment. Isabelle Raynauld's work on early French silent film has revealed how consistently actors can be seen mouthing lines from relevant surviving screenplays; she highlights Gene Gauntier's remark in 1907 that 'If the director wished certain words to register, they were enunciated slowly and distinctly, leaving no doubt of what they were in the spectator's mind' (Raynauld 2001: 72-73, 70). In *Edgar Allen Poe*, it is rhythm that registers, more than words, and rhythm that Griffith seems most interested in helping audiences hear.

Was Griffith interested in all this nineteenth-century poetry as a means to overcome the technological limitations of his medium? In 1917, he lamented in *Moving Picture Classic*:

> There can be no gay, rippling laughter, nor solemn tones of warning; no sad, sweet, pleasant tones; no shrieks of fear – not a sound can help the movie actor. He must express every emotion with his face and hands and with general gestures and movement of the body. (Geduld 1971: 50-1)

Yet Griffith never believed that such restrictions left his films inaudible. 'Mr Griffith has a strong disapproval of the words "silent drama" as applied to motion pictures', noted Roberta Courtland for *Motion Picture Magazine* in 1915, 'for he says of all mediums of expressing thought the Motion Picture is the loudest' (Slide 2012: 19). Poetry played a part for him in making it so. Consider the next Biograph film he based on a poem: *Pippa Passes; or, The Song of Conscience* (1909), which draws on Browning's verse drama *Pippa Passes* (1841). Gertrude Robinson, playing Pippa, wakes as the sun rises off screen and is seen to address it, lips moving and arm raised. She picks up a guitar, and finds a piece of paper on the windowsill. An unusual intertitle flashes up – some sheet music setting a quotation from the Browning: 'God's in his heaven, All's right with the world!' – before we return to Robinson, now visibly singing rather than speaking. Yopie Prins describes Pippa in this sequence as a 'figure for song that can only be seen and not really heard', and suggests that although the music, from a popular setting by Amy Beach, was doubtless 'familiar enough to the audience and might even be a cue for the piano accompaniment', 'what is important in the scene is the vision of Pippa's song rather than its audibility' (Prins 2008: 225). But the ubiquity of illustrated songs in the period's nickelodeon programmes suggests that the intertitle probably had a more practical function, as a prompt for audiences to start singing themselves. As Gunning explains, 'the "song slide" was an important side attraction to motion picture shows' in the first decade of the century, featuring lantern slides with illustrated lyrics accompanied by live performances that 'fostered communal participation' (Gunning 1991: 86-7). Jean Châteauvert and André Gaudreault have shown that when producers started releasing film adaptations of songs, they relied on 'vocal participation on the part of spectators' in a similar way (Châteauvert and Gaudreault 2001: 189). The subtitle and sheet-music intertitle of *Pippa Passes; or, The Song of Conscience* would have aligned it with this popular genre, prompting exhibitors who could manage it to have a singer performing Beach's song at appropriate moments, and encouraging audiences to join in.

As Altman and Richard Abel have demonstrated, turn-of-the-century cinema was never simply silent anyway: the variety of accompaniments with which films were exhibited made it 'an unusually complex hybrid medium' from the outset (Abel and Altman 2001: xiii). But as Altman explains elsewhere, accompaniments varied 'according to differences in date, location, film type, exhibition venue, and many other variables', and involved 'an extraordinary range of practices. Evidence remains of music, sound effects, and lectures, produced by live orchestras, stagehands, phonographic recordings, or the human voice', with films regularly 'subjected to what we might call "resident" practices', including screenings with no accompaniment at all (Altman 2004: 12, 87-9). From 1908 on, producers therefore increasingly attempted to 'gain control of the conditions under which their films would be exhibited' (240). Griffith became an important part of that story: in 1915, *The Clansman* toured with its own orchestra, performing music specially compiled by Carli Elinor; later the same year, it opened as *The Birth of a Nation* with an original score by Joseph Carl Breil (292-3). But at the height of the nickelodeon period when Griffith was working for Biograph, exhibition practices were inconsistent, and directors who were interested in sound had to find ways of evoking it within film itself, ways that would elicit something appropriate from whatever lecturer or sound-effects person a nickelodeon had employed, or give an audience enough to go on if they did not.

Griffith's experiments in this line have mostly been understood in relation to his development of the narrative system and the increasing control over exhibition practices that it required. Take the nickelodeon lecture. Lecturers were usually hired to 'hype' films to audiences early in the century, but they were soon encouraged to 'Give the lecture the form of a connected narrative', as popular lecturer W. Stephen Bush put it, and it was not long before directors took the next step: by 1909, Altman notes, the lecturer's function was being 'folded into narrative technique' or 'carried by increasingly frequent and complex intertitles' (142-3); Gunning even describes Griffith's narrative system as 'a sort of interiorized film lecturer' (Gunning 1991: 93). Or consider sound-effect practices. Referring to Griffith's many plots that 'turn on moments when listening is emphasized', Altman notes the growing frequency with which 'virtual sound tracks' were built into nickelodeon-era films, accompanied in exhibition by 'sound practices dedicated to providing synchronized auditory traces of visible sound events' that established 'narrative and spatial connections' (Altman 2004: 214-16). *Pippa Passes; or, The Song of Conscience* is readily understood this way. What links its diverse episodes and locations is, after all, the sound of Pippa's song: three times, potentially tragic action is avoided as characters are seen suddenly to hear the song we are then shown, in repeated shots of Pippa mouthing and strumming as she walks around town with her guitar.

There is something in the very repetitiveness with which such shots recur, however, that takes us beyond the narrative system even as its continuity is reinforced. Their sheer length, with nothing happening beyond Robinson mouthing and strumming as she strolls or stands still, is arresting, and it arrests the onward movement of the inset stories too. So many long shots consisting of so little except mouthing give the sense of something excessive, a dwelling on recitation for its own sake. Moreover, the verse that the intertitles cite is not always in the service of narrative either. The longest intertitle in *Pippa Passes; or, The Song of Conscience*, which is also its longest verse quotation, is barely part of the story at all. Pippa's holiday has ended; we see her re-enter her room, put down her guitar, and pick up her nightdress. Then we see this:

> ALL SERVICE RANKS THE SAME WITH GOD
> IF NOW, AS FORMERLY HE TROD
> PARADISE. HIS PRESENCE FILLS
> OUR EARTH, EACH ONLY AS GOD WILLS
> CAN WORK . . . GOD'S PUPPETS, BEST AND WORST,
> ARE WE, THERE IS NO LAST NOR FIRST[.]

In Browning's verse drama, this is the 'New-year's hymn' that Pippa consoles herself with before setting off and that she reiterates before falling asleep: even there it functions as citation and moral rather than part of the story (Browning 1849: 1.172, 230). In Griffith's film, it is not even clear whether Pippa is supposed to be speaking these lines at all. They punctuate the scene of her return and remain unintegrated: the few words that Robinson is seen uttering at her window after they have disappeared are too brief for us to feel that these lines are what she is saying. That which might seem to be the most consistently narrativising element in film of this period, the intertitle, is here precisely what sends narrative off course.

Something similar happens in the next film Griffith based on a poem: *The Unchanging Sea* (1910). (Although his earlier *Lines of White on a Sullen Sea* [1909] is often described as based on a poem by William Carleton, I have found no evidence for such a poem existing, and the *Biograph Bulletin* only quotes Carleton's prose [Usai 1996-2006: 3.199]). *The Unchanging Sea* was, as its first intertitle declares, 'SUGGESTED BY CHARLES KINGSLEY'S POEM "THE THREE FISHERS"'. A second intertitle follows with the opening lines:

> Three fishers went sailing to the West,
>   Away to the West as the sun went down,
> Each thought on the woman who loved him best,
> And the women stood watching them out of the town.

What comes next seems to confirm the *Biograph Bulletin*'s claim that the poem, first published in 1851, was only used as 'introduction to a story of sympathetic interest' (4.68): not sailing and watching, but happy love scenes between Arvidson and Arthur Johnson, leaving their fisherman's hut, racing along the shore, and being fondly teased by their community before returning home. It is only after the third intertitle, 'OUT TO SEA', that the events promised in the Kingsley quotation take place. Into them breaks another intertitle with the rest of his first stanza:

> For men must work and women must weep,
> And there's little to earn and many to keep,
> Though the harbor bar be moaning.

Like Pippa's hymn, this is a distraction from the story we are starting to see unfold: an unintegrated remark that does not describe what is happening on screen (the launching of Johnson's boat) but seems to be presented for its own sake. What follows extends its moment of pause: a return to the shot that it interrupted, slightly rearranged, with three women in the foreground, a group of men launching the boat in the middle ground, and the sea taking up most of the rest of the screen. The scene empties: two women leave, the boat sets out, and Arvidson is left alone, her back to the camera. Eventually the only movement comes from the flapping of her clothes in the wind, the bobbing of the boats in the distance, and the repetitive crash of the waves. It is those waves that dominate the shot, I think: they are, almost, audible, and to my ears it is the verse intertitle that has made them so. It is as if the interruption of the story by the almost-irrelevant verse – verse that itself describes sound, 'moaning' – has put everything else on hold so we can start listening to the sound of the sea.

As the *Biograph Bulletin* tacitly recognised by quoting all but seven of the twenty-one lines of Kingsley's poem in its advertisement, despite dismissing it as 'simply a preamble' to Griffith's story, there is something that the verse makes us hear in the film that would not be there without it (4.68-70). Take the seventh intertitle:

> Three corpses lay out on the shining sands,
> In the morning gleam as the tide went down,
> And the women are weeping and wringing their hands,
> For those who will never come back to the town.

This precedes the first shot not set around the village and its shoreline: another sea scene, this time with cliffs in the background and three bodies amidst the breakers in the foreground and middle ground. As before, another intertitle follows with the rest of the stanza:

> For men must work and women must weep,
> And the sooner it's over the sooner to sleep;
> And good-bye to the bar and its moaning.

We then return to the previous shot, now with rescuers and a fourth body that is recognisably Johnson's. But as Trotter puts it, even when the intertitles 'resume their matter-of-factness' and the story picks up pace, depicting

Johnson's amnesia, Arvidson's fidelity, the growth of their child, and their eventual reunion, 'the bar and its moaning have not been obliterated; the shot of corpses and debris remains, as an anti-system, a visual counterpart to that element in poetic language which intelligibility cannot exhaust' (Trotter 2007: 66). What interest Trotter are the moments in Griffith's Biograph films when the earth's contingency – that 'residual formlessness of photographed reality' with which Siegfried Kracauer was preoccupied – springs into view, cutting across the abstractions of the narrative system (54). In *The Unchanging Sea*, verse intertitles play a part in such moments, not only by analogy to the ways in which stray matter resists incorporation into a story or symbolic order, but also as a way of prodding us to hear it. Although Kingsley's verse does not return after the eighth intertitle, the waves do, repeatedly, and so does the rhythm of their breaking. It is that rhythm with which the film ends: it crashes behind and measures the agonizing hesitations that draw out Arvidson and Johnson's final reunion. And it is that rhythm to which the verse intertitles first sensitize our hearing.

What we see in *The Unchanging Sea* is Griffith using verse to open his audience's ears to things beyond the verse itself. In *The Song of the Shirt*, *Edgar Allen Poe*, and *Pippa Passes; or, The Song of Conscience*, recitation is part of the story: these films feature characters who sing or recite, and their intertitles would have enabled exhibitors and audiences to replicate the performances being represented. In the final intertitle of *Pippa Passes; or, The Song of Conscience*, however, Griffith began to experiment with other things that verse might do on screen; by *The Unchanging Sea*, he had detached it from diegesis altogether. For although Arvidson and company act out some of the events described in Griffith's quotations from Kingsley, no-one is supposed to be speaking them. And with recitation no longer represented, audiences have to imagine it instead. This opens up a world of other auditory experience in everything that follows.

When *Chambers's Journal* discussed 'Charles Kingsley as a Lyric Poet' in 1855, it remarked on the power with which his verse evokes sound: 'Some of his dainty little lilts of song are so full of melody, they sing of themselves' (Chambers 1855: 378-9). But no poem really does sing of itself, and the nineteenth-century poets to whom Griffith was attracted were aware of this, as Eric Griffiths has shown in his work on what he, alluding to Browning, describes as *The Printed Voice of Victorian Poetry*. 'Print does not give conclusive evidence of a voice', Griffiths explains, for 'it is impossible to notate speech unambiguously in writing'. Yet 'most of the literature we know, though coming to us in print, envisages and reaches towards a rediscovery of some characters of speech': it is an 'act of supplication to an imagined voice' that 'searches out from print [...] prosodic features, tones of absent voice', and thereby 'speaks to us' (Griffiths 1989: 13, 17, 36, 48). I believe that Griffith, like Griffiths, was alert to the delicacy with which nineteenth-century verse summons speech but does not tell you how to speak it.

It is striking, for example, that so many of the poems Griffith used are so metrically variable, at once appealing to our voices and evading certainty about how to voice them. There are Hood's accentual lines, which owe much to Tennyson's: 'Break, break, break' had been published only a year earlier, in Tennyson's *Poems* (1842), and 'Stitch! stitch! stitch!' surely nods to it. Like Tennyson's, Hood's poem sounds like a song yet leaves the questions of timing upon which sung music relies up in the air (how much time should pass between one 'stitch' and another, for example: the same as it takes to say the syllables that separate the three stresses of the line that follows, or less?). There is the earworm that is 'The Raven', whose trochaic thump does not override a suspicion that some of these trochees might be more thumping than others (compare 'rapping' and 'at my'). And there is the dramatic variation that characterises Browning's *Pippa Passes*, as it shifts between prose, blank verse, and various rhyming forms, raising questions about how these shifts should be dramatized in the process. Griffith's love of such variation is felt in the way he misquotes Kingsley's verse: the difference between his 'Three fishers went sailing to the West' and Kingsley's 'Three fishers went sailing out into the West' is the difference between a freer accentual verse that varies the number of syllables in each line and something more strictly accentual-syllabic that gives fewer options in recitation (Kingsley 1851: 239). Metrical variation characterised Griffith's own attempts at poetry too. In early 1907, Arvidson recalled, 'David wrote yards of poetry' and '*Leslie's Weekly* paid the princely sum of six dollars for a poem called "The Wild Duck"' (Arvidson 1925: 24). Although the poem does not make me wish that Griffith had written more, it evinces preoccupations that remained with him for decades, even in its opening lines:

> Look – how beautiful he is!
> Swift his flight as a bullet
> As he comes in from the sea in the morning.
> For the wind is from the sea in the morning. (Schickel 1996: 82)

In Browning's verse drama, Phene asks Jules: 'was't in the tone / Or the words, your power?' (Browning 1849: 1.196). I believe that Griffith was interested in that power that lies in the relationship between them: in the ways in which words in verse evoke tones but do not unambiguously elicit them, calling complex acts of imagination into play.

The next two poems that Griffith drew on certainly fit this bill, although I have not been able to view surviving prints of the films for which he used them. In 1910, he made a version of Tennyson's verse narrative 'The Golden Supper', published in *The Holy Grail and Other Poems* (1869) and reprinted in *The Lover's Tale* (1879). The *Biograph Bulletin* includes quotations from the poem, and Lea Jacobs describes verse in the intertitles too (Usai 1996-2006: 4.228-31). Griffith's 1911 film *The Spanish Gypsy* also draws on a poem – George Eliot's verse drama of the same title, published in 1868 – although to my knowledge no-one has recognised this. Like Griffith's film, Eliot's poem features a troubadour (Juan, whom Griffith renames Jose), and a girl named Pepita who loves him and dances with him in the plaza, although the film's melodramatic narrative is Griffith's own (5.23-5). What both poetic sources share is a fluid blank verse replete with hyper- and hypo-metrical lines.

Griffith's most extensive response to the fluid blank verse of the nineteenth century came in his next poem film, however: *Enoch Arden* (1911). Three years after *After Many Years*, Griffith returned to its source to make his second film to be released in two parts, and his first longer film released under a single title (5.47-52). The film's relationship to the poem was important to Griffith ('FROM THE POEM BY ALFRED LORD TENNYSON', declares his first intertitle). Yet the opening sequence is taken up with narrative business, establishing the love triangle that will shape the story by introducing 'ANNIE LEE', 'PHILIP RAY', and 'ENOCH ARDEN' in intertitles and what Bowser calls 'introductory shots' of Linda Arvidson, Francis J. Grandon, and Wilfred Lucas (Bowser 1990: 145). *Moving Picture World* published a lecture written by Bush to accompany the film, which in many ways follows Tennyson more closely, doing little beyond taking out his line breaks. But where Bush turns Tennyson into prose and uses him to tell a story, Griffith is willing to punctuate the story to allow verse to speak for itself.

Take what each does with Tennyson's account of Philip seeing Enoch and Annie sitting hand in hand:

> Philip look'd,
> And in their eyes and faces read his doom;
> Then, as their faces drew together, groan'd,
> And slipt aside, and like a wounded life
> Crept down into the hollows of the wood[.] (Tennyson 1864: 5)

This is narrated in Bush's 'Scene 7': 'Philip looked and in their eyes and faces read his doom; then, as their faces grew together, groaned and slipped aside, crept down close to the surging billows' (Bush 1911: 1430). Griffith has a shot showing Lucas and Arvidson on the shore, a shot showing Grandon turning in their direction, then an intertitle, with speech marks so we know it for a quotation:

'PHILIP LOOKED, AND
IN THEIR EYES AND
FACES READ HIS DOOM'[.] (Figure 1)

Lucas and Arvidson reappear, now embracing with Grandon unseen behind them (Figure 2). Then we see this:

'HE SLIPT ASIDE, AND LIKE
   A WOUNDED LIFE
CREPT DOWN INTO THE
   HOLLOWS OF THE WOOD'[.] (Figure 3)

We cut to a shot of bushy plants, faintly trembling, into which Grandon moves and sits down. The shot is drawn out, painfully, as he slowly leans deeper into the foliage, periodically opening and closing his mouth ever so slightly, as if sighs are escaping him, or as if he is breathing so as to keep tears at bay (Figure 4). What we see here, I think, is Tennyson's word 'groan'd', which Griffith does not quote but still keeps in the air. As Tennyson's lines intimate, there are things that can be read that are not words – one's doom, for example – and in this sequence of the film, they prompt us to think about reading more expansively. When Griffith, for the first time, quotes Tennyson here, what

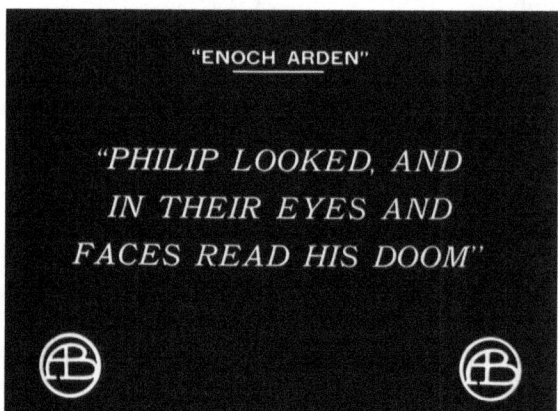

Fig. 1. D.W. Griffith. 2002. *Enoch Arden*. In *Griffith Masterworks*. New York: Kino.

Fig. 2. Griffith. *Enoch Arden*.

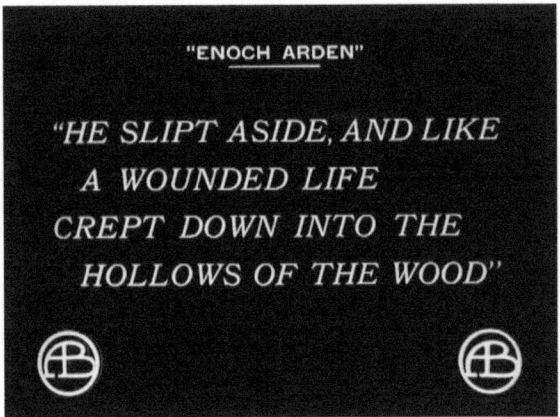

Fig. 3. Griffith. *Enoch Arden*.

Fig. 4. Griffith. *Enoch Arden*.

we start to read, and thereby hear and think about making, are sounds. The sounds that Tennyson's verse so gracefully arranges – 'slipt', 'Crept'; 'aside', 'like', 'life'; 'hollows', 'wood' – seem to bring everything else in this quiet world to auditory life.

'We are coming to pay more and more attention to the words we use on the screen', Griffith told the *New York Times* in 1915 (Slide 2012: 25). Bush would evidently have liked Griffith to use more, and at times he suggests pausing the lecture altogether and asking musicians to cover the gap: while Griffith dwells on Lucas and Arvidson's shoreline farewell, for example, followed by lengthy shots of a ship I suspect he was rather proud of procuring (Bush 1911: 1431). They align again on what Bush calls scene 23 – 'Even to the last deep of the vanishing sail she watched it and departed, weeping for him' – which Griffith differently misquotes Tennyson in titling:

'EV'N TO THE LAST
DIP OF THE VANISHING
SAIL SHE WATCHES IT,
AND DEPARTED
WEEPING FOR HIM'[.]

One imagines Bush then standing in silence again, his patience wearing thin as the next shot drags on. Arvidson is flanked by her children, staring out to sea through a telescope as waves break on the shore; she lowers it, shakes her head, and they plod off-screen. For a moment we are left looking out to sea on our own. It is important to remember that silence could fall in the nickelodeons, Altman insists, quoting O. Winter's description of cinema in 1896: 'Though the waves break upon an imagined shore, they break in a silence which doubles your shrinking from their reality' (Altman 2004: 88-9). By 1911, accompaniments could still be absent or discontinuous, as Bush's lecture text shows. But Griffith was finding other ways to make audible the waves from whose reality Winter shrank. The eddies in Tennyson's verse – the slight hypermetricality of 'vanishing', the extra syllable that overruns the line ending on 'for him', the light rush that follows each inversion ('Ev'n to the last', 'dip of the van-') – reverberate in the storyless sea shot that follows, opening our ears to the breaking we see (Tennyson 1864: 14).

That such processes fascinated Griffith is felt in the fact that the most audible sound in *Enoch Arden* is a sound no-one else hears. After years of doubt, Arvidson has married Grandon; Lucas has been rescued from his desert island, and, having learned his fate from Grace Henderson, gone to look in the window of the new family's home. Tennyson explains it thus:

> Then he, tho' Miriam Lane had told him all,
> Because things seen are mightier than things heard,
> Stagger'd and shook, holding the branch, and fear'd
> To send abroad a shrill and terrible cry,
> Which in one moment, like the blast of doom,
> Would shatter all the happiness of the hearth. (42)

The contradiction is a potent one. Things seen are mightier than things heard, we are told, only to learn that things heard can be more destructive still, for although Enoch is shaken by a sight, the family would be shattered if he made any noise about it. Griffith uses none of these words, but I suspect they were important to him. He cuts from Lucas looking in the window to the family inside, and, just as Arvidson turns toward the window herself (Figure 5), cuts back to Lucas, who seems to cry 'Annie' (Figure 6) before falling back and covering his mouth with his hand (Figure 7). What Griffith achieves here is to open Tennyson's contradiction out so that it can be experienced sequentially. We are invited to hear Enoch cry, and we are shown that things seen are mightier than things heard as he does it, for although there is no sound in

Fig. 5. Griffith. *Enoch Arden.*

Fig. 6. Griffith. *Enoch Arden.*

Fig. 7. Griffith. *Enoch Arden*

this image, we see, beyond doubt, that he calls his wife's name. But then we are shown that he stops himself, and that this cry is just something we have seen: what matters is that no-one has heard it. It is a curious, brilliant moment of simultaneous allusion to and betrayal of the processes by which Griffith brings us to believe in what we hear through what he shows us, and it lays bare how profoundly ambivalent his evocations of sound can be.

In this, Griffith had Tennyson's *Enoch Arden* as precedent. When Annie and Philip marry, the celebrations are repetitively noisy ('So these were wed and merrily rang the bells, / Merrily rang the bells and they were wed'), but Annie's ears remain haunted: 'A footstep seem'd to fall beside her path, / She knew not whence; a whisper on her ear, / She knew not what' (28). Shipwrecked, Enoch is plagued by the sounds of his island, and haunted by the 'babble' of his children and 'the pealing of his parish bells', presumably ringing for Annie's wedding (32-4). This is a poem preoccupied by the experience of half-hearing absent voices. But it is also a poem that generates that experience for its readers, through the lush alliteration, assonance, and irregularity of its blank verse:

> The slender coco's drooping crown of plumes,
> The lightning flash of insect and of bird,
> The lustre of the long convolvuluses
> That coil'd around the stately stems, and ran
> Ev'n to the limit of the land, the glows
> And glories of the broad belt of the world,
> All these he saw; but what he fain had seen
> He could not see, the kindly human face,
> Nor ever hear a kindly voice, but heard
> The myriad shriek of wheeling ocean-fowl,
>   The league-long roller thundering on the reef,
> The moving whisper of huge trees that branch'd
> And blossom'd in the zenith, or the sweep
> Of some precipitous rivulet to the wave[.] (32-3)

Referring to *Enoch Arden* among other poems, Francis Turner Palgrave lamented after Tennyson's death that 'these can never be heard again, no, nor read, to similar advantage. Something of their music, some part of their very essence, has passed with the Maker' (Tennyson 1897: 2.494). But Tennyson hoped there was something audible in the verse itself, as his son recalled:

> when he was reading 'Enoch Arden' he told Miss L– to listen to
> the sound of the sea in the line
> The league-long roller thundering on the reef,
> and to mark Miriam Lane's chatter in
>   He ceased; and Miriam Lane
>   Made such a voluble answer promising all. (2.409-10)

'[T]he voice in the poem is not withdrawn from writing, but into it, preserved by the lines in sight of resuscitation, poised in air', writes Griffiths of Tennyson (Griffiths 1989: 101). *Enoch Arden* may make such resuscitation difficult, oscillating as it does between what Murphet describes as 'sheerly lyrical qualities' and 'ballad-narrative contents' (Murphet 2009: 85). But as Tennyson's remarks to 'Miss L–' suggest, sounds can be summoned by both modes of writing, and the doubt that plagues such summonings was not something of which he was unaware. It is not clear what Tennyson heard as the sound of chatter in his Miriam Lane line – the 'l's, the 'i's, the slight hypermetricality of 'voluble' and 'promising'? – but it is clear that he wrote the experience of feeling doubtful about whether or not one is hearing chatter into his descriptions of Annie and Enoch, so the fact that this experience also troubles his readers is unlikely to be accidental. It is this experience, I believe, that Griffith was most drawn to, and this experience that Tennyson's verse helped him write into his films.

Griffith made a second two-reeler of a Victorian poem not long after – *A Blot in the 'Scutcheon* (1912), based on Browning's verse drama of the same name (1843) – but Russell Merritt is dismissive of its 'semi-coherent Browningese', and I have not been able to view a surviving print to judge for myself (Usai 1996-2006: 5.186-8). Yet Griffith's next poem film shows he was not losing his touch: *The Sands of Dee*, also released in 1912, based on a poem first published in Kingsley's novel *Alton Locke, Tailor and Poet: An Autobiography* (1850). As we have seen, Griffith was not only interested in using verse writing to garner respectability for an ambivalent new technology; he was also interested in the ambivalent technologies of verse writing itself. But verse technologies and filmic technologies were pulling in different directions by 1912, and in *The Sands of Dee*, the last poem film Griffith made for Biograph, he explored their incompatibilities as well as their kinship.

The film opens by quoting the beginning of Kingsley's poem, but most of its story unfolds with melodramatic predictability and little need for intertitles: Bobby Harron loves Mae Marsh, who is tricked into a false marriage with a wealthy artist, rejected, then cast out by her father and mother, played by Charles Hill Mailes and Grace Henderson. But in the closing sequences, verse intertitles suddenly reappear, cutting bafflingly across the inevitable conclusion. After Marsh's dismissal, for example, we see her on the beach, then see the end of Kingsley's first stanza:

THE WESTERN WIND WAS WILD
    AND DANK WI' FOAM,
    AND ALL ALONE WENT SHE.

How are we to interpret what we see next? Henderson fills Harron in on Marsh's plight, and Harron heads shoreward to look for her: if this were happening immediately after the previous shot, Marsh would still be on the beach. She is not: what we see next is her draped, motionless, over a rock amidst breakers. Harron, on the beach a few shots later, seems to see something off screen that is presumably Marsh on the rock, for it is from that rock that he then carries her body in. But what we are shown immediately after he seems to see something is a low shot empty of everything but water running up the sand, followed by Kingsley's second stanza:

> THE CREEPING TIDE CAME UP
> THE SAND, AND O'ER AND O'ER
> THE SAND, AND ROUND AND
> ROUND THE SAND, AND NEVER
>   HOME CAME SHE.

There follows another low shot, of something floating in deeper water (Marsh, perhaps?). But when is this supposed to have occurred? For the next we see of Marsh is when Harron carries her body in from the rock where we earlier saw her slumped. It is as if the shots of Marsh and the verse that accompanies them unfold out of order and outside narrative sequence. Even after everything gathers around Marsh's body for the melodramatic conclusion, she and the intertitles escape again into another kind of time. We see two fishermen, one lifting his hand to his ear, then the end of Kingsley's final stanza:

> BUT STILL THE BOATMEN HEAR
> HER CALL THE CATTLE HOME,
>   ACROSS THE SANDS O' DEE[.]

This explains what we see next – Marsh, hazy on the cliffs, hand by mouth in a calling gesture – before we cut back to the fishermen, who move out of shot, hands to ears, leaving the screen full of waves again as it darkens in a final fade. These closing shots turn the aspects of nineteenth-century poetry with which Griffith had been fascinated since childhood into a narrative subject: they show us what it is like to half-hear sounds that are not literally there, but not not there either. But they also turn narrative itself inside out, thereby offering a resonant summation of his work with verse for Biograph, if not a conclusion to the story.

Decades later, Siegfried Kracauer contemplated the eeriness of silent film, with its 'waves which ripple noiselessly in an inaudible wind'. Music, he wrote, 'lights up the pale silent images on the screen so that they will stay with us', enabling the perception of pattern: 'scattered visual data coalesce and follow a definite course' (Kracauer 1997: 134-5). But that course is not necessarily the course of narrative continuity. The ambivalent music written into Kingsley's verse has other effects. Where Gunning finds that empty shots like that which ends *The Sands of Dee* 'present the world of the story in the process of emptying itself and thereby accomplishing its completeness', I find them replete with something else: they show, not the world of the story, but the world outside story that makes any story necessarily incomplete, that 'world of contingent events and unimportant details' that Gunning suggests the 'filmic narrator' must 'overcome' but that the camera cannot help but record (Gunning 1991: 280, 17). It is this world that the verse in Griffith's Biograph poem films prods us to hear. As Kracauer put it:

> His films are full of fissures traceable to his cinematic instinct rather than technical awkwardness. On the one hand, he certainly aims at establishing dramatic continuity as impressively as possible; on the other, he invariably inserts images which do not just serve to further the action or convey relevant moods but retain a degree of independence of the intrigue and thus succeed in summoning physical existence. In watching these pictures or pictorial configurations, we may indeed forget the drama they punctuate in their own diffuse meanings. (Kracauer 1997: 231)

This is as true of the verse that Griffith cites as it is of the images onto which the verse opens.

Acknowledgements

I am grateful to Jamie Baxendine, who introduced me to Griffith, to David Trotter, with whom I have enjoyed talking about him, and to both for their invaluable comments on this chapter. I am also grateful to students of the Cambridge English Faculty Lyric Paper between 2013 and 2016, who generously discussed this work with me in seminars. All the films I discuss are in the public domain and available on the Internet Archive: https://www.archive.org/.

Works Cited

Abel, Richard, and Rick Altman, editors. 2001. *The Sounds of Early Cinema*. Bloomington: Indiana University Press.

Altman, Rick. 1992. 'Dickens, Griffith, and Film Theory Today'. In *Classical Hollywood Narrative: The Paradigm Wars*, edited by Jane Gaines, 9-47. Durham: Duke University Press.

Altman, Rick. 2004. *Silent Film Sound*. New York: Columbia University Press.

Arvidson, Linda ('Mrs. D.W. Griffith'). 1925. *When the Movies were Young*. New York: E.P. Dutton.

Bowser, Eileen. 1990. *The Transformation of Cinema 1907-1915*. Berkeley: University of California Press.

Brown, Karl. 1988. *Adventures with D.W. Griffith*. Edited by Kevin Brownlow. London: Faber and Faber.

Browning, Robert. 1849. *Poems*. 2 volumes. London: Chapman and Hall.

Bush, W. Stephen. 1911. 'Lectures on Notable Reels'. *The Moving Picture World*, June 24.

Chambers, William, and Robert Chambers, editors. 1855. 'Charles Kingsley as a Lyric Poet'. *Chambers's Journal of Popular Literature*, June 16: 378-9.

Châteauvert, Jean, and André Gaudreault. 2001. 'The Noises of Spectators, or the Spectator as Additive to the Spectacle'. In *The Sounds of Early Cinema*, edited by Richard Abel and Rick Altman, 183-91. Bloomington: Indiana University Press.

Eisenstein, Sergei. 1949. 'Dickens, Griffith, and the Film Today'. In *Film Form: Essays in Film Theory*, edited and translated by Jay Leyda, 195-255. New York: Harcourt, Brace, & World.

Geduld, Harry M., editor. 1971. *Focus on D.W. Griffith*. Englewood Cliffs: Prentice-Hall.

Griffiths, Eric. 1989. *The Printed Voice of Victorian Poetry*. Oxford: Clarendon Press.

Gunning, Tom. 1991. *D.W. Griffith & the Origins of American Narrative Film: The Early Years at Biograph*. Urbana: University of Illinois Press.

Hart, James. 1972. *The Man Who Invented Hollywood: The Autobiography of D.W. Griffith*. Louisville: Touchstone.

Hood, Thomas. 1843. 'The Song of the Shirt'. *Punch, or the London Charivari*, December 16: 260.

Iampolski, Mikhail. 1998. *The Memory of Tiresias: Intertextuality and Film*. Translated by Harsha Ram. Berkeley: University of California Press.

Kingsley, Charles. 1850. *Alton Locke, Tailor and Poet: An Autobiography*. 2 volumes. London: Chapman and Hall.

Kingsley, Charles. 1851. 'Three fishers went sailing'. *The Christian Socialist*, October 11: 239.

Kracauer, Siegfried. 1997. *Theory of Film: The Redemption of Physical Reality*, with an introduction by Miriam Bratu Hansen. Princeton: Princeton University Press.

Murphet, Julian. 2009. *Multimedia Modernism: Literature and the Anglo-American Avant-garde*. Cambridge: Cambridge University Press.

Poe, Edgar Allan. 1845. *The Raven and Other Poems*. New York: Wiley and Putnam.

Prins, Yopie. 2008. 'Robert Browning, Transported by Meter'. In *The Traffic in Poems: Nineteenth-Century Poetry and Transatlantic Exchange*, edited by Meredith L. McGill, 205-230. New Brunswick: Rutgers University Press.

Raynauld, Isabelle. 2001. 'Dialogues in Early Silent Sound Screenplays: What Actors Really Said'. In *The Sounds of Early Cinema*, edited by Richard Abel and Rick Altman, 69-78. Bloomington: Indiana University Press.

Schickel, Richard. 1996. *D.W. Griffith: An American Life*. New York: Limelight.

Slide, Anthony, editor. 2012. *D.W. Griffith Interviews*. Jackson: University Press of Mississippi.

Tennyson, Alfred. 1864. *Enoch Arden, Etc*. London: Edward Moxon.

Tennyson, Hallam. 1897. *Alfred Lord Tennyson: A Memoir by His Son*. 2 volumes. London: Macmillan.

Trotter, David. 2007. *Cinema and Modernism*. Oxford: Blackwell.

Usai, Paolo Cherchi, general editor. 1996-2006. *The Griffith Project*. 12 volumes. London: British Film Institute.

6

Enigma Variations: Mallarmé, Joyce, and the Aesthetics of Encryption

PAUL SHEEHAN

On or about June 2013 human character changed. Democratic governance suddenly became a lot harder to believe in, as Western leaders more or less admitted that the privacy of their citizens was less important than maintaining national security. Calls for greater transparency went unheeded; freedoms that had once been taken for granted began to seem ephemeral; and concerns about technological intrusiveness proliferated. Such, at any rate, was the form taken three years ago by the media response to the revelations of Edward Snowden, a private intelligence contractor who handed over to the world's media thousands of classified documents detailing global surveillance programmes. These documents revealed that the National Security Agency and the so-called Five Eyes – an intelligence alliance comprising Canada, the UK, Australia, and New Zealand, as well as the US – had been running such programmes for years, principally by monitoring telephone, email, and internet use, with little regard for the law.

A flood of dire warnings ensued, predicting the 'end of privacy' and the ubiquity of sinister panoptical technology; the future, heretofore, would be one of compulsory, enforced openness (Knigge 2013; Pierce 2013; Weinberger 2014). In the wider arc of cultural history, however, Snowden's revelations seemed almost like business as usual. Throughout the last century, the right to privacy has more often than not yielded to the pressures of public relations and publicity, as well as more covert practices of state and military surveillance. In fact, these deep-rooted developments have refigured our understanding of the Victorian era. Far from being a period of probity and rectitude, as was once believed, the second half of the nineteenth century now appears to us as the last great Age of Secrecy. Deception, concealment, discretion, and doubling: these storytelling devices all helped to make that Age so compelling, at least in terms of its literary products. Hence the profusion of late-Victorian novels and plays that involve blackmail, often featuring tell-tale documents (the incriminating letter, the elusive property deed); bigamy and hidden or uncertain patrimony; and forbidden desire (whether as sexual impropriety or its decadent twin, sexual transgression). If Charles Dickens presided over this Age, as the unrivalled master of psychological and narrative concealment, then his foil was Oscar Wilde, the arch-poet of secrecy and self-display.

The modernist turn, as we know, involved a complex renegotiation of Victorian precepts and poetics. This shift is particularly critical when it comes to secrecy, because it is marked by an *involution* – not so much a rejection of hidden machinations or an embrace of openness as a turning inwards. Secrets still abide, in the early decades of the twentieth century, but they are no longer seen as primarily social, inter-personal matters. Instead, they are translated into textual concerns, centred around questions of method and technique. My focus in this essay, then, is technographic secrecy – which is to say, the modernist interest in secret languages, in cryptic writing, and in codes and ciphers. By examining this interest, I suggest, we can engage with modernism's difficulty and obliquity, and further our understanding of its hermeneutical ambitions.

The coded word has a long and, as it happens, bloody history – at least by association. Encrypted messages have played a crucial role in the history of warfare, for as long as there have been records of such events. Indeed, if it were not for secret communications, strategies for moving large masses of men into pre-designated positions without enemy awareness would simply not be possible. The Roman historian Suetonius describes how Julius Caesar 'would write in code, changing the order of the letters of the alphabet, so that not a word could be made out' (Suetonius 2000: 28) – an indispensable method for conveying messages to his generals stationed at the war front. The 'manner' in question is now known as the 'Caesar shift', a substitution cipher in which each letter is replaced by another letter further down the alphabet. Poly-alphabetic techniques grew from this – i.e., substitutions that changed alphabets with each letter – first by hand and then, in the twentieth century, more rapidly thanks to what has been called the 'mechanization of secrecy': electro-mechanical, rotor-driven devices that first scramble text and then transmit it using Morse code signals. The best known of these devices is the Enigma enciphering machine, invented by the German engineer Arthur Scherbius in 1918 and used extensively by the Nazi military throughout the Second World War. The fate of the war, as counter-factualist historians like to tell us, hinged on the code-breakers at Bletchley Park. With the help of the 'bombe' deciphering machine (originally designed by Alan Turing) the daily settings of the Enigma machines on the German military network could be established, and the messages intercepted and decoded.

The science that has emerged between these two events, the development of the Caesar shift and the appearance of the Enigma machine, has also expanded accordingly, keeping pace with advancements of the technology. As an instrument for analysing hidden or secret writing, the science of cryptology has two arms: cryptography, the art of making codes and cipher systems; and cryptanalysis, the study of how secret writing can be translated or interpreted.

To read these practices in the context of literary modernism, as I propose to do, is to come up against the perennial problems of difficulty, obscurantism, and unreadability. To put this another way: because it is the art of allusion *par excellence*, modernist writing is determinedly cryptic, even when it is not overtly cryptographic. We need look no further than its anti-revelatory narratives to find signal examples of this tendency – whether it be the dying words of a charismatic but corrupted man, adverting to some unspeakable, inexpressible horror; the enigmatic relationship between a shell-shocked, or perhaps rather schizophrenic, First World War veteran and a politician's wife who is wont to throw extravagant parties; or a tale of adultery, death, and madness recounted by a cuckolded narrator whose limited knowledge and understanding of events make him barely capable of narrating in the first place.

Why were literary modernists compelled to use these modes of evasiveness and unfathomability? Leonard Diepeveen, in *The Difficulties of Modernism* (2003), gives two possible answers. The first, now more or less discredited, is that it was an exclusionary tactic, an imperious gesture to keep understanding in the hands of the privileged few. The counter-argument, which still has some purchase today, is no less high-minded: modernist textual opacity bespeaks the desire to move beyond language, beyond rationality, even beyond form (Diepeveen 2003: 126-35). Though versions of this argument are still in circulation, it has a quasi-mystical character that makes it difficult to see modernist texts as linguistic constructs. I want to suggest, by contrast, something much more straightforward and pragmatic. The coding and encipherment undertaken by some literary works do not just provide the pleasures of puzzle-solving, which can more readily be obtained from non-literary sources; they also yield significant aesthetic returns, in the economy of meaning. There is, in other words, an *aesthetics of encryption* that can be gleaned from modernism's poetics of elusiveness.

Such an aesthetics, I suggest, is founded on a two-sided promise – the promise of a key, and the withholding of a solution. Think of the notes appended to *The Waste Land*, which promise to unlock the mysteries of Eliot's recondite poem but, of course, do nothing of the sort; as Louis Menand notes, the rationale of Eliot's interpretive method means that they become 'simply another riddle [...] to be solved' (Menand 2007: 89). Nevertheless, their supplementary existence affects how the work is read, prompting the hope that its radical discontinuities might *themselves* contain a logic of coherence and (hence) a secret aesthetic schema.

In his magisterial study of *The Cryptographic Imagination*, Shawn Rosenheim describes how such hopes are inculcated. As well as texts that explicitly include ciphers or codes, Rosenheim brings to our attention

> a constellation of literary techniques concerning secrecy in writing. These include private ciphers, acrostics, allusions, hidden signatures, chiasmal framing, etymological reference,

and plagiarism; purloined writing and disappearing inks; and the thematic consequences – anonymity, doubling, identification, and the like – that follow from cryptographic texts. (Rosenheim 1997: 2)

Rosenheim is suggesting that cryptographic techniques can be seen as a part of wider literary-critical procedures; extrapolating from this, we might conclude that they also have aesthetic uses.

However, there is one critical practice that raises questions. Cryptography has a relationship with the theory of textuality that is problematic, or at the very least uncertain. To attend to textuality is to acknowledge that a literary work has a future, as well as the past and present inscribed in it at the time of its birth. It is the recognition that its meanings do not stop with the author or with its contemporary context, but will continue to be produced across time, as its circumstances change. By contrast, to read a text cryptanalytically, so to speak – to discern a clear-cut pattern or a systematic manipulation of literary codes – is to disclose an act of deliberation, to see up close the powers of authorial agency. Cryptographic clues in a modernist text mean that *un*readability is displaced by *self*-readability, in which the cipher, or structuring algorithm, works as a kind of paratext – albeit one that is embedded in the work itself. Consequently, a cryptanalyst, or a cryptanalytical critic, cannot resort to the textual unconscious as support for his or her interpretive propositions.

I will address this clash between cryptographic and textualist readings further on. At this point, I want to suggest that the cryptic and the cryptographic meet most distinctively – on equal terms, as it were – in the novels of James Joyce. These works provide compelling aesthetic and heuristic justifications for the practice of 'secret writing' – as a method, a technique, a technography. To set the scene for Joyce, let us look back to the mid-to-late nineteenth century, and the literary genesis of cryptography.

Poe / Mallarmé: The Number of the Stars

Rosenheim locates the foundations of the cryptographic imagination in the detective story – which means, effectively, Edgar Allan Poe's Auguste Dupin tales, the works that gave birth to the genre. Poe himself was an enthusiast of cryptographic puzzles; in fact, he coined the term 'cryptograph', and even produced a kind of mini-treatise on 'secret writing'. Part history, part how-to guide, it contains this astute observation:

The reader should bear in mind that the basis of the whole art of solution [i.e., decryption], as far as regards these matters, is found in the general principles of the formation of language itself, and thus is altogether independent of the particular laws which govern any cipher, or the construction of its key. (Poe 1841: 34)

Even a secret language must adhere to wider rules that govern all languages – rules concerning regularity, consistency, and necessary repetitions – in order to be intelligible. This means, in turn, that the cipher text bears a relationship to its original or plain text that goes beyond simply the algorithm used for the encryption process.

It is elucidations such as these that endeared Poe to the French Symbolist poets, also concerned with the 'formation of language itself' and with how its general principles might be reconceived. Charles Baudelaire was, of course, Poe's great French champion, but he was followed closely in this by Stéphane Mallarmé, Baudelaire's admirer and one-time disciple. As well as translating several of Poe's texts into French, including *The Raven*, Mallarmé composed (at the invitation of A.C. Swinburne) an elegy to mark the twenty-fifth anniversary of Poe's death. Entitled 'Le Tombeau d'Edgar Poe', it has been read as nothing less than a declaration of Symbolist principles (Wilson 19): 'Donner un sens plus pur aux mots de la tribu' ('[To bestow] purer sense on the phrases of the crowd' [Mallarmé 2006: 70-1]).

It is with Mallarmé that the rarefied sub-category of 'cryptographic modernism' comes into being. To approach the poet through French theory, however, is to confront a very different kind of progenitor. For Maurice Blanchot, writing in the 1940s, Mallarmé is first a destroyer and then a creator: the thinker (and poet) who grasped the absence and silence at the heart of language, and saw it as literature's negative capability, its radically unfixable condition (Blanchot 1995: 27-42). Similar analyses are undertaken throughout the 1960s, in the pages of *Tel Quel*, by Gérard Genette, Philippe Sollers, and Pierre Rottenberg, for whom Mallarmé is *the* exemplar of literary modernity. That enterprise culminates with the publication of Jacques Derrida's 'La Double séance' in 1970. Derrida's Mallarmé disturbs the mimetic hierarchies that Plato sets up so carefully in *Ion* and *The Republic*, making the distinction between *imitator* and *imitated* inoperable. Referring only to its own articulation, the poet's writing is both inside and out, both ideal image and material object (Derrida 1970a: 18-23; 1981: 198-206).

In the 1990s, Mallarmé remains in the vanguard of French theoretical discourse. Alain Badiou gives him pride of place in his Age of Poets – a sequence that runs from Hölderlin to Celan – in which poetry takes over the functions of philosophy. Mallarmé represents for Badiou the fulfillment of this annexation, by showing how the poem can be not just a mode of saying but also a form of thinking (Badiou 2014: 5). And Jacques Rancière seeks to rescue Mallarmé from the shadows of 'obscurity', by which he means secrecy, hermeticism, ineffability. Far from being an 'ivory tower' aesthete, says Rancière, Mallarmé was worldly and community-minded, and fully attuned to art's place in the social and political economy (Rancière 2011:

xv-xvi). None of these writers sees Mallarmé's work as particularly rarefied or coded, nor as rife with private associations and esoteric symbols that need to be deciphered. Blanchot implicitly repudiates such views in an early piece entitled 'Is Mallarmé's Poetry Obscure?' (The short answer: 'no' [Blanchot 2001: 110].) And Rancière states outright that 'Mallarmé is not a hermetic author; he is a difficult author' (Rancière 2011: xiv).

The most recent addition to this canon – a 'fourth generation', as it were – is Quentin Meillassoux's 2011 study, *Le Nombre et la sirène*. The subtitle of this work is *Un déchiffrage du* Coup de dés *de Mallarmé* – 'un déchiffrage' being a decipherment or decoding. Meillassoux only engages superficially with the line of descent I have just cited, briefly (but firmly) taking issue with Blanchot and Rancière. Instead, he draws on a different French critical tradition – that of Mitsou Ronat and Jacques Roubaud, who restrict themselves to a small part of the poem. In the wake of a shipwreck, a hand clutches two dice, and is on the verge of rolling them:

		au poing qui l'étreindrait
	comme on menace	un destin les vents
l'unique Nombre qui ne peut pas		être un autre

		in the fist that seeks to grasp it
	as you threaten	some destiny and also the winds
the one and only Number that cannot		be any other[.]
(Mallarmé 2006: 166-7)		

For Ronat and Roubaud, the 'one and only Number' both structures and co-ordinates Mallarmé's poem, and it is twelve: the alexandrine poetic metre, comprising twelve syllables; the twelve double-pages of the text, in twelve-point type; and the thirty six lines – three multiples of twelve – that make up each page (Meillassoux 2012: 26-7).

Meillassoux argues that Mallarmé himself refutes the 'twelve' hypothesis on the *Un Coup de dés* manuscript, in his instructions for printing the poem. Meillassoux's study is, then, a strange kind of hybrid – at once sensitive to the evidential nuances of 'secret writing', yet establishing many of its claims through the methods of critical theory: puns and etymologies, counterintuitive rationales, and sly metonymical shifts. For Meillassoux, the 'one and only Number' of the poem is seven. He finds support for this in other Mallarmé works; and in cosmology. Because the poet regarded the night sky as a celestial symbol of chance, Meillassoux argues that the Little Bear constellation – which contains the pole star – is significant; and the Little Bear contains seven stars. The momentous last line of the poem – 'Toute Pensée émet un Coup de Dés' ('Every thought emits a throw of dice') – consists of seven words. And the number *sept* is an anagram for Mallarmé's first name – or at least the first four letters (45-51). Meillassoux eventually arrives at the 'unique number' of 707 – the total number of words in *Un Coup de dés* (68-79). The pieces of 'evidence' that he cites to reach this point are not equally robust, but he is at least aware that the encrypted number cannot be treated as an end in itself:

> it is true that a code, in itself, is basically something rather puerile, whatever its complexity; something devoid of literary value, in any case. [...] To introduce such games into such a beautiful work, with such weighty stakes: How could Mallarmé have done this to us? (10-11)

As far as Meillassoux is concerned, the real question, or questions, are: '*Why* encrypt the *Coup de dés* [and] why encrypt it in *this way*?' (11). These questions get to the heart of cryptographic modernism, and to its aesthetical underpinnings. Keeping in mind both Mallarmé's technical virtuosity and Meillassoux's line of enquiry, I will now move on to Joyce.

Joyce's Enigmatics: Reading for the Secret

Mallarmés talismanic number – at least as interpreted by Meillassoux – also strikes a chord with the Joyce of *Ulysses*. Just before Stephen embarks on a discussion about *Hamlet*, in the 'Scylla and Charybdis' episode, he is asked if he has found the 'six brave medicals' to whom he might dictate his work. Stephen replies: 'I feel you would need one more for *Hamlet*. Seven is dear to the mystic mind. The shining seven W.B. calls them.' (Joyce 1986: 151) Seven is, indeed, a luminous number in esoteric lore, as Joyce and Yeats were both aware. And in keeping with this belief, *Ulysses* is laden with 'shining seven[s]': the seventh gravedigger who sidles up to Bloom in 'Hades'; the gorgonzola sandwich that he purchases in 'Lestrygonians', costing seven pence; Robert Emmett's seven last words, recalled by Bloom in 'Sirens'; and the sudden appearance of Edward VII in 'Circe', precipitating the English soldier's attack on Stephen. Seen in this light, it is no coincidence that Molly and Leopold Bloom live at 7 Eccles Street.

But Joyce's interest in numerology is not the only thing that links him to Mallarmé. In the mid-1950s, David Hayman suggested that a 'Mallarmé code' was operating in *Finnegans Wake*. His key instance is on the novel's second page:

> Where the Baddelaries partisans are still out to mathmaster Malachus Micgranes and the Verdons catapelting the camibalistics out of the Whoyteboyce of Hoodie Head. (Joyce 1975a: 4)

Debates about symbolist poetry are restaged as struggles between factions, followers of Baudelaire versus the 'mathmaster' Stéphane Mallarmé, with Verlaine's followers struggling against the rest of the world. From this initial 'key', Hayman traces out the 'double m' insignia as a coded allusion to Mallarmé in play throughout the *Wake*: 'Mohomadhawn Mike', 'Tomatoes malmalaid', 'Montmalency', and the like. But Haymen's cryptotextual analysis does not stop with these arch, semi-facetious examples. His far more contentious claim is that Joyce's text is nothing less than a 'recryption' of *Un Coup de dés*, using the same universal symbols to depict the same truths, and then conveying them in the same way (Hayman 1956: 37). Hayman has amassed a welter of correspondences to support the claim, but what is perhaps most noteworthy about his approach is that he is on Joyce's side. Over the years, similarly totalizing claims about the *Wake* have often ended in dismissal, as if the entire text were a monstrous cryptogram for which only the author possessed the key.

Rather than get lost in determining what that key, or those keys, might be, I will instead turn back to the more tractable *Ulysses*. Bloom himself is acquainted with at least one cryptographic technique. In the 'Ithaca' chapter, he enters the front room of his house, which contains a locked drawer. The punctilious narrator then reveals to us the (fairly considerable) contents of that drawer, including two pornographic postcards, two condoms, and some amorous correspondence from Martha Clifford. Alongside Martha's three letters, Bloom keeps to hand

> the transliterated name and address of the addresser of the 3 letters in reserved alphabetic boustrophedontic punctuated quadrilinear cryptogram (vowels suppressed) N. IGS./WI.UU. OX/W. OKS. MH/Y. IM. (Joyce 1986: 592)

The cryptogram is based on a bi-directional alphabet – A-Z mapped onto Z-A – which when decoded (vowels still suppressed) reads as follows: 'M.RTH./ DR.FF.LC/D.LPH.NS/ B.RN'. Both cryptogram and decoded message, each taking four lines, are 'quadrilinear'. This moment is set up thirteen chapters earlier, in 'Calypso' – the Homeric name for 'the Concealer'. In that chapter, the Blooms keep textual secrets from each other: Molly receives a letter from her impresario Blazes Boylan, and Leopold prepares to collect a fourth amorous letter from Martha Clifford. The cryptogram in 'Ithaca' is thus emblematic of Bloom's penchant for schemes and secrecy, and makes perfect sense in the context of his role as a 'concealer'.

A more consequential form of secrecy is alluded to in the 'Syclla and Charybdis' chapter, set in the National Library, via an instance of what could be termed meta-cryptography. The authorship of Shakespeare's plays is put in question by John Eglinton, who invokes the theory that they are really the work of Francis Bacon. The need for secrecy here might have been political or it might have been religious; in either case, encryption was needed. And the best way to prove it, as Ignatius Donnelly tried to do, was by locating a cipher in Bacon's writing and then applying it to the First Folio (Donnelly 1887); phrases or letters indicating Bacon's authorship would then be revealed. For Stephen's narrating consciousness this is more like popular entertainment than serious scholarship: 'Cypherjugglers going the highroads. Seekers on the great quest. What town, good masters?' (160).

These examples are fairly overt cryptographic details or flourishes. In terms of the book's architecture, exhibit A is the table of times, organs, arts, and technics that Joyce gave to his friend Carlo Linati as, in his words, 'a sort of summary – key – skeleton – scheme (for home use only)' (Joyce 1975b: 271). The Linati schema, like the 'notes' to *The Waste Land*, does indeed hold out the promise of a key, and like the 'notes' it does not actually explain or solve any of the work's deeper mysteries. There is, however, a much bigger promise made to the reader, before she has even opened the book. The Homeric parallel, we might say, is a kind of cipher, an algorithm for understanding, amongst other occurrences, the cryptic relationship between Stephen and Bloom.

The title, in fact, promises everything: a rewriting of Homer's epic account of wandering and return, a translation, and a translocation, from larger-than-life exploits in the Ancient Mediterranean to quotidian life in turn-of-the-century Ireland. But although the text only fulfils a small part of this promise, that did not prevent Eliot and Stuart Gilbert from aggrandizing the Homeric parallels, and the 'mythical method' that they ostensively spawned. By contrast, a later generation of critics, writing during and after the Second World War, was more circumspect. Harry Levin, in his 1941 critical introduction to Joyce, downplayed the Homeric precedent, emphasizing instead the ways in which *Ulysses* parts company with *The Odyssey* (Levin 1941: 72). A decade later, Hugh Kenner went even further. Without actually blaming Joyce, he argued that the parallels with Homer have been followed too slavishly and too methodically, to the detriment of the field of Joyce studies (Kenner 1952: 92-100). And a few years after that, A. Walton Litz suggested that the 'trivial details of the Homeric correspondence' were important for Joyce's exploration of his materials, not as 'clues for future readers' (Litz 1961: 39).

Is Joyce to blame for this state of affairs? Or perhaps we should ask: what's in a title? Being restricted to a single one is contrary to the spirit of the book, and its polyphonic, heteroglossial energies. We might wonder, then, what the effect would be if Joyce had chosen a more neutral, less mythologically weighted title; a title such as, say, *Bloom*. (This is not entirely fanciful because, as we know, the *Portrait* was translated into French and Italian under the title *Dedalus*, and the most recent, 2003 film adaptation of *Ulysses* was re-titled *Bloom*.) Though this would be unfair to Stephen and Molly, and to their narrating consciousnesses, how would it affect the way we read the novel

– would the Homeric parallels stabilize, recede, or disappear from the text altogether?

Mallarmé objected to the weight of significance granted a title, and its power to (over)determine meaning. '[W]e must forget the title', he said, 'for it is too resounding' (Mallarmé 1956: 33). But if the book-title *Ulysses* is a cipher, as I am suggesting, then it is readily exchangeable for other literary precursors. Consider, for example, that in 1907, when Joyce was planning to conclude *Dubliners* with a story entitled 'Ulysses in Dublin', he was also looking ahead to his modern anti-epic. His model for that work-to-come was, however, not Homer but Goethe. In a letter to his brother Stanislaus, Joyce declared that his novel 'would depict an Irish Faust, heroic and full of presumption' (Hayman 1982: 67). If this sounds a lot like 'Stephen Hero', we should note that even in his later, actual incarnation, as Bloom's spiritual son, Stephen possesses an unmistakably Faustian temper. Hayman notes the absorption of abstruse lore, the elevation of spirit over flesh, the acute disillusionment, and Stephen's general unworldliness and asceticism (69). Additionally, we might note that his boisterous and underhanded house-mate – or rather, tower-mate – Buck Mulligan is, as Richard Ellmann points out, more than a little Mephistophelean (Ellmann 1977: 20-21). Ellmann also notes the 'parallel nocturnal settings' of Bella Cohen's brothel in 'Circe' and the Brocken in *Faust*, a place of German legend haunted by witches and devils (20).

In naming his novel *Ulysses* Joyce is, of course, risking bathos, with the implied juxtaposition of mythical hero and modern anti-hero. But this is not all that is going on here. The author of *Ulysses* is asking us to bridge the gap imaginatively, to consider how the two might be brought into alignment, and, having done so, to see that the outcome is not a perfectly analogical relationship, a sustained and unwavering parallel. Rather, it is as if making this leap between extremes opens us up to the book's *other* intertextual affiliations, and to the panoply of alternative titles that might correspond to those affiliations: *Faust, Peer Gynt, Hamlet, The Divine Comedy, Bouvard et Pécuchet, Sweets of Sin*, and on and on. A cipher, for Joyce, is not just a cipher, a process of conversion; it is also an engine for expansion, for multiplying possibilities rather than narrowing them.

For my final example of Joycean encryption, let us go back for a moment to Meillassoux. I noted earlier that the subtitle of his book, *Un déchiffrage du Coup de dés*, roughly means a 'decryption' or 'decipherment' of the poem, as the English translation has it. Meillassoux himself points out that, strictly speaking, a decipherment would be *un déchiffrement*, whilst *un déchiffrage* can also connote a 'sight-reading', in the sense in which a musician sight-reads a score, without rehearsal (Meillassoux 2012: 68). At the same time, the very notion of 'reading a score', through sight or through practice, is a kind of decoding. We are by now all too familiar with the notion of zeroes and ones, the binary code of the digital age. But just as rigorous and exacting is this other form of 'encipherment': the staves, notes, and intervals of the musical code, a 'secret language' known only to trained musicians.

Bearing this in mind, let us consider the 'Sirens' chapter of *Ulysses*. Much has been written about the ways in which Joyce attempts to translate musical forms into literary forms, to create an eight-part fugue out of words alone. Only one person, however, has actually attempted a bar-by-bar notation that explains how he did this. In the late 1980s Margaret Rogers, a musician and composer, transposed the chapter's sixty opening fragments or motifs into music, using some pre-determined principles. The letters of the alphabet from A to G are treated as musical notes. So the chapter's first line, '**B**ron**ze** b**y** **g**ol**d** h**e**ar**d** the **h**oo**f**irons st**ee**lyrin**g**in**g**', could be translated as: b-e-b-g-d-e-a-d-e-f-e-e-g-g. In addition, wherever the suffix *-ing* appears, it is interpreted as 'in *g*', as in, in the key of g. Finally, lower-case letters are in the key of the music, and upper-case letters indicate accidentals, i.e., sharps or flats (Rogers 1999: 264-6).

Rogers has produced the kind of hyper-technical analysis that only a professional musician or composer could come up with. But therein, I think, lies the problem. In its earnest literal-mindedness, this analysis is a misconstrual of what Joyce is doing in 'Sirens' – which is not dissimilar to what Mallarmé wanted to do with poetry. For Paul Valéry, Symbolist poetry meant one thing: poets 'taking back from Music what properly belonged to them' (Austin 1959: 19). Instrumental music could only produce vague meanings and emotive responses, and adding lyrics to it, as in opera, was no solution, because it merely juxtaposed two parallel forms, libretto and score. Poetry, on the other hand – Mallarmé's *poésie pure* – sought to unite suggestion and evocation with clarity and intelligibility. Such a union, in the poet's estimation, if achieved, would be inherently superior to music. At the same time, what counted as 'poetry' wasn't just metrical writing. Mallarmé praised Villiers de l'Isle Adam for elevating prose to the heights of music. Ezra Pound held a similar, albeit less proprietorial, view to Valéry, asserting that 'poetry begins to atrophy when it gets too far from music' (Pound 1934: 14).

In Joyce's 'Sirens' literature and music are united, it is true. But those mysterious opening fragments, the 'overture' to the chapter, are not all from the English language; they are renditions of street and other sounds, imposing, even overwhelming, in their sonorous materiality. Ingenious as Rogers's decoding – or recoding – is, it amounts to a kind of kind of domestication, even a desecration, in its undercutting of the obdurate strangeness of the passage. As Alan Shockley notes, Rogers's fugal (re)compositions 'seem to have very little to do with Joyce's text, and raise more questions than answers' (Shockley 2009: 60) – the chief question being whether such an explicit and overdetermined code accords with the spirit of the text or contravenes it.

In one of the very few discussions of Joyce and cryptology, Hugh Staples avers that the 'art of James Joyce is both arcane and radiant' (Staples 1965: 167). The truth in this statement, I think, is the 'and', which makes the two terms co-dependent: Joyce's writing conceals *as* it shines forth. Sam Slote makes a similar observation about the *Wake*. He considers Joyce's writing to be compulsively indeterminate, describing it as 'the writing which encrypts as it proceeds [and which] hides as it comes' (Slote 1998: 115). And Meillassoux sees *Un Coup de dés* in related terms: 'The text will not be completely illuminated once its cipher is elucidated, but will obscure itself otherwise, cloaking itself in unsuspected shadows' (Meillassoux 2012: 11).

Modernism initiated a new regime of secrecy, as I noted at the start. But what underlies modernist writing at its most difficult, oblique, and uncompromising is not just the notion that literature itself can be a form of secrecy, but that occlusion and revelation go hand in hand, that they are more tightly bonded to each other here than in any literary epoch before or since. It is Meillassoux's 'unsuspected shadows' that are, finally, what cryptographic modernism is really about. And it is the encrypted text – as well as, alongside of – the more straightforwardly *cryptic* text, that gives modernist secrecy its resilience.

The fundamental deficiency of the German military Enigma machine was that it could encrypt no letter as itself; it was this flaw that enabled Turing and his team to crack the code. Yet this is the real strength and power of literary modernism: its enigma machines do not simply occlude or hide or disguise, so that they can be decoded. Their encipherments evolve and mutate, propagating meaning and proffering semantic richness, yielding textual artefacts that can never be fully decrypted or exhaustively elucidated.

Works Cited

Austin, J.L. 1959. 'Mallarmé on Music and Letters'. *Bulletin of the John Rylands Library* 42: 19-39.

Badiou, Alain. 2014. *The Age of the Poets and Other Writings on Twentieth-Century Poetry and Prose*. Edited and translated by Bruno Bosteels. London: Verso.

Blanchot, Maurice. 1995. *The Work of Fire*. Translated by Charlotte Mandell. Stanford: Stanford University Press.

Blanchot, Maurice. 2001. *Faux Pas*. Translated by Charlotte Mandell. Stanford: Stanford University Press.

Derrida, Jacques. 1970a. 'La Double séance'. *Tel Quel* 41: 3-43.

Derrida, Jacques. 1970b. 'La Double séance'. *Tel Quel* 42: 3-45.

Derrida, Jacques. 1981. *Dissemination*. Translated by Barbara Johnson. London: Athlone.

Diepeveen, Leonard. 2003. *The Difficulties of Modernism*. London: Routledge.

Donnelly, Ignatius. 1887. *The Great Cryptogram: Francis Bacon's Cipher in the So-Called Shakespeare Plays*. Chicago: R.S. Peale & Co.

Ellmann, Richard. 1977. *The Consciousness of Joyce*. Oxford: Oxford University Press.

Genette, Gérard. 1962. 'Bonheur de Mallarmé?' *Tel Quel* 10: 61-5.

Hayman, David. 1956. *Joyce et Mallarmé*. Volume 1. Paris: Lettres Modernes.

Hayman, David. 1982. *'Ulysses': The Mechanics of Meaning*. Madison: University of Wisconsin Press.

Joyce, James. 1975a. *Finnegans Wake*. London: Faber & Faber.

Joyce, James. 1975b. *Selected Letters of James Joyce*. Edited by Richard Ellmann. New York: Viking.

Joyce, James. 1986. *Ulysses*. Harmondsworth: Penguin.

Kenner, Hugh. 1952. 'Joyce's *Ulysses*: Homer and Hamlet'. *Essays in Criticism* 2: 85-104.

Knigge, Michael. 2013. 'Opinion: The End of Privacy'. *Deutsche Wille*, September 6. http://www.dw.com/en/opinion-the-end-of-privacy/a-17071351.

Levin, Harry. 1944. *James Joyce: A Critical Introduction*. London: Faber.

Litz, A. Walton. 1961. *The Art of James Joyce: Design and Method in* Ulysses *and* Finnegans Wake. Oxford: Oxford University Press.

Mallarmé, Stéphane. 1956. *Mallarmé: Selected Prose Poems, Essays and Letters*. Translated by Bradford Cook. Baltimore: The Johns Hopkins Press.

Mallarmé, Stéphane. 2006. *Collected Poems and Other Verse*. Translated by E.H. and A.M. Blackmore. Oxford: World's Classics.

Meillassoux, Quentin. 2012. *The Number and the Siren: A Decipherment of Mallarmé's* Coup de dés. Translated by Robin Mackay. Falmouth: Urbanomic.

Menand, Louis. 2007. *Discovering Modernism: T.S. Eliot and His Context*. 2nd ed. Oxford: Oxford University Press.

Pierce, Charles P. 2013. 'The Snowden Effect, Continued'. *Esquire*, September 6. http://www.esquire.com/news-politics/politics/a19430/the-snowden-effect-and-the-end-of-privacy/.

Poe, Edgar Allan. 1841. 'A Few Words on Secret Writing'. *Graham's Magazine* 19: 33-8.

Pound, Ezra. 1934. *ABC of Reading*. London: Faber & Faber.

Rancière, Jacques. 2011. *Mallarmé: The Politics of the Siren*. Translated by Steven Corcoran. London: Continuum.

Rogers, Margaret. 1999. 'Mining the Ore of "Sirens": An Investigation of Structural Components'. In *Bronze by Gold: The Music of Joyce*, edited by Sebastian D.G. Knowles, 263-76. New York: Garland.

Rosenheim, Shawn. 1997. *The Cryptographic Imagination: Secret Writing from Edgar Poe to the Internet.* Baltimore: The Johns Hopkins University Press.

Rottenberg, Pierre. 1969. 'Une Lecture d'Igitur'. *Tel Quel* 37: 74-94.

Shockley, Alan. 2009. *Music in the Words: Musical Form and Counterpoint in the Twentieth-Century Novel.* Farnham: Ashgate.

Slote, Sam. 1998. '"Did God Be Come?": The Definitive Exgenesis of HCE'. In *Writing its Own Wrunes for Ever: Essais de génétique joycienne / Essays in Joycean Genetics*, edited by Daniel Ferrer, 103-117. Tusson: Du Lérot.

Sollers, Philippe. 1966. 'Littérature et totalité'. *Tel Quel* 26: 81-95.

Staples, Hugh B. 1965. 'Joyce and Cryptology: Some Speculations'. *James Joyce Quarterly* 2: 167-73.

Suetonius. 2000. *The Lives of the Caesars.* Translated by Catharine Edwards. Oxford: World's Classics.

Weinberger, Sharon. 2014. 'Edward Snowden, the NSA, and the Never-Ending End of Privacy'. *Discover*, January 7. http://discovermagazine.com/2014/jan-feb/04-the-never-ending-end-of-privacy.

Wilson, Edmund. 1993. *Axel's Castle: A Study in the Imaginative Literature of 1870-1930.* Harmondsworth: Penguin.

7

Teletype

JAMES PURDON

> And so it is with written words; you might think they
> spoke as if they had intelligence, but if you question
> them, wishing to know about their sayings, they always
> say only one and the same thing.
>
> Plato, *Phaedrus*

The tap of the telegraph key inaugurates the age of electronic signalling; the telephone's insistent ring marks the beginning of audible telecommunications. Yet for most of the twentieth century there existed another communications medium as distinctive as either the telegraph or the telephone. In the interim between Morse-click and mouse-click, the incessant mechanical clatter of the teletypewriter and the teleprinter sounded through offices, newsrooms, government ministries, and other sites of networked labour. These devices became an object of fascination for writers as diverse as William Saroyan and Don DeLillo, and a common trope in films ranging from the suspense classics of Alfred Hitchcock and Fritz Lang to the paranoid thrillers of the 1970s. How to explain the fact that this ubiquitous medium has remained invisible to cultural history even as the scholarly study of twentieth-century multimedia has flourished?

True, teletype was used primarily by offices of state, public institutions, and private corporations. It carried traffic between bureaucrats, military officials, law-enforcement officers, clerks, and other professional administrators. When teletype machines were used by post offices or telegram services to transmit private traffic, they were generally operated by professionals rather than those whose messages they carried, and before teletype became a vital part of Second World War military communications, it was of interest to a relatively small number of operators. Still, the same could be said of earlier forms of telegraphy. The Cooke-Wheatstone and Morse telegraph systems, with their highly sophisticated codes, required extensive training and were also operated by specialists, yet several studies have demonstrated the importance to an extensive field of nineteenth-century culture not only of telegraphy as a medium but of the specific features (visible, acoustic, haptic) of telegraphic equipment itself (Standage 1998; Otis 2001; Menke 2008; Wenzlhuemer 2013). By contrast, the history of the transformation of tele-graphing into tele-typing remains decidedly hazy despite the astonishing rapidity with which that transition took place. To put things in perspective: in 1927, according to Post Office estimates, teletype machines handled four and a half per cent of all British domestic telegraph traffic; within six years that share had increased to well over seventy per cent.

This essay sketches the history of teletype's development and adoption and attempts to account for the relative invisibility of the medium in studies of telecommunications culture. It argues that teletype has been misconstrued as a straightforward combination of existing technologies rather than as a distinct medium giving rise to unique conventions of transmission and reception as well as unique forms of attention and affect. From a technical point of view, teletype machines did indeed combine elements of the telegraph and the typewriter. But to begin from sheer technical fact is to overlook how advertising, technical descriptions, and cultural appearances in fiction and film shaped the common understanding of teletype as a new and distinctive communications technology. Notwithstanding its individual components, teletype was promoted and imagined less as a fusion of telegraph and typewriter than as a supplement to that other thoroughly modern medium, the telephone. Over time, however, it evolved its own rituals and rules of procedure. In the newsflash – teletype's characteristic form or genre – it created a new kind of communicative temporality, one that depended as much on a rhythmic process of inscription as on the eventual permanence of the printed text, and helped to reconfigure twentieth-century media around the idea that an instantaneous 'live' transmission could also, and simultaneously, stand as a verifiable historical record.

Almost from its invention, the new technology was seen not merely as uniting two formerly distinct devices, but as transecting several formerly distinct modes of communication: vocal and textual, receptive and interactive, instantaneous and permanent, private and public. For this reason, it is not adequately accounted for by media theories that stress the relative orality or literacy of media, their discursivity or materiality, their heat or coolness, their connective or representational functions, or their capacities for transmission or storage.

Audiovisibility

Alfred Hitchcock's *The Lodger* (1927) has been described, with good reason, as 'the noisiest silent picture ever made' (Spoto 1992: 5). For although *Blackmail* (1929) is usually regarded as the first British sound film, the earlier 'silent' picture is by some measure the more clamorous production. From the film's

Fig. 1. Alfred Hitchcock. 2012. *The Lodger*. London: Network.

opening close-up of a woman's silent scream to the justly celebrated sequence in which the suspicious pacing of Ivor Novello's shady lodger is filmed from below through a floor made of reinforced glass, Hitchcock everywhere seeks, and generally finds, visual equivalents for audible phenomena. If these striking effects do not yet inaugurate the audio-*visual* attractions of sound cinema proper, they nonetheless contribute to an effect of audio-*visibility* that both anticipates the forthcoming era of the talking picture and marks the apex of silent cinema's experiments with visible sound. *Blackmail* may have been Hitchcock's first official 'talkie', but it was *The Lodger* that demonstrated technology's capacity to reproduce speech in the cinema.

    I am thinking here of a third audio-visible moment, between the screaming girl and the glass ceiling, which has not attracted anything like the same degree of critical attention. As the film begins, the corpse of a young woman has been discovered: the latest victim of the serial killer known as The Avenger. Among the crowd surrounding the body is a newspaper reporter, who heads to a telephone booth to call in his story. Hitchcock gave his own account of the sequence to François Truffaut:

> First, the item is typed out on a wire-service machine so that we are able to read a few sentences. Then it is forwarded on the teletypes. People in clubs learn the news. Then there is a radio announcement, with people tuned in to the broadcast. Finally,

Fig. 2. Alfred Hitchcock. *The Lodger.*

it is flashed on an electric news sign – you know, like on Times Square. And each time, we give additional information, so that you learn more about the crime. (Truffaut 1983: 45)

As the reporter calls in his copy from a nearby telephone box, Hitchcock cuts to the desk-bound copy-taker who passes the written sheet off-screen, before it reappears, after a back-and-forth cut to the reporter, on top of a printing telegraph transmitter unit. The operator duly begins keying in the dispatch on an early form of teletype transmitter (Figure 1), whereupon another cut takes us to the receiving end of the device: a teleprinter in a glass case printed with the livery of The Exchange Telegraph Company (Figure 2). There is a dissolve to close-up as the machine rattles off the text (Figure 3):

> 8 20 P M THE SEVENTH GOLDEN HAIRED
> VICTIM OF THE MYSTERIOUS MURDERER
> KNOWN AS THE AVENGER WAS DISCOVERED
> ON THE EMBANKMENT EARLY THIS EVENING
> A WOMAN WITNESS DESCRIBED THE
> MURDERER AS WEARING A SCARF COVERING
> THE LOWER HALF OF HIS FACE AND[.]

Between the voice of the reporter and the fixity of newsprint, word of The Avenger's latest crime passes through an intermediate stage in which we are

Fig. 3. Alfred Hitchcock. *The Lodger.*

invited to watch not one but two teletechnic transformations: first that of the telephone's analogue transmission of voice and then the literally digital fingerings that encode the text of the message as a signal to be reconstituted by the teleprinter.

Medium here conditions message in a very specific way. The intervening presence of the printing apparatus traverses the page, blocking it from view while gradually producing, in a precisely controlled rhythmic movement, the text read by the cinema audience. This is an odd sort of intertitle. Rather than flashing up complete, it proceeds letter by letter, imprinting the message and concealing it at the same time: as the type basket moves across the face of the page to produce new letters, the existing text is obscured by the rollers that keep the paper in place and by the bar on which the printing apparatus is mounted. Instead of waiting for the audience to assimilate an immediately visible on-screen text, the teleprinter requires the audience to process a sequential text that appears according to its own rhythm. The teleprinter controls not only the temporality of printing, but the temporality of attention, and unifies an audience in the need to keep pace with a visible text before it disappears out of focus or out of visibility. Speed-readers lose their advantage. The shot ends with the teleprinter hammering out a tantalizing 'AND', directing attention back to the action of the film while introducing the thematic of partial knowledge that governs its development.

Film criticism of the 1920s had shown signs of dissatisfaction with the intertitle even before the introduction of sound. The pages of *Photoplay, Screenland, Picture Play, Moving Picture World*, and other fan magazines abounded with complaints about verbose, hackneyed, or mis-spelled title cards, while the critic Iris Barry complained that she could only enjoy Lang's *Die Nibelungen* if she shut her eyes when the titles appeared. For Barry, title cards were most necessary when they gave what film as yet could not: speech. 'At a flash-point of the emotions,' she wrote, 'a sub-title is needed, unless the actors can let us, by their bearing or by lip-reading, get what their words must inevitably be' (Barry 1926: 78-9).

In *The Lodger*, we know what the reporter's words must inevitably be because we see them transcribed twice over: first by a human copy-taker and then by a machine. Speech becomes visible. One might take this as early evidence of Hitchcock's preference for diegetic economy: just as all the music in *Rear Window* (1954) can be attributed to a source within the housebound protagonist's earshot, *The Lodger* keeps the audience within the story-world while the teleprinter accomplishes the formal function of a written title card in representing speech.

The term of art for such a diegetically integrated shot is an 'insert'. Inserts, in the form of letters, telegrams, cheques, and other written or typed documents had long been a common device in silent film, but such shots were usually static, representing the written or printed word. The added visual interest of *The Lodger*'s teleprinter arises precisely from its movement, inasmuch as it represents the immediacy of a spoken news report. Hitchcock, himself a former title designer, was particularly attentive to the intertitles of *The Lodger*, hiring the artist E. McKnight Kauffer to jazz them up. And it seems more than coincidental that the teleprinter insert immediately precedes the famous shot of the director himself in his first cameo, centred among typewriters, talking on the telephone. It begins to seem as if Hitchcock not only placed himself at the centre of a teletechnic media apparatus, but acknowledged the readiness of the machine to take over his old job.

The New Telegraphy

Fantasies of using an ordinary typewriter as a real-time communications medium had been in circulation at least since 1899, when the narrator of John Kendrick Bangs's *The Enchanted Type-Writer*, having discovered a dusty typewriter in his attic among 'old bill-files and collections of Atlantic cable-ends', finds to his shock that the device has a supernatural direct line to the shade of James Boswell (Bangs 1899: 11). The development of a working teletype for mundane uses took rather longer.

The precise timeline of teleprinter development is not easy to reconstruct, filled as it is with examples of trial-and-error, simultaneous independent discoveries, and differing solutions to similar problems. A Canadian inventor by the name of Royal Earl House had already developed an ingenious mechanical printing telegraph by the mid-1840s. House's system, a precursor of teletype, required messages to be entered on a 'composing-machine' consisting of a piano-like keyboard, where each key corresponded to a single letter of the alphabet and input was conveyed to the transmitter by means of a fiendishly complicated mechanical system (House 1846). It could transmit around forty words per minute to be printed automatically at the receiving terminal, but required rigorous training, was difficult to manufacture, and was liable to lose contact between its two terminals unless great care was taken to keep them synchronized. In 1854, an Englishman, David Edward Hughes, invented a rival system while working as a professor of music in Kentucky. He returned to England shortly afterwards, and successfully marketed his invention to European telegraph companies. Like House's system, it required a great deal of skill, as well as a sense of timing: because of the arrangement of the keys and the print wheel, signals had to be sent in a regular tempo in order to register properly.

In contrast with one-to-one key-to-signal systems like those of House and Hughes, the system invented by Émile Baudot in the 1870s for the French telegraph service relied on operators to learn a new and highly complex coding language which was, in the literal sense, digital. Baudot built his machine around a five-bit code, with a transmitter consisting of a set of five parallel keys. Each letter input was assigned to a combination of fingers – two on the left hand and three on the right – formed simultaneously, like a chord on a piano. So, for instance, to send an 'A', the operator would typically depress the left middle and index fingers; to send a 'G', he or she would depress the left index finger along with the right middle and ring fingers, and so on. To compose a message of any length on such a device demanded a prodigious memory, extensive training, and considerable physical endurance.

All of these systems, from House to Baudot, relied upon the labour of highly skilled operators trained to perform repetitive actions of a very specialized kind. A major advance came at the turn of the twentieth century with the development of new keyboard-based printing telegraphs. Several versions of typewriter-based systems were developed independently by inventors working on three continents. They were Frederick George Creed, a Canadian telegraph operator living in Glasgow; Donald Murray, a New Zealand farmer and newspaper print worker; father-and-son team Charles and Howard Krum in Chicago; and Ernst Kleinschmidt, a German-American inventor who was later to become the Krums' business partner (Huurdeman 2003).

Creed was probably the first to develop a functional prototype of a standard QWERTY-style transmitter around 1897. His 'high speed automatic printing telegraph system' consisted of a typewriter keyboard connected to a perforating device which punched holes in a moving tape, a transmitting device which transformed the punch-marks on the tape into electrical signals, and a receiving device which produced identical punch-marks on another length of tape. This tape could then be fed into a letter-printer to produce text. Creed was successful in promoting his device: in 1902 the Post Office bought a dozen, and within a few years Creed & Co. were supplying printing telegraph machines to the *Glasgow Herald*, the *Daily Mail*, and the Press Association. Creed may have supplied the teleprinter that propels the narrative of *The Lodger* – one of their clients was the Exchange Telegraph Company, whose branding is clearly visible on the printer's glass case in the film – although the transmitting terminal looks like a Hughes keyboard of an earlier vintage (Creed & Co. *c.*1934).

Murray's system, in prototype by 1901, worked in a similar way to Creed's, but Murray also made modifications on the software side. Recognizing that the introduction of the QWERTY keyboard had made operator fatigue a less pressing problem than mechanical fatigue, he re-mapped Baudot's five-bit code in order to optimize the efficiency and durability of the machine. At the same time, he added new code sequences to control non-printing operations such as carriage-returns. In 1925, Creed & Co. bought the patent to Murray's code, and successfully pressed for its adoption as the international teletype standard.

The Krums' major innovations were to improve the synchronization of printing telegraph systems by developing an additional start-and-stop signal between transmitted characters, and to produce the first integrated teleprinter by eliminating the need for a perforator: their device converted electrical signals directly into printed text without the intervening stage of a punched tape. (Creed & Co. promptly redesigned their machines along similar lines.) The Krums began supplying teletype systems to the US Postal Service in 1910, and two years later installed six circuits for Western Union. After merging with Kleinschmidt in 1928, they rebranded their company as the Teletype Corporation (Teletype Corporation 1958).

By the mid-1920s, these independent innovations had begun to cohere into a recognisably new technology, with Donald Murray as its most determined and eloquent champion. In a paper on 'The New Telegraphy' delivered to the Institute of Electrical Engineers in 1924, Murray emphasised the game-changing features of teletype by invoking another technological triumph, the mass-produced automobile: 'It can work at from forty to eighty words a minute over any distance from 100 feet to 5000 miles, and any girl typist can use it. This is the business-man's printing telegraph – the Ford car of telegraphy' (Murray 1924: 245). And there was more. The new telegraphy didn't just improve on the old telegraphy; it was even better in some respects than that modern marvel, the telephone:

> The telephone has great advantages over the telegraph, but a perfected telegraph network would have other great compensating advantages over the telephone. We must type as well as talk; we

must teletype as well as teletalk. A telephone message is a voice, and nothing more – a sound leaving no record. Nothing is more evanescent. There are sound-recording machines, but the sounds are still sounds, and there is no conceivable mechanism, outside the human brain, that will translate a sound-message into a sight-message. (247-8)

Through Murray's advocacy, the 'new telegraphy' pitched itself as telephony's material supplement, promising to combine talkativeness with textuality in its ability to record, in indelible and easily-legible alphabetic signs, the precise message it transmitted at speeds rapid enough to pass for conversation. That hybridity – of sound-message and sight-message – became teletype's major selling point. The promotional booklets produced for Creed & Co. promised 'a private communication service, combining the personal touch of the telephone with the permanency of the telegraphed message', and the frontispiece of one such booklet shows a lightning-flash incarnated in a pair of hands supplied with Mercury-wings reaching out to a stylized keyboard (Figure 4).

Although Murray distinguishes between 'teletyping' and the 'teletalking' enabled by telephony, he repeatedly associates teletype with spoken communications rather than with print. The talkativeness of the new medium reappears in his suggestion that a network of teletype machines could be used by businessmen to conduct secure conferences at a distance, with the conversation happening in real time and the teletypes automatically producing a verbatim record:

> There would be no overhearing or eavesdropping. The teletype language is spoken and understood only by teletypes, and the code-bars can be mixed at will to scramble the messages and make them doubly secure against overhearing by outsiders. There is something deeply impressive about this idea of a conference taking place between men hundreds or even thousands of miles apart, with no sound but the slight tapping of the typebars, and the men in silence, each alone, watching the words being recorded, or transmitting on his keyboard. (257)

Murray's prophetic fantasy of silent men and talkative teletypes gives on to the dizzying perspective of the future, our own present: an information society in which machines communicate with other machines on behalf of human agents who look on, suspecting that their own obsolescence may be just around the corner.

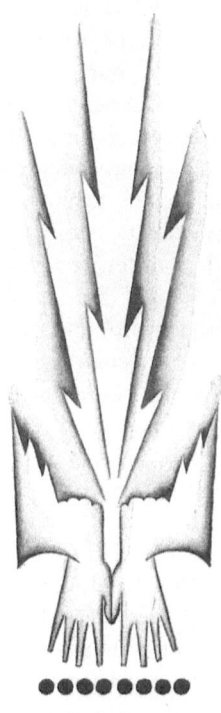

Fig. 4. Creed & Co. c.1934. *Typewriting Over Wires*. Frontispiece. Croydon: Creed & Co.

Teletalk

The ability to talk silently at a distance was not without compensating attractions. Mr Romano, the narrator of William Saroyan's short story '1, 2, 3, 4, 5, 6, 7, 8' (1934) is a nineteen-year-old teletype operator whose job requires him 'to send important telegrams to important people accurately'. The teletype machine, he explains, is 'a great mechanical triumph [...] a great stroke of efficiency, the perfection of the machine', though like most strokes of efficiency it comes at a cost. For one thing, 'old time telegraphers', formerly on a wage of a dollar an hour, have been replaced by young teletypists like him, earning twenty-eight cents an hour for handling twice as much traffic (Saroyan 1939: 50-51). Worse still, the machine has the disagreeable effect of attuning his body and mind to its own rhythms: 'I seemed to feel that they had gotten me so deeply into the mechanical idea of the age that I was doomed eventually to become a fragment of a machine myself' (44).

The teletype is not the only such mechanism in Romano's life, however. At home, he listens with intermittent obsessiveness to phonograph records. 'The phonograph was pretty much himself. He had gotten into the machine and come out of it, singing, or being a symphony, or a wild jazz composition' (43). Jazz above all seems to speak to Romano's awareness of being integrated into the rhythms of a particular time and place: 'He had learned something about machinery, American machines working, through jazz' (46). One record in particular moves him in this way. 'There was one passage of syncopation in this record that was tremendously interesting to me. [...] It was eight swift chords on the banjo, repeated fourteen times, while the melody grew in emotional intensity, reached a climax, and then dwindled to silence. *One two three four five six seven eight*, swiftly, fourteen times. The sound was wiry' (49).

Saroyan's narrator, evidently, has internalized the repetitive, syncopated rhythm of the teletype machine, and the passage stays with him long after he has put the records away and returned from their wiry sounds to the wired texts that occupy his working hours. If he regards the phonograph as a space to inhabit, he feels no such connection to the teletype machine – at least as long as it handles only official business. Things begin to change when the machine becomes a medium not for exchanging messages, but for conducting conversations:

> One Sunday morning, after a long silence, my machine began to function, so I went over to it to receive and check the message, but it was not a message, not a regular telegram. I read the words, *hello hello hello*. I had never thought of the machine as being related in any way to me. It was there for the messages of other people, and the tapping of this greeting to me seemed very startling. For one thing, it was strictly against company rules to use the machine for anything other than the transmission of

regular business. [...] I typed the word *hello*, and we began a conversation.

The party at the other end of the line is (of course) a love-interest. 'I talked with the other operator for about an hour. It was a girl, and she was working in the operating room at the main office' (51-2). Text-message romance blossoms.

Clandestinity adds to the thrill: the teletype lovers have to conduct their trysts in between visits from a watchful wire-chief. But the real excitement arises from their unsanctioned use of teletype itself, which is thereby transformed from a medium used to send and receive official 'messages' into a medium for unofficial, real-time 'conversation'. (The same trajectory, according to which an institutional medium develops into a popular one by way of unsanctioned private use, has been characteristic of new communications media from the telephone to the internet.) For Romano, teletype reconfigures 'talking' as a form of symbolic exchange defined not with reference to its oral/aural qualities, but as a matter of sequence (it appears gradually rather than all at once), fluency (it requires no decoding), and continuity (the channel remains open until one or other party signs off). Romano may conduct his flirtation at a distance by text, but he *thinks* of teletype conversation as possessing all the presence and plenitude that has traditionally been associated with speech. In the enforced gaps between conversations – that pesky wire chief – he begins to hear the insistent strumming of his syncopated banjo tune again, bridging the gap between machinic staccato and emotional melody. He thinks of inviting the girl to move with him to a house in the countryside, a place of 'meaning and fullness' (52).

For the teletypists, that plenitude proves illusory. They drift apart; the house in the country never materializes. So far, so conventional: modernity does for another pair of machine-crossed lovers. And, naturally, if Romano were able to analyse the arc of his storyline as easily as he breaks down his jazz records, he would see it coming. The swelling love theme dwindles into silence while the teletype carries on its own relentless rhythmic output. But I am interested here less in Saroyan's depiction of machine-age alienation than in the connection his story establishes between the rhythms of real-time text conversation and the *feeling* of immediacy. For Romano, the medium appears to drop away so that he imagines himself to be talking, rather than merely sending and receiving messages. There are risks to such an imaginative leap, as he discovers to his cost: like any digital medium, the teletype involves a wager that doesn't always pay out. Yet it can't be said simply that teletype communication fails Mr Romano. Far from it. The lovers drift apart not because they can't connect by digital means, but because that apparent digital connection proves unsustainable in the world of (apparent) bodily presence. What fails is not the digital transmission that might be expected to prove a poor substitute for speech, but speech itself: 'I myself had stopped talking about the house. I myself had stopped hearing the music, and suddenly the silence had returned'. An incompatibility has been discovered (or disguised) through the operation of a technological medium. So complete is Romano's integration with the mechanical idea of the age that the shared presence offered by bodily proximity seems no more authentic than teletype's transgressive promise of intimacy at a distance. Indeed, it seems less so.

The medium did not always appear to drop away. During the Second World War, teletype, as the primary form of military communications, became visible to an army of new users, including the young signals clerk Catherine Saxon, heroine of Edith Pargeter's *She Goes to War* (1942). Visibility was the least of it: Catherine's first impression of the Signal Office teleprinter room is 'of a demoniac, unremitting, inhuman noise; [...] for besides the staccato effect of the keys there is the deep hum of the power which drives the machines; and if the one hammering on your senses from outside doesn't drive you crazy, the other will sneak in and complete the work from inside' (Pargeter 1989: 22). But Catherine Saxon is too live a wire in her own right to allow herself to become subdued to the rhythms of the teleprinter after the manner of Mr Romano. The end of the novel will find her resolved to turn herself into a left-wing journalist-activist, and her technological struggles give an early indication of her lack of fit with the apparatus of the war machine:

> They're such intriguing things, too; they have character, and differ from one another in the most startling ways. They purr when they're pleased with life, they rattle and grow hot when they're angry, and I believe that once, exasperated beyond all endurance, one of our most ill-used specimens burst into flames. I find them impatient with incompetence; they let me tap my slow and cautious way along a whole line, and then carriage return violently and spit a series of X's and figures across the paper, or cast up the answer-back of the station to which I'm transmitting [...] to the accompaniment of a wildly ringing bell. (28)

Catherine comes to regard her 'teles' not as points of access to a transparent conversational medium, but as unknowable entities with an agency of their own. 'One gets into the habit of regarding them as sentient, malicious, fascinating beings, and talking to them accordingly'. Then as now, talking to machines generally means berating them, as the teleprinter girls discover: 'Myra, working at the end machine, finally got sick of the irritating noise, and addressed it in a few pungent words which should have silenced it forever. Teleprinters have that effect on one's language, I find' (74).

One fantasy – the fantasy of talking *through* machines – has been replaced with another more subversive idea: the fantasy of talking *to* machines. Catherine's teles can't answer back, but in another part of the wartime communications apparatus, someone was wondering what they might say if they could:

> You are alone in the room, except for two computer terminals flickering in the dim light. You use the terminals to communicate with two entities in another room, whom you cannot see. Relying solely on their responses to your questions, you must decide which is the man, which the woman. Or, in another version of the famous 'imitation game' proposed by Alan Turing in his classic 1950 paper 'Computer Machinery and Intelligence', you use the responses to decide which is the human, which the machine. (Hayles 1999: xi)

Turing's famous 'imitation game' has long since taken on the status of an origin myth for the era of digital computing, and like all origin myths it has been altered in the course of repeated tellings. As N. Katherine Hayles points out in *How We Became Posthuman*, Turing's original description of the thought-experiment begins not with the task of distinguishing between a man and a computer, but of distinguishing between a man and a woman. Restoring the significance of gender, Hayles argues persuasively that the test is more than just a method for assessing machine intelligence; more radically, it implies the possibility of a fundamental discordance between the fleshly body and its own electronically-mediated self-image. Whatever the outcome of the test, she suggests, Turing's subjects are already integrated into circuits of distributed cognition where they flicker as post-human ghosts in digital machines (xv).

'Flickering' – a key term which appears in both the first and last sentences of the prologue to *How We Became Posthuman* – is the word used by Hayles to express the idea that unstable digital symbols have replaced writing in the age of virtual displays, as well as the claim that such virtual realities usher in a new mode of existence: 'As you gaze at the flickering signifiers scrolling down the computer screens, no matter what identifications you assign to the embodied entities that you cannot see, you have already become posthuman' (xiv).

The objection I wish to raise here has to do not with Hayles's conclusions about the stakes of the imitation game, nor with her wider analysis of the key role played by post-war cybernetics in the transformation of human subjectivity. Rather – in the spirit of her own description of Turing's test as a 'magic trick' that 'relies on getting you to accept at an early stage assumptions that will determine how you interpret what you see later' – it has to do with one assumption in particular which leads her to link Turing's test with post-human subjectivity. That objection is easily stated: Turing's text didn't flicker.

In Turing's thought experiment, the electronically mediated text did not appear on a flickering terminal, for the simple reason that the cathode ray tube had not yet been adapted for use with electronic computers. Turing's test subjects are instead invited to communicate by means of a tried and tested communications device: 'The ideal arrangement is to have a teleprinter communicating between the two rooms' (Turing 1950: 433-60). At the same time as she restores gender to the entities involved in the Turing Test, Hayles obscures another feature of its embodied form: the nature of the technology which mediates the conversation. The plain white sheet of the teleprinter becomes a virtual ghost.

Of course, Hayles is not alone in recalling Turing's test through the technological framework of a later era equipped with VDUs and microprocessors. The image of an individual sitting before a desktop monitor and pinging messages off to invisible interlocutors has become a common illustration of the thought experiment and a staple of undergraduate introductions to artificial intelligence in disciplines ranging from computer science to philosophy of mind. But it seems to me that this moment of medium-blindness matters for Hayles's argument, which hinges on the relationship between virtuality and material embodiment. Hayles wants to claim that the flickering signifiers of electronic computing mark a qualitative transformation in the nature of the human subject. But what if that transformation was less a sudden shift into distributed cognitive virtuality than a gradual reconfiguration of the space of conversation? If Saroyan's Mr Romano feels himself to be talking intimately with another human being through a textual machine, and Pargeter's Catherine Saxon begins to feel as if her teletype machines are lifelike enough to require a good talking to, perhaps the time was ripe for a theory of conversation that could extend that space beyond the norms of (masculine) communication. The prospect of machine-conversation tests the limits of political subjectivity, and does so in specifically textual terms.

The model of the signifier assumed by Turing, here at the conceptual origin of digital computing, is not yet destabilized by a flickering virtuality. But neither is it exactly analogous to the stable symbolic structure that Hayles seems to have in mind as exemplary of traditional texts. Between the 'durable inscription' of print and the 'constantly refreshed image' of virtuality intervenes a third moment of semi-stability as text unfolds in linear time, a conversable temporality in which statements may be made and modified. It is this unfolding temporality that permits the Turing test – and permits all human-machine interaction – to take place. The 'imitation' aspect of Turing's imitation game doesn't extend beyond semantic content: tone of voice, intonation, rhythm, and other features of communication are ruled out of court before the test begins. As John Durham Peters remarks, 'Turing gives us communication as if bodies did not matter [...] "communication" allows him to equate a teleprinter and a breathing human presence as doppelgängers. He had learned to equate the proxy sent at a distance with its bodily origin' (Peters 1999: 237).

Turing could make this assumption, I want to suggest, because of teletype's pre-existing conceptual proximity to the informal immediacy of conversation rather than the formality of the printed word. The teleprinter is not a neutral conversational medium. (No medium is ever that.) But it is possible that Turing's choice of teletype as his 'ideal arrangement' can be ascribed in part to features of the medium that must be understood both technically and culturally, in light of a complex history of marketing campaigns, protocols of operation, informal conventions, and the unique modulations of temporality and symbolic exchange established by the device itself.

Such technographic details should matter to us, not least because teletype was of primary importance to advances in computing technology after the Second World War. The abstract machine that Turing had already hypothesized in his paper 'On Computable Numbers' was modelled on a tape-based teleprinter apparatus, and the findings of that paper formed the basis both of his work in decipherment at Bletchley Park and the subsequent development of digital computers (Turing 1936). Early mainframes used paper-based teletypes for input and output; the command-line familiar to anyone who has used an MS-DOS machine or a UNIX terminal is the direct descendant of these devices. The forms taken by our interactions with computers, and our interactions with other humans through computer-mediated networks, have been determined in part by assumptions and decisions that were engineered into teletype long before the semiconductor revolution, while the concepts and vocabularies we draw on in describing those interactions have been shaped by a century of real-time textual telecommunications. The technography of teletype, in other words, is a technography of all contemporary telemedia. We are all teletypists now.

Works Cited

Bangs, John K. 1899. *The Enchanted Type-Writer*. New York: Harper & Brothers.

Barry, Iris. 1926. *Let's Go to the Pictures*. London: Chatto & Windus.

Creed & Co. c.1934. *Typewriting Over Wires*. Croydon: Creed & Co.

Hayles, N. Katherine. 1999. *How We Became Posthuman: Virtual Bodies in Cybernetics, Literature, and Informatics*. Chicago: University of Chicago Press.

House, Royal E. 1846. 'Printing Telegraph'. US Patent No. 4464.

Huurdeman, Anton A. 2003. *The Worldwide History of Telecommunications*. Oxford: Wiley.

Menke, Richard. 2008. *Telegraphic Realism: Victorian Fiction and Other Information Systems*. Stanford: Stanford University Press.

Murray, Donald. 1924. 'Speeding Up The Telegraphs: A Forecast of the New Telegraphy'. *Journal of the Institution of Electrical Engineers* 63: 245-72.

Otis, Laura. 2001. *Networking: Communicating with Bodies and Machines in the Nineteenth Century*. Ann Arbor: University of Michigan Press.

Pargeter, Edith. 1989. *She Goes to War*. London: Headline.

Peters, John Durham. 1999. *Speaking Into the Air: A History of the Idea of Communication.* Chicago: University of Chicago Press.

Saroyan, William. 1939. *The Daring Young Man on the Flying Trapeze.* London: Penguin.

Spoto Donald. 1992. *The Art of Alfred Hitchcock.* New York: Doubleday.

Standage, Tom. 1998. *The Victorian Internet: The Remarkable Story of the Telegraph and the Nineteenth Century's On-Line Pioneers.* New York: Walker & Co.

Teletype Corporation. 1958. *The Teletype Story.* Chicago: The Teletype Corporation.

Truffaut, Francois. 1983. *Hitchcock/Truffaut.* Revised edition. New York: Simon & Schuster.

Turing, Alan. 1936. 'On Computable Numbers, With an Application to the Entscheidungsproblem'. *Proceedings of the London Mathematical Society* 2: 230-65.

Turing, Alan. 1950. 'Computing Machinery and Intelligence'. *Mind* 59: 433-460.

Wenzlhuemer, Roland. 2013. *Connecting the Nineteenth-Century World: The Telegraph and Globalization.* Cambridge: Cambridge University Press.

8

Ticker Tape and the Superhuman Reader

Robbie Moore

The New York Stock Exchange at 11 Wall Street is more a TV studio than a financial hub. Thirty broadcasters report from the trading floor every day, and the former Trading Post 9 is now a permanent studio set for CNBC. In terms of hard news gathering, the presence of TV cameras is pointless. The action happens elsewhere. Crashes no longer play out as a wave of trading-floor panic among knee-high piles of paper; rather, crashes play out silently in digital code, triggered by quirks in automatic trading software. For this reason, the website *MarketWatch* announced in 2014 that they'd no longer use photos of traders to illustrate their stock market reports. These photographs are a nostalgic fiction, *MarketWatch* said, when trading is 'done almost entirely by computers piping algorithmic playbooks into a fortress of servers in Mahwah [New Jersey]' (Olshan 2014).

This moment has been a long time coming. The process of automation and mediatisation of stock trading has been underway for 150 years, at least since the arrival of the stock ticker in 1867. The stock ticker was both a network and a machine. As a network, the ticker connected the New York Stock Exchange with hundreds (in the 1870s) and then thousands (by the turn of the century) of brokerage firms, banks, private offices, and upscale institutions like the Waldorf Astoria and Delmonico's, along with sub-networks of saloons and bucket shops (Preda 2009: 127; Hochfelder 2006: 340). Similar networks were established nationally and internationally, radiating from trading centres like Chicago and London. Ticker networks delivered a more or less continuous and more or less live stream of trading data to its members. Each receiver in the network had a stock ticker machine that converted the telegraphic signal into marks on paper. The machine also had a decorative and totemic function: often literally placed on a pedestal at the centre of an office or lobby, the early-model ticker was topped with an oracular glass dome, around which crowds gathered to watch the tape unfurl. The ticker machinery comprised two printing wheels, one with letters and one with numerals and fractions, which printed the name, price, and volume of stocks onto spools of ticker tape. Each data point was in itself almost meaningless.

The reader of the ticker looked for the relations between ticks, seeking not a discrete piece of information but a direction, a pattern. It was a reading practice which yearned towards the future, a reading practice whose ultimate goal was not to understand the message sent, but to anticipate the message yet to be sent. There was clearly an amnesiac quality to the quick movement of the tape, especially as the machine was almost always poised above a wastepaper basket, so that each message was only ever a few ticks away from trash. The present of the ticker rapidly faded.

By the turn of the twentieth century, the ticker had been absorbed into American culture. Some commentators asserted an affinity between literary and ticker-tape storytelling technologies. '[T]here is no more interesting or exciting serial story than the stock ticker tells', wrote the banker Henry Clews (Zimmerman 2006: 223). The stockbroker and writer Edwin Lefèvre, who advised Frank Norris on the inner workings of the wheat market for *The Pit*, believed that ticker tape was pure, distilled narrative: 'A foot was a book; a yard, a history' (Lefèvre 1907: 2). The ticker tape reader, who interpreted the narrative encoded on the tape, became a recognisable type in the culture of the Progressive Era. 'It is striking how often the dramas of Wall Street are illustrated (both visually and verbally) not with noisy scenes of crowds and mass hysteria but with small scale scenes of concentrated reading' (Knight 2013: 49). In an increasingly abstract, financialised economy, the tape reader functioned as a medium: a human embodiment of a disembodied system, able to read and interpret the signs of spectral capital. Tape readers were part human, part mechanical in their sensitivity to market vibrations. The hero of Edwin Lefèvre's *Sampson Rock of Wall Street* (1907), for instance, has to evacuate his humanity in order to be at one with the rhythm of the tape, even as he asserts his human mastery over the prosthetic machine: 'an elbow resting on one corner of the ticker-stand, tense, immobile, something less than human, something more than human about him, his eyes fixed hypnotically on the tape' (Lefèvre 1907: 54). Ticker-tape readers were a symptom of, but also a potential remedy for, the abstraction of capital: heroic figures who could, it was argued, imagine capital in its totality through deep reading of the tape. This chapter traces the concept of the tape reader as a superhuman reader of reality, from Frank Norris to two technographic experiments in the 1930s: Archibald MacLeish's tickerised verse drama *Panic* and Bob Brown's ticker-inspired reading machine, in which literature looks to machinery as a means of renewing the language and revitalising the practice of reading itself.

The rising prominence of the ticker coincided with a crisis in the literary representation of capitalism. Frank Norris's 'Epic of the Wheat' novels, dealing with huge, interlocking economic systems, foreground the limits of their own representational capacities. David A Zimmerman describes the 'economic sublime' in Norris's fiction: 'the idea that commercial events or operations, because of their speed, complexity, or abstractness, terrify and oppress the individual who witnesses them' (Zimmerman 2006: 142). In Norris's *The*

Octopus (1901), the corporation – with its diffuse, suprahuman 'personhood' – eludes traditional mimetic strategies:

> The corporation might be the absent center of this naturalist novel; it cannot be made manifest by anyone, from president to poet. [...] *The Octopus* is finally a novel of displacements in which representations proliferate, split, metastasize, and then disappear entirely because accurate representation itself is untenable under the corporate form. (Mrozowski 2011: 180)

The stock ticker installed at the Derricks' wheat ranch offers Norris a way of apprehending the corporate octopus: drawing a web of connections that joins the farmers to the San Francisco exchange, 'and through that city with Minneapolis, Duluth, Chicago, New York, and at last, and most important of all, with Liverpool' (Norris 1986: 619). The ticker is introduced in the novel's second chapter; here, Norris sketches the geographic reach of the network:

> no doubt, the most significant object in the office was the ticker. [...] During a flurry in the Chicago wheat pits in the August of that year, which had affected even the San Francisco market, Harran and Magnus had sat up nearly half of one night watching the strip of white tape jerking unsteadily from the reel. At such moments they no longer felt their individuality. The ranch became merely the part of an enormous whole, a unit in the vast agglomeration of wheat land the whole world round, feeling the effects of causes thousands of miles distant – a drought on the prairies of Dakota, a rain on the plains of India, a frost on the Russian steppes, a hot wind on the llanos of the Argentine. (619-20)

Ticker tape used a simplified syntax of company name, price, and volume of stock traded, which the ticker reader interpreted as noun, verb (up or down), and adverb (up or down a lot or a little). Norris mimics the ticker's syntax in his repeated evocation of 'a [weather event] on the [ecosystem] of [region]'. Here, ecosystems are rendered as interchangeable nouns that are acted upon by a positive or negative variable (a weather event). Up or down; drought or rain. That the ecosystems are almost all exotically particularised (prairie, steppe, llanos) actually has the effect of hollowing out their spatial specificity, drawing attention to the signifier itself as an empty geocultural cliché. Norris's tickerised syntax doesn't so much map the global wheat market as rhetorically replicate the way territories are incorporated and reified by the market. The effect is all the more striking coming immediately after the novel's first chapter, in which the travelling writer Presley surveys the Californian landscape from a hilltop and summons the spirits of the epic poets to rhapsodise the immensity of rural life that surrounds him: 'the imagination itself expanded under the stimulus of that measureless range of vision' (613). In displacing the first chapter's thick descriptions of place, Norris's tickerised catalogue signals a new form of epic vision, able to gesture toward capitalism's immensities even as it admits the impossibility of representation beyond the generic.

To look through Norris's ticker-eye is to become wraith-like, hovering over howling empty expanses. In Lefèvre's *Sampson Rock of Wall Street* – described by one reviewer as 'Four hundred pages of unrelieved tape and ticker, ticker and tape' ('Review of the Season's Fiction' 1907: 761) – the ticker-eye grants the hero a more romantic form of epic vision. In a passage dense with mixed metaphors, Lefèvre's ticker collapses the boundary between representation and reality, labour and capital, body and system:

> He approached the ticker and gazed intently on the printed letters and numbers of the tape, so intently that they ceased to be numerals and became living figures. [...] The tape-characters were like little soldier-ants, bringing precious loads to this New York office, tiny gold nuggets from a thousand stockholders, men and women and children, rich and poor, to the feet of Sampson Rock. [...] the entire State of Virginia was spread before him in miniature, like an outrolled map, glowing and glittering polychromatically in a flood of sunshine. And through this map ran a line, not a ticker-tape, with towns instead of abbreviations or bridges instead of dashes, but a vein; and it was not a vein of human blood or of human tears, but of human sweat, a living thing, born of work, stretching tentacle-like arms everywhither[;] the same net-work of life-giving and life-creating veins extending to the Great River and the Great Lakes. (Lefèvre 1907: 16-17)

The panoramic perspective of the ticker brings 'Order out of chaos' (17) and restores wholeness to a fractured society. Through the ticker, Sampson occupies the necessarily imaginary centre of capitalism's decentred network: the 'veins' of this body politic radiate outward from himself. In constituting a fantasised centre, Sampson imposes a feudal conception of an organised social totality onto capitalist relations of production. He becomes the ruler of a capitalist kingdom, in which ticker-numerals deliver supplicatory tributes to his feet. The lofty vantage of the ticker here acts like the enchanted mirror or crystal ball of a sorcerer-monarch. The fantasy points to the *Übermensch* complex common to many representations of the ticker-tape reader in this period: as Alex Preda notes, the 'myth of superhuman powers of the speculator became entrenched in the repertoire of popular culture' (Preda 2009: 207).

Sampson Rock's ability to see through the tape to the world itself is founded on the belief that to read price fluctuations is to take the pulse of social reality. This belief took form in the 'Dow Theory' expounded by the editor of the *Wall Street Journal*, William Peter Hamilton, and in the work of influential financial journalist and banker Charles A. Conant (Ott 2004: 12-13). The latter argued in 1904 that the stock exchange was a 'barometer' for the entire national economy, representing aggregated expert opinion on the true value of assets:

> If a railway is built in the wilderness of Manitoba and proves unprofitable, the investor does not need to hunt up people in Manitoba to ask how much freight and how many passengers it is carrying; he has only to look at the quotations for its bonds or stock on the New York Stock Exchange to know at once what is the judgment of experts on its value as a commercial enterprise. [...] Thus through the publicity of knowledge and prices, the bringing of a multitude of fallible judgments upon this common ground to an average, there is afforded to capital throughout the world an almost unfailing index of the course in which new production should be directed. (Conant 1904: 91-2)

If stock prices are an (almost) unfailing index of present (and future) events, then the flow of prices on a ticker tape is an unedited rendering of that reality in language. This idea was popularised in tape-reading guidebooks: 'The tape tells the news minutes, hours, and days before the news tickers, or newspapers, and before it can become current gossip. Everything from a foreign war to the passing of a dividend; from a Supreme Court decision to the ravages of the boll weevil is reflected primarily upon the tape' (Tape 1910: 11). The ticker's automatic writing, therefore, was a reflection – a transparent representation – of the real. Ticker reading took on a Calvinist attitude toward the holy text as the revealed word of God, through which the natural world may be primarily understood: an electro-Calvinism tempered, in the writings of Lefèvre and others, by the need for a clerical class of hermeneuticians trained in the arts of revelation. As Lefèvre writes in one of his short stories, '[t]here was no god but the ticker, and the brokers were its prophets!' (Lefèvre 1901: 179).

While Norris and Lefèvre think about the ticker-eye in terms of mastery and totality, Will Payne's wire-tapping novel *The Losing Game* (1910) shows a more proletarian way of writing about the ticker. The protagonists of the novel, Emma Raymond and John Pound, are telegraph operators in a stock-ticker sweatshop. Their work is to notate the live ticker feed from the New York Stock Exchange, and to retransmit the data to secondary ticker networks of local brokers and dubious 'bucket shops' (where customers place bets on the movements of the market). This is physical labour: watched by a rheumatic manager, the rows of operators sweat in the heat as they hunch over their machines, producing a 'hard, rapid, senseless clatter' (Payne 1910: 12). Emma and John are strangers who happen to be seated side by side. Their bodies transmit clicking, sparking, telegraphic expressions of desire as they work:

> He merely touched the slips from the top of his pack, making the woman reach an arm's length to get them — which she did silently and steadily, putting them on top of her pack; her fingers touching the keys of her machine. [...] That occasional look through her dark, demure eyelashes seemed to throw off tiny sparks. Twice or thrice, also, her lips parted slightly and, very gently, she clicked her small, white teeth together. (9)

But their seduction stalls and fizzles in the alienated factory environment. Alienation and sexual frustration are fused together in an image of mechanical breakdown: 'Nearly everything in the room seemed trying to do something that it couldn't. The man and woman got to no culminative point in their game; the brass contrivance stirred and sparked, but didn't go; the light no sooner showed in a bulb than it died' (10). They are trapped in a cycle of eternal repetition, telegraphing messages into the ether which will never be reciprocated. The solution, however, is not to escape the machine but to take control of it: to close the circuit and become both sender and receiver in the network. Emma meets John conspiratorially after work, and they discuss ways to escape their predicament. Though they are expert readers and interpreters of the ticker, neither has had any luck playing the market. The game is rigged, they believe, whether by bucket shops or more legitimate exchanges. To win, John argues, 'a fellow must play the game from the inside' (23). John has previous experience tapping wires, while Emma has experience 'tapping' cash registers. They devise a plan to manipulate the ticker. John explains that ticker operators sometimes accidentally neglect to send out a stray stock quote or two and, upon realising their mistake, send out the overlooked quote preceded by the letter 's', which alerts the receiver to the error. John suggests that he can exploit the 's' code to send data out of order, misinforming the ticker sub-network about the true live price of stocks. Emma, watching the ticker tape in a bucket shop, will recognise John's signals and place winning bets on the special stocks he marks out; only she and John will know that these stocks have already risen in price. In exploiting this weakness in the system, Emma and John assert control over the flow of information and are no longer subject to the ticker's temporality. This manipulation of the ticker stands in for scenes of seduction. The barrier to their union is John's 'bottled up' heart: 'At once his heart stirred as though something had pricked it, and he bottled himself up again. By that time she was familiar with the bottling process. He would move only an inch at a time' (21). 'Tapping' the wires becomes a liquid metaphor for unstopping this bottled up desire. The novel doesn't supplant Emma and John's initial telegraphic flirtation with something more authentically human; instead, it imagines love as the smooth transmission and decryption of electric messages.

If *The Losing Game* was written, as one reviewer argued, 'for people with a sneaking admiration for the kind of rascality that it pictures so graphically and so attractively' ('Current Fiction' 1910: 377), such rascality was being stamped out in the 1910s through the consolidation of the network and the professionalisation of tape reading. This process would further elevate and masculinise the image of the ticker reader. Before the process of consolidation, access to the ticker through bucket shops and other informal establishments was widespread. One New York broker complained in 1889 that 'indiscriminate distribution of stock quotations to every liquor-saloon and other places has done much to interfere with business. Any person could step in a saloon and see the quotations' (Hochfelder 2006: 340). While legitimate brokerages were exclusive, the *Chicago Tribune* suggested in 1879 that bucket shops had a clientele drawn from across races, genders and classes: 'any person, man or woman [...] white, black, yellow, or bronze can deal directly' (341). In 1892, *The Sun* reported on one of Chicago's women-only bucket shops, filled mostly with 'elderly maidens and widows, with an occasional married woman who dabbles in stocks without the knowledge of any one but her broker' ('Interesting Information' 1892: 18). The article suggests that women 'feel the pulse of the market much quicker than men', though they must pay a higher moral price, becoming 'oblivious to sentiment and careless of personal appearance, and absurdly superstitious' (18). From the 1880s, the New York Stock Exchange began to pursue legal, political, and economic strategies to limit ticker access and curtail amateur tape readers (Preda 2009: 139-40; Hochfelder 2006: 350-55). Wires were ripped out of walls by the police. *The Sun* reported in 1894 that Boston police had ordered all stock and news tickers out of saloons, hotels, and restaurants; the police refused to name the statute under which they were acting ('Ordered Out the Tickers' 1894: 1). The Chicago Exchange enforced an information blackout in 1890, trying to starve the bucket shops out of business (Hochfelder 2006: 352). Finally, the New York exchange took on the Western Union telegraph monopoly, which was profiting handsomely from bucket shops. By 1892, Western Union was obliged to install tickers only in brokerages owned by members of the New York Stock Exchange (Preda 2009: 140).

As bucket shops slowly died out and the ticker network solidified in the 1910s, tape reading was increasingly restricted to professionals. A 1931 article described tape readers as '[m]ore times than not [...] a graduate from some Stock Exchange activity, customers' man, in a brokerage office, or statistician for some firm in the Street' (Greason 1931: 25). Through trade journals, financial newspapers, and guidebooks, ticker readers defined themselves as a profession that required precision, masculine clear-headedness, privacy, and study. These publications set high bars for the tape reader to surmount.

First, the tape reader should be physically and aurally insulated from everyday life. Richard Wyckoff, a trader and magazine editor who published under the name of Rollo Tape, offers this advice in *Studies in Tape Reading*:

> For perfect concentration as a protection from the tips, gossip, and other influences which abound in a broker's office, he should, if possible, seclude himself. A tiny room with a ticker, a desk, and a private telephone connection with his broker's office are all the facilities required. The work requires such delicate balance of the facilities that the slightest influence either way may throw the result against the trader. (Tape 1910: 17)

Second, the ticker reader must perform a close reading of the tape itself. Other contextual documents were a distraction from the truths of the primary text. The 'most expert type of tape-reader [...] carries no memorandums, and seldom refers to fluctuation records. The tape whispers to him, talks to him' (Tape 1908: 34). Third, ticker readers must be without affect. The economics professor Charles Amos Dice advises that 'the trader must develop a dispassionate attitude toward the tape, so that he is not affected by his hopes and fears' (Dice 1926: 284). Rollo Tape writes,

> The Tape Reader evolves himself into an automaton which takes note of a situation, weighs it, decides upon a course, and gives an order. There is no quickening of the pulse, no nerves, no hopes or fears. [...] The Tape Reader is like a Pullman coach, which travels smoothly and steadily along the roadbed of the tape, acquiring direction and speed from the market engine, and being influenced by nothing whatever. (Tape 1910: 15-16)

Fourth, ticker readers must concentrate and they must practice, submitting themselves to a new time economy and a new regime of attentiveness:

> The tape reader spends every day at the ticker watching the tape with most careful attention. Any moment the tape may show the beginning of a move upward or downward which is weighted with opportunities for making money. The tape reader, to be successful, should devote his whole time to studying the tape. He should have no business calling other than watching the tape. (Dice 1926: 280)

Some writers recommended taking home the day's expired tape to study it.

They insisted on something else, too: a special sensitivity, or what Rollo Tape calls a 'sixth sense' (Tape 1910: 7), which cannot be learnt. Lefèvre, ghostwriting the autobiography of Wall Street trader Jesse Livermore, suggests that the divination of the tape reader represents 'the subconscious mind, which is the creative mind, at work. That is the mind which makes artists do things without their knowing how they came to do them' (Lefèvre 1923: 76). But there was a fine line, it seems, between sensitivity to the ticker and susceptibility to the ticker. One pro-Wall Street journalist describes the ticker as a 'narcotic' (Wamsley 1921: 54); Lefèvre describes a man with 'ticker fever', whose right forefinger 'shook [...] with a hammering motion' (Lefèvre 1901: 94, 98), as if his body were becoming the machine it services; and a doctor writing for the *Medical Times* describes the illness of 'tickeritis':

> I have long held the theory that the constant ticking of the instruments in the broker's office throws the majority of traders into a state of self-hypnosis, in which they become automatons [...] Patients have been able to throw themselves into a hypnotic state by watching the light from revolving mirrors. Why should not the constant ticking have the same effect on the brain of the trader through his ears? (Howe-Adams 1904: 162)

The ticker-reading hero of Norris's *The Pit* succumbs to the mesmeric power of the market; according to Zimmerman, the crumbling of his faculties 'registers what the New Psychology understood to be the potential danger of entrancement: an instrument of titanic powers, he is ultimately only their instrument' (Zimmerman 2006: 139). If these accounts challenge the tape reader's reputation for rational self-possession, defenders of Wall Street argued that this was precisely why readers needed to be licensed experts and not hysterical amateurs. In 1934, in the wake of a banking meltdown, the liberal think tank The Twentieth Century Fund suggested that 'the financial and moral standing' of amateur traders was a major concern that threatened the stability of the market. The Fund argued that morally weak buyers can be overawed by stock tickers, in the same way that they might be overawed by the movies:

> One of the most powerful stimuli to stock market gambling on the part of the outside public is the easy and pleasant access to the market provided by the stock ticker [...] especially since recent inventions like the electric board and the translux tape. The feverish and exciting atmosphere created by these devices [...] kindles and magnifies the urge for gambling. (Clark, Dewhurst, Bernheim, and Grant 1934: 181)

The report concluded that the general public needed to be educated in order to speculate rationally.

The New York Stock Exchange itself helped to propagate the image of the ticker reader as a rational actor in an efficient marketplace. From the 1910s, the Exchange's Committee on Library administered a campaign to restore trust in trading and to distance legitimate traders from amateur bucket shop gamblers. The Committee crafted a vision of the Exchange as a smooth mechanism. An official illustrated history published in 1919 offered 'photographs of empty, tidy trading floors and small groups of neatly attired clerks calmly operating pneumatic tubes, tickers, and telephones' (Ott 2004:

7). Committee secretary William Van Antwerp highlighted the ticker and its 'mechanical efficiency' as a central achievement of the New York Exchange (Antwerp 1914: 342). In tandem, the Committee challenged cultural representations of trading that they regarded as fallacious and outdated. A 1914 film adaptation of Frank Norris's *The Pit* was threatened with a libel suit because it represented the trading floor as a scene of collective frenzy. Changes to the film were secured after the threat was issued (Ott 2009: 44). In this manner, the Exchange established a false though rhetorically seductive dichotomy: the bucket-shop gambler, the amateur, the crowd, the hysteric, and market panic were positioned as the abject Other in relation to the professional tape reader, whose part-mechanical subjectivity was cool, self-regulating, and immune to panic.

The panic of October 1929, however, exposed the limitations of the ticker machine itself. The tape could not keep up with the volume of sales and continued to tick hours after the market had closed. The President of the New York Stock Exchange admitted that the 'mechanical limitations of the ticker system [...] considerably aggravated the public hysteria' (Meeker 1930: 599). The out-of-control ticker became visual shorthand for the crash, as in the erupting ticker tape in Pare Lorentz's *The Plow That Broke the Plains* (1936). Yet Bob Brown's *The Readies* (1930) and Archibald MacLeish's *Panic* (1935) kept alive the myth of the masterful tape reader, while asserting a precarious alliance between the technocratic expert and the mass.

Macleish's verse drama, *Panic*, which premiered with a young Orson Welles as the financier McGafferty (as well as crowd choreography by Martha Graham and music by Virgil Thomson), features two kinds of ticker machines in supporting roles. In the street, the scene is '*faintly lighted by the jerking flashes*' of the Times Square news ticker (MacLeish 1935: 3). Like the Trans-Lux Movie Ticker installed in the New York Stock Exchange in 1923, which projected an image of the paper ticker tape onto a translucent screen in real time, the Times Square ticker turned live news feeds into a public spectacle (Preda 2009: 131). In McGafferty's office, the room is dominated by a more old-fashioned, private news ticker, its spools of tape chronicling an accelerating financial panic. In stage directions, MacLeish notes that the '*whir of the mechanism*' and the '*beat of the type* [...] *comes in intervals of sound over intervals of silence: a rhythm parallel to the rhythm of the verse*' (MacLeish 1935: 8). At other times the ticker is said to '*beat in counter rhythm*' under the sound of an actor's voice (66).

MacLeish's verse is marked by the rhythm of the machine with which it duets. In an introductory note, MacLeish rejects the English blank verse common to verse drama. Blank verse, he writes, is so 'even', 'toneless', 'relaxed', and 'free' as to 'leave the audience doubtful whether it is prose or verse' (ix). Instead, MacLeish adopts an accentual, percussive, and implicitly tickerised metre, rejecting the iamb in favour of the trochee, the dactyl, and the spondee. This more closely approaches the 'rhythms of the spoken language of our country', MacLeish claims. Twentieth-century American speech 'is a language of accents. Its most marked characteristic is its accentual strength'. MacLeish's feet deploy stressed syllables in a way, he claims, that imitates the 'voices of men talking intently to each other in the offices or the mills or on the streets of this country' (viii). The poet's search for a means of representing the authentic voice of the people leads him to the nervous rhythm of ticker tape.

Yet mastery of this machine language is distributed unequally in *Panic*. McGafferty unfurls his thoughts in pentameter, while the crowd in the street outside McGafferty's office, moving in unison like a Greek chorus, speak in a more cramped, clipped trimeter, frequently with one concrete image per line. Their visions of economic collapse are thereby rendered like the enjambed, spasmodic flashes of the Times Square ticker from which they read:

> A YOUNG MAN
> Rigs rusting at pit-heads:
> Pumps frozen: switches
> Green with the rain: the oil
> Thickened: scale in boilers –
> [...]
> A WOMAN
> Drought – not in the springs!
> Rot – not from the rain! (5-8)

Replicating the news ticker's rhythm, the crowd is represented as the mouthpiece of the machine. They read their fate, but are unable to comprehend or alter it: 'What shadow hidden or / Unseen hand in our midst / Ceaselessly touches our faces?' (8) McGafferty's longer lines sing like a bravura soloist over the remorseless ostinato of the crowd. While the crowd speaks of confusion and panic, he speaks of choice and agency:

> God you talk like girls that see a ghost!
> There's only men and weather in this world: –
> The rest is wishing. You can stand and fight or
> Run and not fight but your choice will choose it. (13)

McGafferty promises to be a superhuman reader of capital. He believes the financial crisis is ultimately legible. Signs reliably point to a reality beyond themselves, a reality that can be acted upon: 'There's nothing secret – mysterious: / Nothing men with human brains can't handle. / Smoke's a sign of fire: we can find it' (10). At the heart of this play is the desire for a master tape reader to soothe the general panic. MacLeish knows this mythic reader to be impossible, yet still evokes him as the only solution for American capitalism in crisis. The Sophoclean tragedy of *Panic* hinges on McGafferty's inability to live up to this heroic promise. As he succumbs to the machinery of fate, McGafferty hurls curses at the ticker, his former lyrical fluency replaced by a mechanical stutter:

> God! Will the thing stop! Is the groping world
> Mechanical and grinds on like a gear-nest –
> Ignorant in the sullen oil – that drives the
> Wheels toward nothing – anything – nothing – death – but
> Drives them! Drives them! Drives them! Always drives them! (73)

MacLeish wrote *Panic* while working at the business magazine *Fortune*. During the depths of the Depression, the magazine had made a shift from capitalist hagiography toward a left-liberal position that regarded American business leadership with scepticism, took the labour movement seriously, and welcomed New Deal reforms. *Fortune*'s journalists were largely young bohemians and aspiring poets: 'it is easier to turn poets into business journalists than to turn bookkeepers into writers' claimed the media magnate and *Fortune* founder Henry Luce (Vanderlan 2010: 94). The journalists, and MacLeish in particular, played a large role in *Fortune*'s political renovation (Reilly 1999: 214-8). MacLeish's own political renovation occurred simultaneously in his poetry and in the pages of *Fortune*. His disillusion with corporate titans and his rejection of romantic individualism in poetry – 'The individual is no longer the unit, the sacred integer, the solemn end' (Barber 1988: 37) – led not toward socialism, but toward a kind of corporate liberalism. The collective mattered, but it was the responsibility of individuals in power – whether it be Roosevelt, Morgan, or MacLeish – to provide the collective with its form and its direction. In an open letter in 1932 'To the Young Men of Wall Street', MacLeish argued that business leaders had 'ignored the necessity of giving the economic order shape and structure and human hope'. A new generation of leaders was required to 'create an idea of capitalism which men will support with their hope rather than their despair' (Vanderlan 2010: 107). If capitalists were incapable of supplying the collective with vision, then the poet must step in to finish the job. Writing in 1931 about poetry after *The Waste Land*, MacLeish argued that it was the duty of the poet to create a motivating 'image of mankind in which men can again believe' (Barber 1988: 31). In MacLeish's ideal polity, the superhuman reader of the ticker and the superhuman poet of the people would be two sides of the same coin.

A similar conflation of the business elite and the cultural elite occurs in the post-crash manifesto of the obscure American modernist Bob Brown. In *The Readies* (1930) and *Readies for Bob Brown's Machine* (1931), Brown proposes a ticker-like reading machine with a spool of tape that rapidly whizzes through novels and poems one word at a time:

> Why wasn't there a man-made machine like the running tape-of-thought device in the mind which would carry words endlessly to all reading eyes in one unbroken line, a reading machine as rapid and refreshing as thought, to take the place of the antiquated word-dribbling book? I wanted a reading machine to bring the

words of others faster into my mind. [...] I conceived that with such a machine to represent them fully, writers might find a new urge to write more vividly, or at least differently, to approach closer to the hieroglyphic mysteries that have streamed across their gossamer braintapes from the beginning of time to infinity.
(Brown 1931: 168)

Brown's imagined machine, which never got beyond a prototype, would be something he could 'carry or move around, attach to any old electric light plug, and read hundred thousand word novels in ten minutes if I want to, and I want to' (Brown 2014: 28). There would be a bulb for illumination, a built-in magnifying glass to magnify the tiny font, an ability to accelerate or decelerate the tape, and perhaps even tinted paper or coloured lighting effects to delight the eye. Brown's two inspirations, he claims, were reading Gertrude Stein and working on Wall Street. 'The Wall Street ticker is a reading machine', he writes (Brown 1931: 166). 'A heavy didactic market came along, must be Henry James at the helm. A wave of joss-stick chop-stick jazz made the tape toss choppily in a Conrad sea. [...] Might be interesting like Gertrude Stein if you read it backward and left out the figures' (166-7).

Brown convinced a number of poets including Stein herself, Ezra Pound, William Carlos Williams, and Filippo Tommaso Marinetti, to contribute to his 1931 anthology *Readies for Bob Brown's Machine*. Many, however, submitted old work, while Williams submitted a weak two-line gag, and most regarded Brown and the whole business with a cocked eyebrow, as even Brown himself admitted (Stephens 2011: 159-60). By asserting that this was no ordinary reading machine, but a *modernist* reading machine, Brown was reserving his invention for a select cadre of readers. Yet Brown also suggests that the reading machine is a means of collapsing the opposition between modernism and mass culture, expert and average Joe. His vision drags high modernism into a sleepless, accelerated, 24-hour marketplace:

> The Book of the Day or Book of the Hour Club could sell its output in clips of a dozen ready to slip into the reading machine. [...] Reading by machinery will be as simple and painless as shaving with a Schick razor and refills may be had at corner drug stores, cigar stores, or telephone booths from dawn to midnight.
> (Brown 2014: 30-31)

The name 'Readies' is itself a riff on mass culture: machine-reading would become, Brown writes, 'a moving type spectacle [...] a method of enjoying literature in a manner as up to date as the lively talkies' (27). Modernist culture's resistance to commodification would be broken down simply by routing it through a novel delivery mechanism. Through sheer speed of projection, Brown imagined modernist texts becoming a luminescent substance, beaming directly to the mind. Yet it is a technocrat, and not an everyday reader, that Brown imagines working his machine. The machine-reader would require careful training of the kind required by expert ticker-tape readers. Brown talks of the 'practiced reading eye' and the 'intelligent, experienced eye' (36, 51). By adapting to the machine, the eye will be 'soothed and civilized and eventually become ashamed of its former nakedness' (33). The duality of high and low, dissolved in Brown's conflation of modernism and mass culture, is reconstituted in his racialised rhetoric of expertise. He suggests that the Readie expert will slough away her barbarian self in the process of becoming prostheticised.

Brown believed that America outpaced the reader's ability to read it. 'To continue reading at today's speed', Brown writes, 'I must have a machine' (28). The complexity of modernity necessitated heroic readers: technocrats with mastery over machines, who were themselves part-machine. Brown's heroic reader could finish a 300,000-word novel in ten minutes; Norris's heroic reader could instantly apprehend the global marketplace; MacLeish's heroic reader might save us from panic. Built upon the mythology of Wall Street, the superhuman reader was a remarkably persistent fantasy, an imaginary solution to real contradictions in the era of high finance.

Works Cited

Antwerp, William C. Van. 1914. *The Stock Exchange from Within*. New York: Doubleday.

Barber, David. 1988. 'In Search of an "Image of Mankind": The Public Poetry and Prose of Archibald MacLeish'. *American Studies* 29: 31-56.

Brown, Bob. 1931. *Readies for Bob Brown's Machine*. Cagnes-sur-Mer: Roving Eye Press.

Brown, Bob. 2014. *The Readies*. Edited by Craig Saper. Baltimore: Roving Eye Press.

Conant, Charles A. 1904. *Wall Street and the Country: A Study of Recent Financial Tendencies*. New York: G.P. Putnam's Sons.

'Current Fiction'. 1910. *Nation* 90: 376-7.

Dice, Charles Amos. 1926. *The Stock Market*. New York: A.W. Shaw Company.

Clark, Evans, J. Frederic Dewhurst, Alfred L. Bernheim, and Margaret Grant. 1934. *Stock Market Control; A Summary of the Research Findings and Recommendations of the Security Markets Survey Staff of the Twentieth Century Fund, Inc*. New York: D. Appleton-Century Company.

Greason, Al. 1931. 'Ticker Readers – Old and New'. *Variety*, December 29.

Hochfelder, David. 2006. '"Where the Common People Could Speculate": The Ticker, Bucket Shops, and the Origins of Popular Participation in Financial Markets, 1880-1920'. *Journal of American History* 93: 335-58.

Howe-Adams, J. 1908. 'Concerning the Physician's Finances'. *Medical Times* 32: 161-8.

'Interesting Information'. 1892. *Sun*, February 14: 18.

Knight, Peter. 2013. 'Reading the Ticker Tape in the Late Nineteenth-Century American Market'. *Journal of Cultural Economy* 6: 45-62.

Lefèvre, Edwin. 1901. *Wall Street Stories*. New York: McLure, Phillips & Co.

Lefèvre, Edwin. 1907. *Sampson Rock of Wall Street: A Novel*. New York: Harper & Brothers.

Lefèvre, Edwin. 1923. *Reminiscences of a Stock Operator*. New York: George H. Doran Company.

Meeker, J. Edward. 1930. *The Work of the Stock Exchange*. New York: Ronald Press Company.

MacLeish, Archibald. 1935. *Panic: A Play in Verse*. Boston: Riverside Press.

Mrozowski, Daniel J. 2011. 'How to Kill a Corporation: Frank Norris's *The Octopus* and the Embodiment of American Business'. *Studies in American Naturalism* 6:161-84.

Norris, Frank. 1986. *Novels and Essays*. Edited by Donald Pizer. New York: Library of America.

Olshan, Jeremy. 2014. 'This is the Last Photo We'll Ever Run of the NYSE Trading Floor'. *MarketWatch*, October 1. http://www.marketwatch.com/story/this-is-the-last-photo-well-ever-run-of-the-nyse-trading-floor-2014-10-01.

'Ordered Out the Tickers'. 1894. *Sun*, June 22: 1.

Ott, Julia. 2004. 'The "Free and Open" "People's Market": Public Relations at the New York Stock Exchange, 1913-1929'. *Business and Economic History* 2: 1-43.

Ott, Julia. 2009. '"The Free and Open People's Market": Political Ideology and Retail Brokerage at the New York Stock Exchange, 1913–1933'. *Journal of American History* 96: 44-71.

Payne, Will. 1910. *The Losing Game*. New York: G.W. Dillingham Company.

Preda, Alex. 2009. *Framing Finance: The Boundaries of Markets and Modern Capitalism*. Chicago: University of Chicago Press.

'A Review of the Season's Fiction'. 1907. *American Monthly Review of Reviews* 35: 760-8.

Reilly, Kevin S. 1999. 'Dilettantes at the Gate: *Fortune* Magazine and the Cultural Politics of Business Journalism in the 1930s'. *Business and Economic History* 28: 213-22.

Stephens, Paul. 2011. 'Bob Brown, "Inforg": The "Readies" at the Limits of Modernist Cosmopolitanism'. *Journal of Modern Literature* 35: 143-64.

Tape, Rollo. 1908. 'Market Lectures'. *Ticker* 1: 33-5.

Tape, Rollo. 1910. *Studies in Tape Reading*. New York: Traders Press.

Vanderlan, Robert. 2010. *Intellectuals Incorporated: Politics, Art, and Ideas Inside Henry Luce's Media Empire*. Philadelphia: University of Pennsylvania Press.

Wamsley, Wilbur. 1921. 'The Stock Ticker, the Pulse of Wall Street'. *Manse's Magazine* 73: 54-9.

Zimmerman, David A. 2006. *Panic! Markets, Crises, and Crowds in American Fiction*. Chapel Hill: University of North Carolina Press.

9

Bibliographic Technography: Ezra Pound's *Cantos* as Philological Machine

Mark Byron

Ezra Pound's modernist epic *The Cantos* asserts itself as a primer in historical bibliography. The famous opening – 'And then went down to the ship, / Set keel to breakers, forth on the godly sea, and / We set up mast and sail of that swart ship' (Pound 1996: 3) – deploys an Anglo-Saxon vocabulary and alliterative versification to represent the *Nekyia* episode from Book XI of the *Odyssey*, in which Odysseus journeys to the underworld. Pound believed the *Nekyia* to be the most archaic episode in the entire Homeric corpus, but instead of drawing on Homer's Greek, he took the episode from a Latin translation by Andreas Divus – 'In officina Wecheli, 1538, out of Homer' (5) – a book he had picked up 'on the Quais in Paris' (Pound 1968: 265). This palimpsest effect, overlaying classical Greek, Anglo-Saxon, Renaissance Latin, and modern English with an antiquarian bent, brings together related literary and textual journeys across languages and epochs, including the author's own journey to Paris. As a whole *The Cantos* ranges across personal, literary, political, and intellectual histories, not to mention philosophy, geography, and economics; it aspires to be encyclopaedic. But though the diversity of Pound's sources is remarkable, the poem is even more impressive for the way in which it deals with those sources imaginatively, incorporating their various textual structures into its own fabric and presenting the history of textual technologies as an ongoing poetic enterprise.

The Cantos presents the materiality of diverse texts on its surface: multiple poetic genres and modes, parliamentary speeches, Papal encyclicals, ancient Chinese bone inscriptions, imperial decrees, epistles, hymns, and musical scores – all in an array of languages and scripts, and complemented by such textual apparatus as citations, glosses, and annotations. The poem emulates the forms and techniques of the texts upon which it draws, engaging textual history and bibliography as means for preserving and transmitting precious cultural cargo. This materialist poetics is a powerful technography, in which technologies of writing are made evident in the formal arrangements of text on the page.

GOD SAVE LIBERTY THE CONGRESS AND ADAMS

Fig. 1. Pound 1996: 371

Pound's complex deployment of sources performs a history of writing, which he takes to its limit in the documentary method of the two decades of Cantos composed in the years leading up to the Second World War. The first of these decads, the so-called China Cantos, comprises for the most part selected excerpts translated from Joseph de Maille's thirteen-book *Histoire Générale de la Chine* (1777-1785). In taking this approach, Pound conforms to the Imperial Court's version of history as relayed to a French Jesuit diplomat in the late eighteenth century. A monumental 耀 (yao) ideogram functions as a frontispiece or epigraph for the decad, supplemented by a chronological table of contents and a brief editorial rationale for the transliteration of names (Pound 1996: 254-6). The ideogram preserves the image and the memory of a hand-written script in a mechanically produced volume. Though the semi-mythic Emperor Yao's reign in the third millennium BCE preceded the emergence of early Chinese writing in the Shang Dynasty, in the second half of the second millennium BCE, and though the ideogram 耀 signifies little by itself, Pound uses it to indicate Yao as the progenitor of the durable information technology of writing at the heart of Chinese dynastic history.

The following decad, the Adams Cantos, in turn excerpts and rearranges passages from the ten-volume *Works of John Adams* (1850–1856), edited by Charles Francis Adams. David Ten Eyck has shown how this poetic technique, combined with Pound's selection of subject matter, shifts the focus from a Jeffersonian Republic to a version of American polity and international diplomacy in keeping with his idiosyncratic vision of Fascist Italy (Ten Eyck 2012). At the same time, the physical layout of the page in these cantos foregrounds textual materiality. A vertical bar appears in the margin of two cantos (Pound 1996: 377, 416) and oversized ideograms are placed strategically throughout the sequence. When quoting the phrase 'God save the Congress, Liberty and Adams' (Adams 1850-1856: 3.120), Pound rearranges its terms, capitalises it, substitutes spacing for its punctuation, and arches it across the page, as if forming a celebratory banner (Figure 1).

Later, in the decad's final canto, Pound adapts Adams's reflection that he desires 'no other inscription over my gravestone than: "Here lies John Adams, who took upon himself the responsibility of the peace with France in the year 1800"' (Adams 1850-1856: 10.113). Pound's poem generalises the commitment to peace, capitalises the text, and frames it on the page in imitation of an epitaph (Figure 2).

> JOHN ADAMS
> FOR PEACE
> 1800

Fig. 2. Pound 1996: 418

Both the China Cantos and the Adams Cantos, therefore, deploy source texts to promote specific arguments about cultural and political legitimacy, and they do so by drawing attention to the material production and reproduction of text.

Late Classical and Medieval Textuality

In the 1930s, Pound also pursued an interest in late classical and medieval forms of textuality, each with its own material technologies and intellectual conventions. Pound was particularly invested in technographic transformations: moments at which the conservation and the distribution of accumulated knowledge were altered by enhanced means of textual production and transmission. The shift from late classical to early medieval and Carolingian textuality, for instance, is important because it established the pre-eminence of the codex and the codification of scholarly techniques such as glossing and annotation. So, too, such classical encyclopaedic works as those of Eusebius, Pliny the Elder, Vitruvius, and Varro were emulated in the encyclopaedic texts of Martianus Capella (fl. 410-420), Pseudo-Dionysius (late fifth to early sixth century), John Scottus Eriugena (c. 815- c. 877), and others. These works were designed to function as books of instruction, either as epitomes of classical thought or as schematic accounts of everything in existence. They were glossed, copied, and abbreviated in the monastic schoolroom and passed down to later generations of students and clerics. These early medieval encyclopaedic texts also established a functional relation between reader and page space, which gave the reader an interlocutory and critical role. This, in turn, is the textual scene emulated in Pound's *Cantos*, whose reader must at the same time negotiate a dizzying array of authoritative sources and the dispersed space of a poetic text which includes indexical elements such as Chinese ideograms, musical scores, and pictographs. Pound attempts to produce not so much an encyclopaedic poem, as a poem of encyclopaedism.

But perhaps the greatest influence on Pound's poetics, in this regard, was the careful philological work he pursued on the manuscript heritage of Dante's contemporary Guido Cavalcanti. Pound's interest in Cavalcanti began during his education at Hamilton College and the University of Pennsylvania, where he undertook intensive study of medieval literature with a focus on the troubadours of twelfth-century Provence. William T. Paden argues that Pound's early and enduring philological investments are essential to an understanding of his poetic aims: 'Since he wielded his erudition as an instrument of hermeneutic compression and aesthetic impact, the general understanding of his art stands to benefit from a study of his performance as a Provençal philologist' (Paden 1980: 402). Pound's research into the troubadours initially relied upon textbooks, probably those prescribed by his Professors: William P. Shepard, at Hamilton; and Hugo Rennert, at Pennsylvania (403-4). But Pound later devoted considerable time and resources to the first-hand study of Provençal manuscripts in the Biblioteca Ambrosiana in Milan and the Bibliothèque Nationale in Paris, particularly in 1911 and 1912 while working on his essay 'Troubadours – Their Sorts and Conditions' (1913). Pound's scholarly ambition to update Provençal philology provided source material and technographic guides for his subsequent poetic enterprises: 'Pound was a serious, competent, and fitfully industrious student of the troubadours [...] He used Provençal manuscripts for the two essential purposes of philology – once to rediscover the past and once to enlarge the present' (410-11).

From 1925 to 1931, Pound examined every extant Cavalcanti manuscript in Italy, aiming to produce a definitive edition of Cavalcanti's *Rime*. He conducted this extensive textual and codicological research in the Biblioteca Laurenziana in Florence, the Vatican Library, the Biblioteca Communale in Siena, and elsewhere. He recorded details relating to textual variants of long-standing notoriety in the history of Cavalcanti scholarship, as well as empirical data such as the relative frequency of particular poems within and across manuscripts (Pound 1925-1932a). He also made copious notes keying poems or lines of poems to potential sources or influences, as well as to relevant critical works. Pound knew this critical tradition well, making frequent mention of such commentators and editors as Dino del Garbo, Egidio Colonna, Egidio Romano, Celso Cittadini, Girolamo Frachetta, Antonio Cicciaporci, and Ercole Rivalta. He also notes a wide range of sources and successors, from Avicenna's commentary on Aristotle's *De anima* to Dante's *Divina commedia*, all of which were to inform his edition of the *Rime*. This edition would offer both a philological reconstruction of Cavalcanti's poetic corpus, with facing-page translations, and an evaluation of the critical tradition. Pound tried to have it published with at least three different presses: *Sonnets and Ballate of Guido Cavalcanti* with Small, Maynard, and Company in Boston in 1912; *Complete Works of Guido Cavalcanti* with the Aquila Press in London in 1929, aborted when Aquila declared bankruptcy after only 500 unbounded sets of sheets had been printed; and *Guido Cavalcanti Rime* with Marsano in Genoa in 1932. After the failure of this third edition, Pound's critical apparatus and commentaries, which had been variously published in journals during the 1910s, were finally collected in the essay 'Cavalcanti' (Pound 1934).

Pound's serial attempts to produce a philologically rigorous edition of Cavalcanti's *Rime*, while ultimately compromised, demonstrate the alignment of two potent elements in his technography: the intellectual machinery of textual scholarship, on the one hand, and the physical machines used to generate mechanical reproductions, on the other. First, Pound was committed to untangling long-standing problems of source attribution and intellectual lineage. Cavalcanti functioned for him as an entry point into the earlier Middle Ages. In Canto XXXVI, for example, he turns from a translation of the thirteenth-century 'Donna mi prega' to the thirteenth-century Papal condemnation of Eriugena, and then to that ninth-century philosopher's own thinking: 'Authority comes from right reason' (Pound 1996: 179; see Bush 2013; Byron 2014: 30-45). And while Cavalcanti's poem seems to meditate on the nature of *amor* in the customary fashion of the *dolce stil nuovo* ('sweet new style'), Pound claims in an extended gloss on it that Cavalcanti deploys a vocabulary derived from ancient fertility rites, as well as one amalgamating Aristotelian ontology with Neoplatonic cosmology and transmitted by medieval Islamic philosophers (Pound 1934). He sought to establish these links in extended correspondence with the medievalists Étienne Gilson and Otto Bird. In a letter of 13 March 1938 Bird remarked that 'all those Italians knew the Arabian treatises backwards and forewords [sic]' (Bird 1938). In this way, Pound's translation in Canto XXXVI presents love in fundamentally different terms from those in which Dante presents his love for Beatrice: here a masculine *amor* is the active subject and vehicle of mystical knowledge, conveyed to its 'knowers' in a schematic conceptual system of 'virtu', the 'diafan' of light, and the 'intellect possible' (Pound 1996: 177). For Pound, a linguistic and etymological study of manuscripts allows us to identify otherwise obscured intellectual lineages.

Second, in addition to his assiduous if sometimes unconventional research, Pound engaged with manuscripts by embracing newly developing information technologies. At the same time as he was researching Cavalcanti's poetry, he played an important role in salvaging a vast quantity of neglected manuscripts of the music of Antonio Vivaldi. With Olga Rudge, he uncovered hundreds of these works in Dresden, Turin, and Venice. At the time Rudge was engaged as Guido Chigi Saracini's personal secretary, assisting with the establishment of the Fondazione Accademia Chigiana in Siena. The Palazzo Chigi Saracini had held concerts of classical and avant-garde music during the 1920s, but the scholarly business of retrieving and assessing Vivaldi's forgotten works began in earnest with the inauguration of the Fondazione in 1932. Rudge and Pound visited Turin and Venice, and were able to secure microfilm of the Dresden manuscripts. Seeing the enormous potential in this relatively novel technology of information preservation and distribution, both became advocates of microfilm in manuscript studies. Pound and Rudge wrote a number of unpublished essays on the subject (Pound and Rudge n.d.), and during the 1930s Rudge continued to advocate the preservation of Vivaldi's manuscripts on microfilm.

This enthusiasm for the microfilming of music was matched by Pound's commitment to the photographic reproduction of manuscripts of poetry. He had dozens of high-quality photographic plates of Cavalcanti manuscripts produced, all intended for inclusion in the 1929 Aquila edition of the *Rime* or in the 1932 Marsano edition (Pound 1925-1932b). Most of these photographs record Cavalcanti's poems as transcribed into literary compendia, and in several cases they allow the careful reader to identify specific issues in a poem's stemmatic history. Occasionally a high-quality photograph magnifies the ambiguity of a particular scribal hand (especially when it comes to recording critical vowels in such poems as 'Donna mi prega'), or indicates damage to the manuscript page that obscures a word or letter. Pound also took photographs of illustrations in several manuscripts taken during a visit to the Vatican Library in 1928. One page, for instance, derives from the volume Barberiniano Latina 3593 (Figure 3) and is glossed by Pound in a notebook as 'disegno amore sofia un cavallo ed altre figure' ('drawing of amore, sofia [wisdom], a cavalier and another figure') (Pound 1925-1932a). This schema of major allegorical types appealed to Pound because, he thought, it supported his argument that Neoplatonism had influenced Cavalcanti. He clearly wanted to give the image pride of place in the ill-fated Aquila edition. Pound believed that photographic intervention had the potential to resolve or clarify longstanding philological issues, especially in the case of a poetic and manuscript heritage extending over 600 years. Furthermore, surviving page proofs and setting copy of both the Aquila and Marsano editions (Pound 1929b; Pound 1929-1932; Pound 1932), as well as numerous sheets of the Aquila edition on rag paper and on vellum (Pound 1929a), demonstrate Pound's direct involvement with the design and layout of the various editions. His ubiquitous marginal directives and suggestions are particularly telling. This material archive shows, when put alongside his endorsement of photographic facsimiles as an interpretive tool, that Pound was as concerned with the physical as with the intellectual and formal machinery of textual production.

Pound's Aldine Epic

In addition to medieval manuscripts, Pound attended throughout his career to the technographic transformation represented by early modern printing, and in particular its implications for textual transmission. Venice, Italy's first city in the age of printing, and Aldus Manutius, its most famous printer and publisher, appear at pivotal points in *The Cantos*. Pound's long association with Venice traverses his career: from his first volume of poetry, *A Lume Spento*, published in Venice in 1908, to his burial at San Michele in 1972. Far more than a context and theme, Venice shapes the textual and bibliographical dimensions of Pound's poetry, primarily with respect to Aldus. Pound owned

Bibliographic Technography: Ezra Pound's *Cantos* as Philological Machine 159

Fig. 3. 'Symbolic design. Ms Ba'. Manuscript Barberiniano Latina 3593, f. 126. Photographic plate, black and white, 23.3 x 16.9 cm. Beinecke Rare Book and Manuscript Library, Yale University. YCAL MSS 43, Box 82, Folder 3591.
Reproduced by permission of Mary de Rachewiltz.

several Aldine editions: a 1514 edition of Petrarch, a 1536 edition of Lorenzo Valla, and a 1562 edition of Catullus, Tibullus, and Propertius. He went to considerable lengths to understand the historical context and value of book design and typography, as is evident in his Aldine editions as well as in his small collection of incunabulae and early sixteenth-century texts.

The Aldine pivot on which Pound's modern typography revolves represents the critical moment at which printing transformed an erstwhile manuscript culture, providing scholars and publishers with new technical means to conserve and disseminate what they considered to be the sum of knowledge and literary achievement. For Aldus this meant preserving the best of Greek classical literature (his edition of Aristotle is a case in point), as well as introducing a number of technical innovations for which his name and publishing house gained significant fame: a normalised system of punctuation; the italic font designed by Francesco Griffo and used in a 1501 edition of Virgil's *Opera*, the first classical work Aldus published in octavo (see Updike 2001: 125-32); the famous dolphin and anchor insignia; and the publication of cheaper octavo volumes that gave access to a wider readership. Aldus personally edited many of the classical works he produced, including a wide range of Latin classics and a posthumously published edition of the Septuagint. That Pound was attracted to such a potent figure in cultural production and technical innovation is no surprise. Aldus embodies a deep respect for classical knowledge and aligns his publishing aesthetic with its preservation. His sensitivity toward the past is equalled by an ambitious futurity in his own publishing and editing regime, whereby classical culture is made to live anew in sixteenth-century Italy. The Aldine revolution was founded in the machinery of the printing press, but it is the τέχναι of bibliography and of textual transmission, together with book design's capacity to preserve and invigorate classical knowledge, that ignite Pound's interest and lead him to offer his own homage to Aldus.

But before considering that homage, we need to remember that the first three major instalments of *The Cantos* were published as deluxe editions with illustrated capitals, in direct homage to the traditions of medieval manuscript production and of its emulation in early printed texts such as those of Aldus: the whole apparatus amounting to a pointed rejection of conventional Victorian textual production (McGann 1993: 80). The capitalisation in these deluxe editions varies from medieval chivalric imagery to Renaissance cameo portraiture to Vorticist images of modern warfare. *A Draft of XVI. Cantos* was published in Paris by William Bird's Three Mountains Press in 1925, with capitals by Henry Strater. Rebecca Beasley sees in Strater's capitals 'a visual analogy for the poem's classicist values and its specific arguments' (Beasley 2007: 206; see Culver 1983: 448-78). Illustrations also serve as tailpieces to numerous cantos. John Rodker then published *A Draft of the Cantos 17-27* in London in 1928, with capitals by Gladys Hynes, and in 1930 Nancy Cunard's

Hours Press published the third instalment, *A Draft of XXX Cantos*. George Bornstein calls this volume

> a halfway house between the gaudy originals [*A Draft of XVI. Cantos* and *A Draft of the Cantos 17-27*] and the quotidian current form of the text; it offers the same typeface but smaller pages, and in place of the elaborate nearly pre-Raphaelite early capitals a set of more modern Vorticist ones designed by Pound's wife Dorothy. (Bornstein 2001: 37)

Jerome McGann describes the three deluxe editions as acts of 'bibliographical homage and allusion' to William Morris's Kelmscott Press, founded in March 1891 (McGann 1991: 138). Pound, like Morris, deployed the technologies of print to emulate manuscript design, much as Gutenberg, Aldus, and other pioneering printers had done in the first decades of printing.

Moreover, Pound's Aldine preoccupations offer an exemplary model for the way he critically absorbs and reimagines the texts and textual structures of the past. *The Cantos* functions as an extended propaedeutic: a detailed and sometimes recondite referential apparatus exists within its fabric of images, allusions, and prosodic experiments. Pound's habits of dense reference take us into complex zones of intertextuality, so that often he will cite from a text with a contested transmission history in order to send the reader back to the source or sources. The poem asks us to rethink the relations between textual immanence, the vestiges of transmission, and the notion of authority. Returning to the opening lines of Canto I, we are given the source text for the canto's chosen episode from Homer's *Odyssey*: 'Lie quiet Divus. I mean, that is Andreas Divus, / In officina Wecheli, 1538, out of Homer' (Pound 1996: 5). Pound devotes an extended section of his essay 'Translators of Greek: Early Translators of Homer' (1918) to the bibliographic importance of the Divus translation of the *Odyssey*:

> In the year of grace 1906, 1908, or 1910 I picked up from the Paris quais a Latin version of the *Odyssey* by Andreas Divus Justinopolitanus (Parisiis, In officina Christiani Wecheli, MDXXXVIII), the volume containing also the *Batrachomyomachia*, by Aldus Manutius, and the *Hymni Deorum* rendered by Georgius Dartona Cretensis. (Pound 1968: 259)

Pound goes on, a few pages later, to provide the bibliographical context of his Divus edition and to speculate about its possible connection to the printing house of Aldus Manutius:

> The first Aldine Greek Iliads appeared I think in 1504, Odyssey possibly later. My edition of Divus is 1538, and as it contains Aldus's own translation of the Frog-fight, it may indicate that

> Divus was in touch with Aldus in Italy, or quite possibly the
> French edition is pirated from an earlier Italian printing. (265)

It is fitting, then, that Aldus and his fellow printers become a point of focus at the end of *A Draft of XXX Cantos*. They appear here partly as a way of measuring the transmission of knowledge within networks of patronage and political power.

Following a number of extended allusions to Venice, *A Draft of XXX Cantos* concludes in Canto XXX with the union of two political dynasties in the form of Lucretia Borgia's marriage to Alfonso d'Este in late 1501 (the publication date of the Aldine Virgil). Lucretia leaves her father, Rodrigo Borgia (Pope Alexander VI), and travels in a procession from Rome to Ferrara. She stops in the town of Fano, within the territory of her brother Cesare Borgia, at which point the reader is regaled with a short history of Italian printing:

> ...and here have I brought cutters of letters
> and printers not vile and vulgar
>   (in Fano Caesaris)
> notable and sufficient compositors
> and a die-cutter for greek fonts and hebrew
> named Messire Francesco da Bologna
> not only of the usual types but he hath excogitated
> a new form called cursive or chancellry letters
> nor was it Aldous nor any other but it was
> this Messire Francesco who hath cut all Aldous his letters
> with such grace and charm as is known
>   Hieronymous Soncinus 7th July 1503.
> and as for the text we have taken it
> from that of Messire Laurentius
> and from a codex once of the Lords Malatesta... (Pound 1996: 148-149)

In 1501 the Jewish printer Hieronymous Soncino had brought Griffo, also known as Francesco da Bologna, to Fano as part of his enterprise to publish books in Hebrew, Greek, Latin, and Italian. This remarkably cosmopolitan venture draws Pound's narrator back into the Aldine sphere: the early years of movable type and the font-cutters, compositors, and printers of northern Italy.

Pound's allusion to Lucretia Borgia's procession and its brief hiatus in Fano thus produces a thread of bibliographical history that leads to Venice and its most famous printer. The concluding lines of the canto draw together Soncino and Aldus in the early print culture of northern Italy, in counterpoint to the excesses of political and papal power of the Borgias. The final lines then cite the quattrocento statesmen Lorenzo de' Medici and Sigismundo Malatesta, patrons of the arts and founders of learned libraries. Reaching back into the world of the illuminated codex, Pound's narrator seals this bibliographical homage to the manuscript culture of medieval Europe, to the print culture of early modern Europe, and to the revolutionary transformation of the one into the other. Attention will turn to Chinese history and its textual embodiment soon enough in Pound's poem, yet the bibliographical iconicity of these early cantos stands as testimony to the central role of Venice and its most famous printer in enabling the curation and dissemination of ancient and modern knowledge. Venice is the place of beginnings and endings for Pound. As a place of births and deaths, symbolic and actual, Venice is also the place of rebirths preserved and transmitted in Aldine texts, in the modern culture of printing, and in Pound's subsequent reimagining of this revolution of the word. *The Cantos* calls up these earlier transformations in the machinery of textual production as a kind of technology of nostalgia, at the same time as it looks to new ways of furthering the information flows upon which a culture relies.

Conclusion

Pound's deployment in *The Cantos* of medieval and early modern printed texts performs a hermeneutics both of summation and prolepsis. By drawing on a number of encyclopaedic texts at strategic points, Pound's 'poem including history' enjoins the reader to discern how the rising hegemony of the codex form in the late classical epoch operated to preserve all existing knowledge thought to be worth keeping from classical Greece and Rome, as well as from the Patristic corpus. Within the emergent centres of learning, the Carolingian techniques of glossing, annotation, and schoolroom transcription also provided a model for the European university in the twelfth century, and a number of early medieval texts came to exert enormous influence upon later learning and literary production. This history, much of whose detail has been lost or obscured, functions for Pound as the sacred thread joining the ancient world to the High Middle Ages. This was the epoch in which the poetic corpus and techniques of the troubadours and the poets of the *dolce stil nuovo* emerge, and they in turn formed an integral part of Pound's own poetic education. This education would focus in particular on the poetry of Guido Cavalcanti, resulting in the translation of 'Donna mi prega' incorporated into Canto XXXVI, as well as in Pound's attempts to publish a critical edition of Cavalcanti's *Rime* enabled by new technologies of textual reproduction.

The early stages of Pound's epic also draw upon the themes and techniques of early printing, commemorating the ways in which the great Venetian printer Aldus Manutius and his texts replicate antecedent manuscript cultures in a cognate attempt to preserve and transmit the best of human knowledge and cultural expression. Pound's poem, in turn, emulates the physical properties of Aldine texts in the printed capitals of deluxe editions and in an ostentatious textual apparatus. These gestures of deference to early Venetian printing also imply an awareness of all that was to unfold from the new textuality of the early modern epoch: a proleptic gesture towards modern knowledge production and transmission. Pound's interests in photographic facsimile and microfilm demonstrate an unlikely precocity, marshalling the mechanisms of an evolving information culture. The combination of technical accuracy and reproducibility, on the one hand, and acute scholarly attention to textual minutiae, on the other, enables the kind of access to and interpretation of texts for which Pound advocated throughout his career. This is where his bibliographic technography comes into its own: Pound was not so much anticipating the culture of information saturation to come, as he was already responding to that culture in its first formations.

Works Cited

Adams, John. 1850-1856. *The Works of John Adams*. Edited by Charles Francis Adams. 10 volumes. Boston: Charles C. Little and James Brown.

Beasley, Rebecca. 2007. *Ezra Pound and the Visual Culture of Modernism*. Cambridge: Cambridge University Press.

Bird, Otto. 1938. Letter to Ezra Pound. Beinecke Rare Books and Manuscript Library, YCAL MSS 43, Box 4, Folder 190.

Bornstein, George. 2001. *Material Modernism: The Politics of the Page*. Cambridge: Cambridge University Press.

Bush, Ronald. 2013. 'Between Religion and Science: Ezra Pound, Scotus Erigena, and the Beginnings of a Twentieth-Century Paradise'. *Rivista di Letterature d'America* 32: 95-124.

Byron, Mark. 2014. *Ezra Pound's Eriugena*. London: Bloomsbury.

Culver, Michael. 1983. 'The Art of Henry Strater: An Examination of the Illustrations for Pound's *A Draft of XVI. Cantos*'. *Paideuma* 12: 448-78.

McGann, Jerome J. 1991. *The Textual Condition*. Princeton: Princeton University Press.

McGann, Jerome J. 1993. *Black Riders: The Visible Language of Modernism*. Princeton: Princeton University Press.

Paden, William T., Jr. 1980. 'Pound's Use of Troubadour Manuscripts'. *Comparative Literature* 32: 402-412.

Pound, Ezra. 1925-1932a. Notebooks for *Cavalcanti Rime*. Beinecke Rare Book and Manuscript Library at Yale University. YCAL MSS 43, Box 114, Folders 4889-4891 and Box 115, Folders 4892-4894.

Pound, Ezra. 1925-1932b. Photos of Cavalcanti manuscripts. Beinecke Rare Book and Manuscript Library at Yale University. YCAL MSS 43, Box 82, Folders 3591-3593.

Pound, Ezra. 1929a. English sheets (on rag paper and on vellum) for Aquila Press edition of *Cavalcanti Rime*. Beinecke Rare Book and Manuscript Library at Yale University. YCAL MSS 43, Box 81, Folders 3565-3568.

Pound, Ezra. 1929b. Page proofs for Aquila Press edition of *Cavalcanti Rime*. Beinecke Rare Book and Manuscript Library at Yale University. YCAL MSS 43, Box 81, Folders 3563-3564.

Pound, Ezra. 1929-1932. Page proofs for the Marsano and Aquila editions of *Cavalcanti Rime*. Beinecke Rare Book and Manuscript Library at Yale University. YCAL MSS 43, Box 236, Folders 3-7.

Pound, Ezra. 1932. Setting copy for the Marsano edition of *Cavalcanti Rime*. Beinecke Rare Book and Manuscript Library at Yale University. YCAL MSS 43, Box 81, Folders 3583-3584.

Pound, Ezra. 1934. *Make It New*. London: Faber.

Pound, Ezra. 1968. 'Translators of Greek: Early Translators of Homer'. In *Literary Essays of Ezra Pound*, edited by T. S. Eliot, 94-108. New York: New Directions.

Pound, Ezra. 1996. *The Cantos*. New York: New Directions.

Pound, Ezra, and Olga Rudge. n.d. 'La Giro', 'La Possibilita della microphotographia', and 'Microphotographic Front'. Beinecke Rare Book and Manuscript Library at Yale University. YCAL MSS 54, Box 146, Folders 3446-3447.

Ten Eyck, David. 2012. *Ezra Pound's Adams Cantos*. London: Bloomsbury.

Updike, Daniel Berkeley. 2001. *Printing Types: Their History, Forms, and Use*. New Castle: Oak Knoll.

10

Modernist Measure: Poetry and Calculation

SEAN PRYOR

In the summer of 1938, W.B. Yeats began to think again about measure. 'Measurement began our might', he announced in 'Under Ben Bulben': 'Forms a stark Egyptian thought, / Forms that gentler Phidias wrought' (Yeats 1966: 638). In another poem written that summer, 'The Statues', he praised the Greek sculptors who 'with a mallet or a chisel modelled [...] Calculations that look but casual flesh' (610). So successful was their modelling of the human body, Yeats says, that Greek girls and boys 'pressed at midnight in some public place / Live lips upon a plummet-measured face'. Amorous adolescents kissed cold statues, thanks to mathematics. When the late Yeats thinks about calculation, number, and measurement, in poems which denounce the 'formless' tide of modernity (611), he thinks about ancient precedent and ancient instruments: the Greeks and their plumb bobs.

When Yeats dies the following winter and W.H. Auden writes an elegy, he thinks about thermometers and photometers:

> He disappeared in the dead of winter:
> The brooks were frozen, the air-ports almost deserted,
> And snow disfigured the public statues;
> The mercury sank in the mouth of the dying day.
> O all the instruments agree
> The day of his death was a dark cold day. (Auden 1988: 241)

Auden's modern instruments measure light and heat; they quantify the weather on January 28, 1939, which was indeed a dark cold day. It reached 36 degrees Fahrenheit and was cloudy in New York, where Auden wrote the poem, and it reached 52 degrees Fahrenheit and was unsettled on the French Riviera, where Yeats died ('The Weather' 1939). But Auden's instruments also measure grief, the thoughts and the feelings that accompany loss, and so his line measures the legitimacy of poetry which makes low temperatures and heavy clouds share and express grief. To measure the pathetic fallacy with a thermometer is, it seems, to measure the distance between quantity and quality.

When Auden revised the poem, he changed the fifth line from 'O all the instruments agree' to 'What instruments we have agree' (Auden 1991: 247). He shifted from bardic exclamation to plainspoken qualification: the instruments *we* have are limited, and give only provisional measurements. The revised line includes us: it makes us reconsider the instruments we have; and the revised line returns upon itself: it makes us ask which instruments the poem has. It makes us think of Auden's other instrument, verse, which measures Yeats's achievement by rising from the first section's loose, mostly unrhymed lines to the third section's resounding tetrameter couplets:

> In the deserts of the heart
> Let the healing fountain start. (249)

This is precisely the metre or measure in which Yeats had, some six months earlier, declared that 'Measurement began our might'. Auden rises to Yeats's measure. This instrument does not agree that the day of Yeats's death was a dark cold day, or not simply so: it heralds that healing fountain, even in the prison of mortality. How then, is the measurement of heat and light related to the measurement of syllables, stresses, and lines? This is my question here: how can we understand the relation between measuring instruments and verse measures in modernism?

The problem can be approached in three ways. The first is simple: to consider the representation of measuring devices, old and new, in modernist poetry. The second is to consider the emergence in the late nineteenth and early twentieth centuries of a materialist metrics, which saw acoustic scientists seeking to graph or image poetic rhythm and metre with sophisticated new measuring instruments. These scientists wanted to understand what makes poetry poetry, and what separates it from prose. But we do not have to think either of measuring instruments or of poems merely as objects to be represented. Both instruments and poems are also modes of representation, and they are both forms or manifestations of subjectivity. For this reason, the significance of modernist measure emerges only when, third, we allow poetry to be a measurement technology too.

To do that means to reflect theoretically on modernist verse, and to remember the necessary and mutual mediation of quantity and quality. It is certainly not the case that scientific instruments are concerned only with quantity, nor that poetry is concerned only with quality. Without counting, said William Carlos Williams, there is no verse, only prose (Williams 1959: 145). But the separation seemed straightforward to some. In 1893 the American psychologist James McKeen Cattell proclaimed that we 'no longer speak of the boundless sea and the innumerable host of the Argives. We ask, how many? how much?' (Cattell 1893: 317). Having sung of the Fenians' 'swift innumerable spears' in *The Wanderings of Oisin* (Yeats 1966: 2), Yeats would surely have objected. But Cattell was emphatic: the 'history of science is the history of measurement', he wrote.

> Clocks, balances, and foot-rules seem indispensable to our present civilization. Thermometers, barometers, lactometers, etc., are no longer looked upon as scientific instruments, and these and other means of measurement will soon be used by everyone. (Cattell 1893: 316)

This was the modern empiricism against which Yeats, at the height of the fin de siècle, set his poetry. 'Everything that can be seen, touched, measured', he insisted, 'is to the imaginative artist nothing more than a means' (Yeats 2007: 143). By 1927, Joseph Macleod lamented that poets 'have ceased to be prophets' and have instead 'become barometers' (Macleod 1927: 257).

This is a familiar conflict. In the period stretching from the 1890s to the Second World War, there are countless examples of poetry's apparent antipathy to measuring instruments. D.H. Lawrence opposed quantitative measurement to the natural world. '[Y]ou to whom the sun is merely something that makes the thermometer rise!' he cries in 'Oh Wonderful Machine!' (Lawrence 2013: 1.554). In 'Dreams', Walter de le Mare recoiled at the thought that our every action and desire could be gauged quantitatively:

> Nay, is that Prince of the Dust – a man,
> But a tissue of parts, dissectable?
> Lancet, balances, callipers – can
> The least of his actions by human skill
> Be measured as so much Sex, Want, Will? (de la Mare 1979: 237)

Instruments of measurement frequently figure the intrusion of quantitative science into intimate, natural, sacred, political, or aesthetic realms. The science of psychology was a common culprit, as was the science of economics. In this, poets exploited associations made by economic journalists and theorists themselves. The phrase 'business barometer', for instance, appeared in the *New York Times* in 1868 and in London's *Economist* in 1875 ('The Business Barometer' 1868; 'Germany And Austria' 1875); by the 1910s and 1920s it was standard currency (Persons 1916; Gerstenberg 1919: 573-4; 'The Business Barometer' 1922). But for Kenneth Allott, capitalist quantification was a curse: 'Enumerate your riches, get them by heart. [...] The pins in the tidy are numbered off and treasured, / With callipers the width of each twig is measured' (Allott 2008: 48). In a similar vein, Louis MacNeice attacked liberal democracy's 'Moderates', their 'brains a mere barometer', for having sold their 'birthright for a fat / Mess of pottage' (MacNeice 2007: 767). Politics becomes merely the calculation of private gain. Finally there is Hugh Selwyn Mauberley, reduced from out-of-date aesthete to seismographer:

> Unable in the supervening blankness
> To sift TO AGATHON from the chaff
> Until he found his sieve ...
> Ultimately, his seismograph. (Pound 1990: 197)

Mauberley passively records the shockwaves made by others' blasts, the genuine innovations of an Ezra Pound or a Wyndham Lewis. And though callipers are as old as Greek plumb bobs, this, I believe, is the earliest use of the word *seismograph* in poetry in English.

But what really was new, especially in the late nineteenth century, was the graphing of poetry itself. This turned the tables of representation. Building on the work of Hermann von Helmholtz and Wilhelm Wundt, experimental psychologists and phoneticians applied kymographs, ergographs, and phonautographs to the measurement of speech and of poetry (Hall 2009). Edward Wheeler Scripture's 1902 study, *The Elements of Experimental Phonetics*, sought to ground the lofty realm of poetic inspiration and intuition in objective, empirical science. The old debates about classical prosody, and even the musical prosodies of Coventry Patmore and Sidney Lanier, now seemed redundant. But for modernism, perhaps the most important example was William Morrison Patterson's *The Rhythm of Prose* (1916). Harriet Monroe gave Patterson's book an excited review in the April 1918 issue of *Poetry*: 'systems of verse-scansion inherited from our ancestors', Monroe urged, 'are as unscientific and out of date as pre-Galileo astronomy' (Monroe 1918: 31). *The Rhythm of Prose* proved especially exciting because it closes with a discussion of free verse. In order to decide whether free verse is simply prose, genuinely poetry, or some third thing, Patterson had Amy Lowell perform her own and others' works to be measured by his instruments. Lowell in turn described their collaboration in *Tendencies in Modern American Poetry*, offering a detailed analysis of H.D.'s 'Oread' in terms of isochronous 'time units' (Lowell 1917: 264-5). Quantitative calculation could also be turned against experimental forms. In 1931 Max Eastman imagined placing 'two of the most enthusiastic admirers of this poetry' in separate sound-proof chambers and then asking each to read a poem by E.E. Cummings 'in the august presence of a sphygmograph' (Eastman 1935: 62). This machine was 'designed to record in a white line on a black roller the actual pulsations' of what, as Eastman remarks, Paul Rosenfeld called the new poetry's 'rapid, capricious, and melodic line'. Is there any chance, Eastman asks, that the two readers would produce the same curve, and so justify Cummings's typographical experiments? 'Of course they would not.'

Eastman was by no means alone in his objections. John Gould Fletcher complained that we 'cannot measure poetry with a metronome, or even classify it with a phonograph, as Dr Patterson would have us do' (Fletcher 1919: 13). Lascelles Abercrombie protested that investigating the 'physiological or physical origins of metre' is like 'expecting a man to describe a railway journey by telling you [...] how the thermodynamics of the engine may be drawn in a graph' (Abercrombie 1923: 8). And as Jason David Hall has shown, critics such as I.A. Richards and W.K. Wimsatt maintained a 'belief that machines, in spite of their demonstrable sonic sensitivity, could not account for an intuitive aspect of the metrical phenomenon' (Hall 2011: 193).

Works like *The Rhythm of Prose* and *The Elements of Experimental Phonetics* do raise the problem that to measure particular performances, and even, given a large sample of performances, to arrive statistically at some average performance, may not be to measure the poem itself. The poem can seem instead an ideal object, or partly ideal, never wholly material, reducible neither to a single performance nor to performance as such. There is also the problem that a material metrics must decide in advance which features or qualities to quantify. Patterson writes:

> we first of all conceive the rhythm of either prose or verse in the form of a rhythmic tune, combining patterns of time, stress, and, to some extent, pitch. Patterns of tone-color are superimposed, as soon as we consider the actual sounds of the words, and patterns of subjective weight, as soon as we consider the words as vehicles of thought and feeling. (Patterson 1916: 75)

Patterson's and Scripture's phonautographs, which transcribed sound waves as the undulations of a line traced on paper or glass, were sophisticated devices for measuring time, stress, and pitch. But far from being empirical givens, such features must be abstracted in order to be quantified. Patterson's sequence of rhythmic tune, tone-colour, and subjective weight is an abstraction, too: the progression is a fiction that enables and prioritises material measurement. Patterson seems to sense something of this, for he says that we have to listen for tone-colour as soon as we consider the 'actual' sounds of the words. Before that, the phonautograph had been measuring something else.

What, we should also ask, does the poem itself measure? Materialist metrics begs this old question by abstracting time, stress, and pitch. Classical prosody would answer instead that verse measures feet. Spurred by Einstein's theory of relativity, Williams proposed that modern verse counts, or ought to count, relatively equal or 'variable' feet (Williams 1959: 151). But even for metrical verse the answers vary. Two years after Monroe reviewed Patterson, Bliss Perry surveyed the evidence produced by laboratory psychology and concluded that

> The individual's standard of measurement – his poetic foot-rule, so to speak – is very elastic – 'made of rubber' [...] Furthermore, the composers of poetry build it out of very elastic units. They are simply putting syllables of words together into a rhythmical design, and these 'airy syllables', in themselves mere symbols of

ideas and feelings, cannot be weighed by any absolutely correct sound-scales. (Perry 1920: 148)

There are two apparent contradictions here, which both Perry and Patterson struggle to reconcile: the contradiction between quantity and quality, and between matter and spirit. One good modernist solution would be to invoke Bergson's metaphysics. In that case we would have, on the one hand, the extensive magnitudes of matter, of space, and, in our case, of speech measured by scientific instruments. On the other hand we would have intensive magnitudes, which, as Bergson reminds us, are not really magnitudes at all since they cannot be quantified (Bergson 1912: 4). These include the phenomenon of durée, and the ideas and feelings of which spoken sounds are, as Perry puts it, symbols. For Bergson, to measure the grief in Auden's elegy or the healing praise would be to falsify it, illegitimately confusing the intensive and the extensive.

But before looking at the actual measures of some actual poems, I want to suggest that rather than Bergson, we would do well to remember Hegel. Hegel, too, was sceptical about the claims made for quantitative measurement. When 'quantity is not reached through the action of thought, but taken uncritically', he writes, 'the title of exact science is restricted to those sciences the objects of which can be submitted to mathematical calculation' (Hegel 1975b: 146). A scientific understanding of human actions, desires, and works will then be sought only by subjecting them to callipers. Better, for Hegel, is a dialectic of quality, quantity, and measure, and by measure Hegel does not mean simple quantification. If our apprehension of an object begins with its qualitative determination – water, say, which is not milk – quantification abstracts some feature of that object and construes it in terms of identical or equal units. This then allows us to assess the temperature of the water in a saucepan, to 'measure' it, and to compare it to the temperature of the milk in another saucepan on the stove. But at a certain point, the quantitative increase in the water's temperature means a qualitative change: the water boils, and is no longer water. This, for Hegel, is measure as such: 'the qualitative quantum', a quantum 'to which a determinate being or a quality is attached' (157). Measure is the quantity which determines quality. And we only engage in quantitative calculation, says Hegel, for the purposes of measure, even when we fail to recognise that that is what we are doing. If I am working in the field of materialist metrics, I set my phonautograph to image Amy Lowell's performances of free verse precisely so as to decide whether that free verse is prose, poetry, or some third form with its own quality.

Hegel also knows that Amy Lowell's timing and stress and pitch, her material or embodied performances, are always already mediated by spirit. The sounds have sense from the start. He works through this problem by comparing poetry to music. For Hegel, poetry need not be subject, so abstractly as is the case with a musical beat, to an absolutely fixed measure of time for its communication and progress. In music the note is a fading sound without support which imperatively requires a stability like that introduced by the beat; but speech does not need this support, for it has this already in the idea that it expresses, and, furthermore, it does not enter completely and without qualification into the external sphere of sounding and fading but retains precisely the inner idea as its essential artistic medium. For this reason poetry actually finds directly in the ideas and feelings which it puts clearly into words the more substantive determinant for measuring retard, acceleration, lingering, dawdling, and so forth. (Hegel 1975a: 2.1017)

So the substance which poetry measures is at once both matter and spirit, stress and idea, pitch and feeling. What does this mean for modernist poetry, at a time when callipers, seismographs, business barometers, and stock exchanges seemed to some the only mechanisms for apprehending truth or value? And what does measure as qualitative quantum mean at a historical moment when the quantitative study of poetry coincided with poems which ostensibly abandon quantification: poems which replace the calculation of stresses or syllables with the measureless measures of free verse? To conclude, I want to consider two examples.

The first is from Wallace Stevens's *Notes Toward a Supreme Fiction*:

Perhaps there are times of inherent excellence,

As when the cock crows on the left and all
Is well, incalculable balances,
At which a kind of Swiss perfection comes

And a familiar music of the machine
Sets up its Schwärmerei, not balances
That we achieve but balances that happen,

As a man and woman meet and love forthwith. (Stevens 1997: 334)

How are Stevens's pentameters and Swiss chronometers related? Part of the answer lies in the puzzling association of Swiss perfection with incalculable balances, since the balance wheels in Swiss watches are calibrated to produce precise calculations. Then there is the puzzling association of that seemingly inhuman machine with the very human Schwärmerei, swarmings or enthusiasm or eros. The Swiss perfection may accompany or supersede those balances, in accordance with them or in contrast. Then, as if in reverse, the machine's routine music sets up rare or remarkable Schwärmerei, as singular and unprecedented as falling in love. Or, since that music seems to accompany the Swiss perfection and so to be contingent upon those particular times of inherent excellence, maybe the machine's music is itself rare and remarkable. And because the event of falling in love is archetypal it is typical, familiar, even routine. Part of the answer therefore lies in the single deft sentence's constantly shifting balance of measurement and the immeasurable, indifferent iteration and singular event, quantity and quality.

But part of the answer lies in the quality of Stevens's metre. We can be fairly sure that Stevens had encountered materialist metrics, at least in passing and if only at second hand. Stevens read the first volume of Paul Elmer More's *Shelburne Essays* with enthusiasm (Stevens 1977: 220; Stevens 1996: 133), and in his essay on 'The Science of English Verse' More first quotes Helmholtz and then concludes: 'rhythm in verse is a branch of the scientific study of sound, and has nothing to do with grammar or logic or numbers or thought. It is as amenable to law as any other phenomenon within the realm of acoustics' (More 1904: 109). In *Notes Toward a Supreme Fiction*, the familiar law of the iambic pentameter seems a strict timekeeping machine: the metre seems to equate and calculate syllables and stresses. Stevens is certainly counting, but given the heavy enjambments and the mid-line pauses, the poem clearly does not measure isochronous acoustic intervals. The prosody of 'At which a kind of Swiss perfection comes' seems straightforward, and 'As a man and woman meet and love forthwith' offers familiar variations: an extra unstressed short syllable at the beginning and the twin stresses of a compound word at the end. The first two syllables of 'And a familiar music of the machine' are less straightforward. Though neither need carry an emphatic stress, either 'And' or 'a' must constitute the metrical beat, since unlike 'man', the first syllable of 'familiar' cannot do so. 'And a familiar music of the machine' has fewer stresses and more syllables than the line about Swiss perfection, as does 'Perhaps there are times of inherent excellence'. And yet, whether we employ classical scansion or the most recent generative metrics, none of these variations fail or break the poem's measure.

We can think of that measure this way. To speculate abstractly about times of inherent excellence and to offer a simile about falling in love are as qualitatively distinct as milk and water. So, too, the marvellous alliterations which deliver the machine's familiar music are qualitatively distinct from those which declare the cock's crow. Yet Stevens's instrument does quantify the lines' sounds, which is why no line breaks the measure. More importantly, Stevens's instrument quantifies the sense. As single lines, each line is equivalent, and each line offers a unit of thought and feeling, even or especially when heavy enjambment counterpoints syntax: 'Is well, incalculable balances'. Each line is a unit of sound and sense, inseparable. And through this mutual mediation, both matter and spirit are measured.

This measure, as Hegel says, is a return to quality from quantity, and being the measure of the whole poem, it cannot be merely a form for mimicking content. If that were the case, if Stevens's metre merely mimicked Swiss chronometry, the line about the machine's music would presumably need to be as conventionally strict as the line about Swiss perfection. Instead, Stevens's pentameter is a qualitative quantum. A determinate being is attached to each quantum of matter and spirit: it becomes poetry. And this means, crucially, that Stevens's poem takes the measure of Swiss watches and crowing cocks in its qualitative difference from them. In an age of instruments, and in relation to cocks, chronometers, musical beats, and even new love, modernist measure thus becomes newly self-conscious. It understands itself anew as its own form of measurement technology.

It would be customary, here, to remember Pound's famous dictum about composing poetry not in the sequence of a metronome but in the sequence of the musical phrase (Pound 1968: 3). Yet Hegel would object to the distinction because, for him, music as such is bound to the fixed measure of time, or is at least much more tightly bound to that fixed measure than poetry. In Stevens's poem, the machine's timekeeping is presumably quite fixed and more so than Stevens's own measures. At the same time, Stevens's measures are more fixed than most of Pound's, and though Pound's distinction is not between metrical verse and free verse, we should ask what the measureless measures of free verse mean for the dialectic of quality and quantity:

> The apparition of these faces in the crowd;
> Petals on a wet, black bough. (Pound 1990: 111)

'In a Station of the Metro' also provides an opportunity to depart from direct references to measuring instruments. Not that quantitative calculation is absent or unimportant here. The Paris Metro, whose first line opened in 1900, and the rise of the railways in general, obviously relied on and promulgated new technologies for representing and conceiving temporality: timetables, station displays, station clocks. Still, we do not know whether those faces in the crowd await the 3 o'clock from Gare de Lyon or have just stepped off the 2:50 from Châtelet. Nor do we know how many faces or how many petals: they may not be as innumerable as the Fenians' swift spears or the host of the Argives, but they do go unnumbered. The poem only distinguishes plural from singular, faces and petals from crowd and bough and apparition. Yet Pound is counting, too. A line of twelve syllables, Pound's alexandrine measures the distance between his poem in English and its French subject. Its quantum is qualitative. And Pound's second line counts not syllables but consonants and stresses: we shift from a syllabic measure to an accentual measure, and the line's alliteration on the stops /p/ and /b/, not to mention the internal rhyme on /ɛt/, recalls the alliterative four-beat line of Anglo-Saxon verse. This is another qualitative quantum, but qualitatively distinct from the first. You might say that it measures not the distance between languages, but the history of a language.

The effect here is clearly quite different from that of Stevens's poem. Stevens's measure is the measure of the whole poem, a measure which no line breaks. Pound's second line immediately breaks the measure of his first. David Nowell Smith remarks rightly that 'In a Station of the Metro' represents a 'standoff between metricality and nonmetricality' (Nowell Smith 190). Pound's second line has a moment of measurelessness. This is characteristic of modernist free verse as such, whether or not, as they do here, the lines invoke established forms or historical precedents. In modernism, new free-verse lines necessarily mean moments of measurelessness, and every new measureless line becomes in turn its own measure. Or every successful new line must mean a new measure, successfully producing its proper quality. 'These two transitions', says Hegel, 'from quality to quantum, and from the latter back again to quality, may be represented under the image of an infinite progression – as the self-abrogation and restoration of measure in the measureless' (Hegel 1975b: 160). Making that progression audible and visible, insisting that we think and feel that progression in the sensuous, is one of modernism's most interesting responses to the uncritical quantitative calculation that our train is late or that a fat mess of pottage is worth our birthright.

Works Cited

Abercrombie, Lascelles. 1923. *Principles of English Prosody: Part I: The Elements*. London: Martin Secker.

Allott, Kenneth. 2008. *Collected Poems*. Cambridge: Salt.

Auden, W.H. 1986. *The English Auden*. Edited by Edward Mendelson. London: Faber and Faber.

Auden, W.H. 1991. *Collected Poems*. Edited by Edward Mendelson. London: Faber and Faber.

Bergson, Henri. 1912. *Time and Free Will: An Essay on the Immediate Data of Consciousness*. Translated by F.L. Pogson. London: George Allen & Company.

'The Business Barometer'. 1868. *New York Times*, February 28: 4.

'The Business Barometer: A Forecast of Trade in the Future'. 1922. *Manchester Guardian*, April 1: 15.

Cattell, James McKeen. 1893. 'Mental Measurement'. *Philosophical Review* 2: 316-32.

de la Mare, Walter. *Collected Poems*. London: Faber and Faber.

Eastman, Max. 1935. *The Literary Mind: Its Place in an Age of Science*. New York: Charles Scribner's Sons.

Fletcher, John Gould. 1919. 'A Rational Explanation of Vers Libre'. *Dial* 66: 11-13.

'Germany And Austria'. 1875. *Economist*, January 23: 92-3.

Gerstenberg, Charles W. 1919. *Principles of Business*. New York: Prentice-Hall.

Hall, Jason David. 2009. 'Mechanized Metrics: From Verse Science to Laboratory Prosody, 1880-1918'. *Configurations* 17: 285-308.

Hall, Jason David. 2011. 'Materializing Meter: Physiology, Psychology, Prosody'. *Victorian Poetry* 49: 179-97.

Hegel, G.W.F. 1975a. *Aesthetics: Lectures on Fine Art*. Translated by T.M. Knox. 2 volumes. Oxford: Clarendon.

Hegel, G.W.F. 1975b. *Hegel's Logic: Being Part One of 'Encyclopaedia of the Philosophical Sciences' (1830)*. Translated by William Wallace. Oxford: Clarendon.

Lawrence, D.H. 2013. *The Poems*. Edited by Christopher Pollnitz. 2 volumes. Cambridge: Cambridge University Press.

Lowell, Amy. 1917. *Tendencies in Modern American Poetry*. New York: Macmillan.

Macleod, Joseph. 1927. *Beauty and the Beast*. London: Chatto and Windus.

MacNeice, Louis. 2007. *Collected Poems*. Edited by Peter McDonald. London: Faber and Faber.

Monroe, Harriet. 1918. 'Dr Patterson on Rhythm'. *Poetry* 12: 30-36.

More, Paul Elmer. 1904. *Shelburne Essays*. First series. New York: G.P. Putnam's Sons.

Nowell Smith, David. 2013. *Sounding/Silence: Martin Heidegger at the Limits of Poetics*. New York: Fordham University Press.

Patterson, William Morrison. 1916. *The Rhythm of Prose*. New York: Columbia University Press.

Perry, Bliss. 1920. *A Study of Poetry*. Boston: Houghton Mifflin.

Persons, Warren M. 1916. 'Construction of a Business Barometer Based upon Annual Data'. *American Economic Review* 6: 739-69.

Pound, Ezra. 1968. *Literary Essays of Ezra Pound*. Edited by T.S. Eliot. New York: New Directions.

Pound, Ezra. 1990. *Personae: The Shorter Poems of Ezra Pound*. Edited by Lea Baechler and A. Walton Litz. New York: New Directions.

Stevens, Holly. 1977. *Souvenirs and Prophecies: The Young Wallace Stevens*. New York: Alfred A. Knopf.

Stevens, Wallace. 1996. *Letters of Wallace Stevens*. Edited by Holly Stevens. Berkeley: University of California Press.

Stevens, Wallace. 1997. *Collected Poetry and Prose*. Edited by Frank Kermode and Joan Richardson. New York: Library of America.

'The Weather'. 1939. *Times*, January 30: 14.

Williams, William Carlos. 1959. 'Measure'. *Spectrum* 3: 131-57.

Yeats, W.B. 1966. *The Variorum Edition of the Poems of W. B. Yeats*. Edited by Peter Allt and Russell K. Alspach. Corrected 3rd printing. New York: Macmillan.

Yeats, W.B. 2007. *Early Essays*. Edited by George Bornstein and Richard J. Finneran. New York: Scribner.

11

Absolutist Slot Machines

BECI CARVER

In John Steinbeck's depression-era novel, *The Grapes of Wrath* (1939), the contents of the slot machines in a row of roadside shops seem momentarily to suggest the end of privation. The 'wealth in nickels' 'showing through the glass' of the gambling machines and the 'records piled up like pies' in the jukeboxes confront the novel's migrants with a mirage of prosperity. However, the self-conscious fantasy of the simile 'like pies' restores a reality principle, which is reinforced when customers insert nickels into the slots (Steinbeck 2000b: 159). One nickel unlocks a relatively substantial four slugs for Bill's friend at Al & Susy's Place, but the tokens have to be spent in-house, while the nickels deposited in the jukebox buy one song each. Steinbeck writes of the latter machine: 'The nickel [...] has caused Crosby to sing and an orchestra to play [...] This nickel, unlike most money, has actually done a job of work' (164). Here, the human quality of the coins (their capacity to perform a 'job of work') is offset by the determinist nature of their activity: neither their human operators nor they themselves have much agency in shaping the effects they 'cause' (in this instance, Crosby's singing), although they ostensibly control them. Cause relates to effect in so crude a way as to be as likely to produce dissatisfaction as satisfaction. Towards the beginning of the novel, a truck driver who spends his small change in a slot machine is struck by the imperviousness of the mechanism to his expectation: 'The whirling cylinders *gave him* [my italics] no score. "They fix 'em so you can't win nothing"', he said to the waitress' (9). The word 'fix' goes on to be associated with feats of mechanical engineering; the sixteen-year-old Al Joad 'love[s] the guts of a engine' and prides himself on being able to work magic under the bonnets of vans (267). By contrast, the book's slot machines are incapable of being worked upon, or accessed at all, except on their own terms. They at once promise a kind of wealth (in putting their contents on display) and stiffly withhold that wealth, as if specifically to tantalise Steinbeck's drifters.

At the core of Steinbeck's socialist thinking in the 1930s and 1940s was a belief in the capacity of economic communities to adapt to changing circumstances. In *Cannery Row* (1945), as in *The Grapes of Wrath*, this economic pragmatism is applied to the use of machines. Steinbeck's Eddie reflects on the advantage of Henry Ford's signature car: 'There was one nice thing about Model T's. The parts were not only interchangeable, they were unidentifiable' (Steinbeck 2000a: 56). The idea that all the components of the mechanism might be 'unidentifiable' introduces a note of comic foreboding into Eddie's amateur engineering, but the idea that they might be 'interchangeable' recalls the open-mindedness with which characters in the novel are content to exchange whatever they own for whatever they want. Steinbeck writes, with a mix of mockery and approval: 'Frogs *were* [Steinbeck's italics] cash as far as Doc was concerned' (88). It is only slot machines, in Steinbeck, whose economics of predetermined, minimal exchange completely resists adaptation. There is an absolutism to their insistence upon a particular type of transaction.

If Steinbeck had been writing in the eighteenth or early-to-mid nineteenth century, his slot machines might have contributed to *Cannery Row*'s economic pragmatism. The slot machine took its 'earliest form', according to Nic Costa, in the 'Honour Box', which 'released a lever enabling the user to open the compartment containing the tobacco' (Costa 1988: 9). This system required that only coins of a size and shape that fitted the slot could be used, but the user's freedom to serve herself tobacco potentially allowed scope for a flexible relation between coin and commodity: to take much too much tobacco would be a breach of 'honour', but the definition of a pinch might be reasonably generous. However, from the late nineteenth century onwards, as the slot-machine industry evolved into a major site of technological innovation and enterprise, the emphasis on profit produced a new passion for security. Machines were weightier, more resilient, and more comprehensively mechanised, so that attempts to steal from them were conspicuous as vandalism. In a patent of 1885 for a postcard vending machine, the inventor Percival Everitt records his shock at the 'malic[e]' with which 'the slit provided for the admission of the coin' was gummed up, and at how the 'delivery slide' through which postcards would normally be dispensed was manipulated 'in a manner which it is not necessary or expedient to state' (13). Whether or not Everitt's vandals were successful in penetrating his machines, their attitude towards them was emphatically adversarial: the age of slot-machine chivalry was gone. By the 1930s, the interiors of some coin-operated machines seem to have been inaccessible even to local authorities. In Winifred Holtby's fictional Yorkshire town of South Riding, the members of a committee charged to check 'the ethical tone of the penny-in-the-slot machines along the esplanade' are obliged to 'march [...] from one machine to the other, dropping in their pennies, listen[ing] to the tinkle, click and whir as the machine was set in motion, and thoughtfully examin[ing] the revolving picture sequences, which had been advertised by such seductive titles as *Through Winnie's Window* and *What the Butler Winked At* (Holtby 2010: 270). The means by which the mechanism is 'set in motion' is necessarily a fantasy: the 'tinkle', 'click', and 'whir' describe an acoustic environment with which only the sounds themselves interact. From the outset, slot machines acquired private worlds – a kind of subjectivity defined not by the nature of its contents but by the mere existence of those contents in their secret, elaborately barricaded state.

Part of what was attractive about early slot machines was their mysteriousness, and the arbitrary way in which that mysteriousness manifested itself. There was a sense in which the act of triggering the machine might unleash anything, even magic. In H.G. Wells's *The Time Machine* (1895), a machine that broadly resembles a slot machine in its 'metal framework' and miscellaneous glitter of finery (ivory, brass, nickel, quartz), is operated simply by the pressure of a hand on a lever; the Time Traveller explains: 'Presently I am going to press the lever, and off the machine will go' (Wells 2007: 8-9). Towards the end of the novel, when the narrator 'put[s] out [his] hand' to 'touch the lever' and receives a visceral shock as the 'squat substantial mass sway[s] like a bough shaken in the wind', he perhaps anticipates the manner of the Time Traveller's ultimate, mysterious disappearance (89). The book leaves open the question of whether its protagonist's last journey is deliberate or accidental: whether he is the victim of curiosity or technology. This idea of mechanised self-sabotage may also be linked to the birth of the motorcar in the 1890s, although motorcars were few and far between at the time; the first Benzes were too ramshackle to inspire much public faith or aesthetic appetite, lacking the 'obvious commercial value' of Daimlers, which only began to be sold in 1892 (Gregersen 2012: 35). On the other hand, slot machines were everywhere in the 1890s. Moreover, the simplicity of the Time Machine's operation specifically recalls the slot machine – many types of which were triggered by the double pressure of a penny or nickel (dimes were too thin) in a slot, and a hand on a lever (Bueschel 1995: 15) – while Wells's emphasis on the unpredictability of time travel recalls the unknowability of turn-of-the-century slot machines. The Time Traveller may visit the future, but he cannot know contingency as it manifests itself in the behaviour of his vehicle. This knowledge is outside the reach of science: it is a mechanism's secret.

The excitement of late nineteenth-century slot machines derived in part from their association with the larger industry of technological entertainment. Laura Marcus links the conflation of space and time embodied by Wellsian time travel with the emergence of cinema (Marcus 2007: 97), and slot machines could themselves be proto-cinematic or cinematic; Holtby's coin-triggered 'revolving picture sequences' are an example. Wells's Time Machine may thus perhaps either be read as what might have been called a kinetoscope, or mutoscope, or cinemetroscope, or rayoscope, or veriscope, or viveoscope, or animatograph, or projectoscope, or magniscope, or biograph (Nasaw 1999: 142), or as a coin-operated gambling machine. From the invention of the first British gambling machine in 1887 – 'a coin freed horse racing game which mimicked the large Jeu de Course gambling games commonly encountered in the casinos of the nineteenth century' – up until the prohibition of public gambling in Britain in 1930, the majority of slot machines visible to Wells would have been gambling machines (Costa 1988: 37, 59). The notion of 'trickery' in the opening chapter, as an evil to be watchful against in pledging one's trust, also frames the mere act of believing in the 'paradox' of time travel as a gamble (Wells 2007: 8-9, 3). The reader has the luxury of suspending her disbelief – or of exercising a form of belief that puts nothing at stake – whereas the narrator has a gambler's phobia of being 'played upon'; he declares nervously: 'It appears incredible to me that any kind of trick, however subtly conceived and however adroitly done, could have been played upon us under these conditions' (8).

The idea that a slot machine or its manufacturer might be conspiring against one was more likely to gain ground in the 1890s, when slot machines had novelty value (although they were not new); but there were also some late nineteenth-century machines that resisted mystification. When Wells writes in *The History of Mr Polly* (1910) that 'something between a giggle and a gas-meter' rasps in Mr Rusper's throat, he associates the scuttle of a coin in a gas-meter not with mystery as such but with inaccessibility: the true goings on of Mr Rusper's throat are as unaccountable as his name's first vowel ('r*u*sp-' not 'r*a*sp-') (Wells 2010: 114). Coin-operated meters could seem withholding in a practical as well as an epistemic sense. In Elizabeth Bowen's 'Firelight in the Flat' (1934), there is a vivid clash between the self-sustaining quality of memory and the electric fire's reliance on shillings to work. Robertson is himself fuelled by nostalgia, but is unable to rely on the metaphor for his nostalgia to remain in operation: 'the open fire kept something inside alight. Bitterly retrospective, Robertson reached out for the switch. But there was no electricity. He felt round in his pocket: he had no shilling' (Bowen 1999: 435). If the ebbing fire fails as a metaphor for nostalgia, it succeeds instead as a metaphor for Robertson's failure to make his memory matter in the present; Bowen writes: 'Robertson was an ex-officer, as the war kept receding, this counted for less and less.' Yet his experience is still that of someone thwarted: the meter resists him.

In the sense that Robertson expects a mundane state of affairs to continue (the fire to stay alight), he contrasts with George Orwell's George Bowling in *Coming Up For Air* (1939), who looks to 'one of [those] penny-in-the-slot machines that tell your fortune as well as your weight' for reinforcement in his decision to leave his wife and to reinvent himself more generally (Orwell 2000a: 214-15). Bowling is a version of Wells's Mr Polly, who abandons his wife and his best friend Mr Rusper in search of adventure; Orwell announces this debt by having Bowling read *The History of Mr Polly* (124). Wells's description of the sound in Mr Rusper's throat as 'something between a giggle and a gas-meter' is also echoed in Bowling's consciousness of a 'clicking noise somewhere inside' the 'penny-in-the-slot machine' when he deposits his penny (215), and in both texts the mechanism of coin-operated service is unknowable, though it lacks mystique; 'something' becomes 'somewhere' in Orwell: the locus of obscurity spreads. Moreover, in Orwell's account of Bowling's encounter with a slot machine, the inaccessibility of the mechanism is underlined by the uselessly catch-all nature of its instruction: 'Persevere, for you will rise high!' We might argue that the promise 'you will rise high' is ironised and thus contradicted by the immediately subsequent disclosure of Bowling's weight ('14 stone 11 pounds'): Bowling, as his name suggests, is no balloon. On the other hand, there is no way of resolving the ambiguity of 'Persevere'. Bowling began the novel by choosing not to persevere in his old way of life, and his current course of action is also one in which he might choose to persist or not persist. Perseverance may mean entirely opposite things, depending on one's definition of the status quo. Raymond Williams argues in *George Orwell* (1971) that 'most of Orwell's important writing is about someone who tries to get away but fails', and Bowling's brush with the fortune-telling machine may be understood to carry this failure to a metaphysical level (Williams 1971: 39). If there can be no such thing as perseverance for the aspiring radical, there can be no such thing as 'get[ting] away', and if there is no such thing as getting away, there is no escape from disenchantment. Orwell's slot machine defines a kind of existential absolutism.

British slot machines may often have seemed to be resistant to the wishes of their users, but they were also a testimony to the creative licence of European and American inventors. The spectrum of coin-purchasable goods was huge, and bizarre; there were machines that sold ant eggs, others that sold compressed air, and others that offered medical diagnoses. In 1897, when x-ray technology was only two years old, a coin-operated faux x-ray machine appeared, as if to confront technological discovery with technologised make-believe. Slot machines occupied a space somewhere between the prose of functional innovation and the poetry of sheer formal experiment. Waugh chimes with this conception of the slot machine as a mode of formal experimentation in comparing Henry Green's *Living* (1929) to 'those aluminium ribbons one stamps out in railway stations on penny in the slot machines' (Waugh 2009: 44-5). The accretive quality of Waugh's syntax here ('those aluminium ribbons one stamps out *in* railway stations *on* penny in the slot machines') de-emphasises whatever practical function the stamping out of aluminium ribbons might have, presenting the phenomenon instead in terms of a series of effects that prompt curiosity – like Green's series of syntactical shock tactics. However, if early twentieth-century Britain's slot machines could potentially suggest the experimental freedom of modernist writing, American slot machines were more likely to suggest manufactural and distributional constraints. When one of the leading American manufacturers of the coin-operated photo-booth, David McCowan, set out to establish his business, he was warned by Al Capone: 'We run all the vending in this country' (Goranin 2008: 36). Whether or not Capone was as good as his word in this instance is impossible to know, but the fact that he was widely credited with the influence he claimed to possess was enough in itself to consolidate his power. And rumour was occasionally supported by revelation. In 1929, when the police stumbled on 'the center of [Capone's] slot machine racket' in an innocuous looking outhouse in Chicago Heights, they simultaneously defeated Capone and fuelled his legend (Bergreen 1994: 301). The mere act of engaging with an American slot machine could thus be insidiously haunted. Costa writes that even machines imported from America could seem to have Capone 'lurking inside' them (Costa 1988: 81).

In early twentieth-century France, the suspicion of Capone's influence, along with a more general anxiety at the prospect of foul play, meant that 'coin machines of all types had a difficult time' (78). In 1937, the government outlawed all slot machines with a gambling element, with the effect that what remained of coin-operated entertainment could seem cloyingly predictable and over-safe. In *La Nausée* (1938), the slot machine to which Sartre compares everyday conversation is both a metaphor for false consciousness and an extreme instance of a declawed machine: the worst that the anecdotes and wisdom dropped into the delivery slides can do is glue themselves to the teeth like soft caramel (Sartre 2000: 101). Moreover, the idea that slot machines were officiously neutral, that there might be a proactive dimension to their blandness, seems to play behind Alain Robbe-Grillet's account of the coin-operated machines in the automat café in *Les Gommes* (1953). When the detective, Wallas, finds himself at an automat restaurant, the scene provokes one of the novel's riffs on the concept of enforced erasure:

> Revenu sur ses pas, Wallace avise, de l'autre côté de la rue Janeck, un restaurant automatique de dimensions modestes mais équipé des appareils les plus récents. Contre les murs s'alignment les distributeurs nickelés; au fond, la casse ou les consommateurs se munissent de jetons spéciaux. La salle, tout en longeur, est occupée par deux rangées de petites tables rondes, en matière plastique, fixèes au sol. Debout devant ces tables, une quinzaine de personnes – continuellement renouvelées – mangent avec des gestes rapides et précis. (Robbe-Grillet 1953: 160).

'Récents' at the end of the first sentence implicitly posits an equivalence between Wallas's return to la rue Janeck – a site he revisits throughout the book – and the novelty of the automat machines. Return becomes the medium of novelty, or to put it more starkly, return consists paradoxically in a new beginning rather than a reinstatement of the past. There is a continuity between the way the customers 'renew' themselves and the way Wallas returns, although the former is contingent on a disappearance: renewal only looks like return. The idea that Wallas only looks like himself, that he may have lost his personhood (whatever that entails) in the maelstrom of the 'continual' exchange between present and future versions of the same image, is reinforced by the odd elasticity of his visual perspective: he seems at once to be across the street from the café and to be able to see the precise and rapid gestures of customers.

The peculiar, encroaching blankness of Robbe-Grillet's automat café may be explained in part by the long battle to sanitise French slot machines in the first half of the twentieth century, but it may also relate to their Americanness. The walls of the French café are lined with nickel dispensers, without which the diners would be unable to operate the slot machines. There is thus a sense in which the machines occupy their own world with its own currency: an American embassy with no politics or philosophy – simply an imposition of difference. Bueschel writes that the majority of slot machines were 'made for nickel play', so that changing one's money became part of the ritual of using them (Bueschel 1995: 15). There were some machines that promised to be 'Made to work with Coins suitable for all Countries', but this advantage seems not to have been sufficiently profitable to dictate a new norm (189). Moreover, even in America where nickels were a national currency, the necessity of converting one's money in order to use the machines was treated as a limitation and a curiosity. When the American comedian Jack Benny threw his legendary automat parties in the 1960s, he furnished his guests with 'roll[s] of nickels' (Hardart and Diel 2002: 14). It was as if the machines required tokens to be used. In Malcolm Bradbury's *Stepping Westward* (1965), the British-born American professor James Walker is described as 'buy[ing] a handful of nickels' in order to operate an automat machine (Bradbury 1993: 143). Walker exchanges American money which is itself unfamiliar to him for money that has been rendered provisional by its association with a specific activity and space. In entering the world of the automat café, he is doubly foreign, but also foreign in a way that likens him to his American fellow diners: everyone needs change for the machines.

Automat cafés were a staple of American life at midcentury, and could sometimes offer themselves as a metonym for city life. In John Cheever's story, 'O City of Broken Dreams' (1948), when the Malloy family relocate from Wentworth, Indiana – a fictional rural town – to New York, their daily routine centres around the Broadway automat, whose chicken pie, fish cakes, and baked beans are enthrallingly strange for all their pretended homeliness, with a strangeness that somehow constitutes New York. In Cheever's story, this otherworldliness is politicised by its association with the pernicious contemporary myth that automat machines ran by magic, as if the army of staff employed to maintain them did not exist. Alice Malloy enthuses that the automat coffee bursts 'magical[ly]' from its spout and that the glass doors of the food cubicles 'spr[i]ng' open of their own accord (Cheever 2009: 55). Whereas Cheever casually mentions Alice's 'callused hands', the manual care lavished on the restaurant goes unrecorded. David Freeland writes of America's automat machines at midcentury: 'someone had to cook the food, stock the little compartments, keep the floors clean, bus the tables, refill the sugar and condiments, and exchange larger coinage into nickels for a meal' (Freeland 2009: 172). Freeland recounts a half-century long tug-of-war between America's leading automat company, Horn & Hardart, and those of their employees who insisted on the right to unionise – a right which, after its legal consolidation by the Wagner Act of 1935, seemed especially vital. Horn & Hardart stuck to their guns partly because they understood the appeal of their brand to reside in the myth that automat service was magical. However, far from protecting this myth, the effect of their steeliness – the absoluteness of their anti-unionism – and the press attention it attracted, made customers more aware of the workers missing from the picture. Edward Hopper's *Automat* (1927), with its empty chair and the visual echoes between the woman's buttermilk bonnet and the two rows of dully reflected restaurant lights, not only encodes her romantic anticipations and/or nostalgias but points to the actual peoplelessness of the space. Anomalously, she is in public and yet in private. Thirty years later in the Hollywood blockbuster, *That Touch of Mink* (1962), the idea that the backstage dimension of the automat machine might be kept secret was familiar enough to lend irony to a gossipy exchange through a serving hatch between Doris Day and an automat cook. The slot machine encounter imagined here allows Day and her friend to speak freely, as if the machine between them were a medium rather than an object in its own right. Day orders her meal vocally, approaching the stern instruction 'FIRST PRESS BUTTON' not as a requisite for being served (her meal is in another section of the café) but as a mere stage in the process of calling out to her friend. The mechanism becomes a tool, rather than a set of arbitrary protocols: it is humanised out of its absolutism.

American automat machines derived some of their austerity and mystique from their self-containment. In Cheever's story, this self-containment is part of a broader conception of New York as a city that runs by itself, where no one really works. When Alice Malloy is asked whether she is 'Looking for a job' she says no, though she is willing to concede that she is 'going on business' (Cheever 2009: 53). The Malloy family expect to make their fortune in New York simply by selling the first scene of a play whose plot they have plagiarised. They disconnect the idea of achievement or production from any idea of labour, or more specifically, they associate New York with the luxury of being able to transcend all consciousness of labour, both their own and that of other people. Cheever writes of their travelling clothes: 'They were dressed, like the people you sometimes see in Times Square on Saturday night, in clothing that had been saved for their flight' (52). The formulation 'saved for [...] flight' alerts us to the element of magical thinking at the heart of the Malloys' vision of themselves in New York. *For* is promoted from its usual mundane prepositional duties into a vehicle of transformation: the clothes become wings by being saved. Of course, the Malloys are in no frame of mind to feel tyrannised by slot machines, however remote from human influence those machines might appear. Nevertheless, automat machines whose attendants were similarly conspicuous by their absence could sometimes seem so autonomous as to be capable of harbouring their own agendas. In Cornell Woolrich's story, 'Murder at the Automat' (1937), the inveterate automat diner Mr Avram is discovered 'sprawled across [his plate], [with] one arm out, the other hanging limply down toward the floor' – the victim of a poisoned sandwich (Woolrich 2010: 323). Woolrich's tone is comic but there is a bitter edge to the joke. Avram has no means of anticipating this fate, whose perpetrator turns out to be an automat cook – and his wife's boyfriend and accomplice. He thus escapes from his wife's tyranny at home (as he sees it) only to be felled by it in the place he perceives as his refuge: he moves, unknowingly, from the sphere of one kind of absolutism to that of another. For Woolrich as for Sartre, the slot machine is a site of false consciousness.

The absolutism of slot machines could be insidious, or it could be vivid to the customer as a lack of give or grace. When Steinbeck's truck driver finds that the 'whirling cylinders g[i]ve him no score' and goes on to conclude that 'They fix 'em so you can't win nothing', the double move by which 'give' gives something (the score of nil) and gives nothing (fails to give a score) builds a negativity into the very nature of the machine's agency. Likewise, in Bradbury's *Stepping Westward*, the coin-operated phone-booth seems actively ungenerous; in requiring exactly 'four pennies' and in keeping Walker waiting to be connected, it 'mak[es] him nervous', and in making him nervous, it anticipates the effect of his wife's voice on the other end of the line (Bradbury 1979: 38). Part of the humour here lies in an implicit association between Mrs Walker's role in managing a kind of expectation at the maternity ward of a hospital, and the phone-booth's role in managing the expectation of the caller. In writing that 'you practically had to say you were giving birth in the callbox before they would connect you' (37), Bradbury links the two structures of suspense, with the 'connect[ion]' acting as an inverse echo of an umbilical cord's severance. The suggestion is that Walker's wife – 'a dragon in her uniform' (38) – is as unforgiving towards her patients as she is towards Walker, and that both versions of unforgivingness are embodied by the booth. The slot machine is unforgiving on her behalf, as if it were her instrument rather than Walker's. Moreover, in the sense that Bradbury's phone-booth mirrors his protagonist's subordination to his partner, it may recall Orwell's phone-booth in *Keep the Aspidistra Flying* (1936). David Trotter writes of the booth from which Gordon Comstock calls his girlfriend, Rosemary: '[t]he mechanism [...] with its prescribed sequence of actions, at once effects and stages (or restages) [his] capitulation' (Trotter 2013: 58). This machine's 'prescribed sequence of actions' works like a speech act in giving reality to an event (Gordon's 'capitulation') by symbolising it, while, on the other hand, it lacks the speech act's grounding in intention. Gordon treats the call as a foregone conclusion, as opposed to an act he self-consciously intends; when he finds 'exactly two pennies' in his pocket – enough for a call in 1935 – he decides: 'So the die was cast' (Orwell 2000b: 263). All the agency he permits himself is a gambler's submission to chance; the intention he then exercises is almost the machine's.

On one level, Gordon may be said to use the phone-booth to compensate for his indecision, in which case it serves his purpose. He chooses to be forced into a 'sequence of actions' by the machine. Similarly, in Joyce's *Ulysses* (1922), when Leopold Bloom remembers peeping at 'A dream of wellfilled hose' through the coin-operated mutoscope at Capel Street, he chooses to make do with sexual fantasy; 'wellfilled' is not *ful*filled: the false synonym exposes his compromise (Joyce 1992: 480). And again, in John Rodker's *Adolphe 1920* (1929), Dick's fascination with the woman in 'lace-edged drawers, laced boots, and black stockings' he watches through the window of another mutoscope is acknowledged and accepted as self-limiting by the reminder: 'A coin brought her back' (Rodker 1996: 132). The coin 'br[ings] [...] back' what may not be secured: its gift is premised on a loss. Dick, Bloom, and Gordon embrace the unbiddable nature of the slot machines with which they engage, and to an extent this unbiddability is the condition of their interest in the machines. However, the flipside of such acclimatisations to slot machines is a rejection of the very principle of ungivingness. In Louis MacNeice's 'In Lieu' (1962), slot machines belong to a half-century's worth of gradual deterioration in the value of acquirable objects; the synthetic chemicals of modern perfumery, sold from a hypothetical slot machine, are akin to the Eucharistic 'wafers and wine'. (Nigel Groom writes that 'in perfumery "synthetic" does not signify cheapness', but MacNeice would not have been convinced by this quibble [Groom 1997: 260].) His slot machine substitutes undesirable objects for desirable ones:

> Roses with the scent bred out,
> In lieu of which is a long name on a label.
> Dragonflies reverting to grubs,
> Tundra and desert overcrowded,
> And in lieu of a high altar
> Wafers and wine procured by a coin in a slot. (MacNeice 1979: 522)

In the last two lines, substitution itself becomes a substitution. The miracle of transubstantiation associated with the Eucharist is disabled by the use of bread and wine whose cost is visible and negligible (unlike Christ's sacrifice), and which one 'procure[s]' oneself, so that the only relation possible between the slot machine's fare and Christ's blood and body is one of substitution. Not even the Protestant notion of symbolic transubstantiation is feasible under these conditions, where the materialities of transaction are so blatant. The slot machine deprives the Eucharist ceremony of grace: the fact of or capacity for giving more than is warranted. The cheap wafer and wine can be no more than themselves.

MacNeice's aural mirror rhyme (between '*al*tar' and s*lot*') asks to be thought of as another instance of substitution, rhyme being an act of repetition that invites reflection on the fidelity of one word to another. The mechanism of commemoration embodied by the 'high altar' is substituted on a practical level and on the level of sound by the 'coin in a slot'; and both substitutions fall short: less than a mirror rhyme, the echo of 'al' in 'lo' qualifies as a rhyme only by the hairbreadth criteria of its coincidence with line-endings, and by the consonance of 't'. MacNeice was not the first poet to translate a sense of the lack of grace in slot machine transactions into a concept of rhyme. In Elizabeth Bishop's 'The Soldier and the Slot Machine' (1942), the exact rhymes – 'hand'/'land', 'dead'/'head', 'gilt'/'spilt', 'cough'/'off', 'know'/'row', 'through'/'too', 'apart'/'heart', 'sure'/'floor', 'junk'/'drunk', 'afford'/'Award' – reconfigure the poem's characterisation of a gambling machine whose sympathy is felt to be unreachable, by giving the sound back cleanly, without adding anything to it (Bishop 2011: 287-8). There is no excess of unrhymed consonants: no evidence of listening (or mishearing), only of hearing. Or we might say that, if the poem listens, it listens like a machine. The conceptual basis for this reading is offered in the seventh and tenth stanzas:

> Its notions all are preconceived.
>   It tempts one much to tear apart
> The metal frame, to investigate
>   The workings of its metal heart,
>
> And even if generously inclined
>   Its money all will melt, I'm sure,
> And flow like mercury through the cracks
>   And make a pool beneath the floor ...

Both the 'notions' of the rhyme and those of the slot machine are 'preconceived' in the double sense of prejudged and preconstructed, and both these connotations of 'preconceived' happen to have the same outcome: a lack of responsiveness. Moreover, this entanglement of the idea of the implacable slot machine with that of the poem allows the soldier's frustration to be meted out against the form. The fantasy of defeating the machine suggested by 'Its money all will melt, I'm sure, / And flow like mercury through the cracks / And make a pool' pits the soldier's words against the poem's 'preconceived' mechanics, with the 'crack' of the line end acting as a kind of neutered attack. For, rhythmically, the mechanism is unchanged: the pause introduced by the conjunctions is no lighter than a punctuation mark.

Bishop's tone is self-mocking here, and the majority of writers with whom I engage in this essay have no real objection to slot machines – MacNeice perhaps being the exception. There is an inarguable justice to the procedure by which slot machines fulfil a contract, trading a pre-agreed number of coins for a pre-agreed product, whether that product is a particular property or an experience. To balk at the 'preconceived[ness]' of such returns is, in a way, to query a contract having accepted its conditions. Using a slot machine means submitting to its absolutism. However, if we consider slot machines alongside the 'interactive' media that have come to define our own technological era, what twentieth-century writers perceived as their intransigence may seem like a failure of interaction. Erkki Huhtamo designates the coin-operated gambling machine as 'proto-interactive' in its reliance on tactility: 'The tactility of the relationship was essential: to operate the machine, one had to touch it by means of an interface' (Huhtamo 2005: 9). And yet, this act of touch is the end of an interaction rather than the beginning of one, while the mechanism it triggers is only able to respond inflexibly. 'Its notions all are preconceived.' Laureates of the slot machine in twentieth-century literature may not find its modus operandi counterintuitive, but they are conscious of a stiffness in its methods of response. For all their difference of outlook and temperament, Bishop, MacNeice, Rodker, Joyce, Orwell, Bradbury, Steinbeck, Woolrich, Cheever, Robbe-Grillet, Wells, and Bowen have in common a conception of the slot machine as a site of self-displacement: the machine takes over – a 'dragon in [its] uniform', to repurpose Bradbury's description of Mrs Walker. The literary history of the slot machine may thus be read as the fossil of an old and ambivalent appetite for dragons in uniforms.

Works Cited

Bergreen, Laurence. 1994. *Capone: The Man and the Era*. New York: Simon & Schuster.

Bishop, Elizabeth. 2011. *Poems*. New York: Farrar, Straus & Giroux.

Bowen, Elizabeth. 1999. *Collected Stories*. London: Vintage.

Bradbury, Malcolm. 1993. *Stepping Westward*. New York: Open Road.

Bueschel, Richard M. 1995. *The Collector's Guide to Vintage Slot Machines*. Atglen: Schiffer.

Cheever, John. 2009. *Collected Stories and Other Writings*. New York: Library of America.

Costa, Nic. 1988. *Automatic Pleasures: The History of the Coin Machine*. London: Kevin Francis.

Freeland, David. 2009. *Automats, Taxi Dances, and Vaudeville: Excavating Manhattan's Lost Places of Pleasure*. New York: New York University Press.

Goranin, Näkki. 2008. *American Photobooth*. New York: Norton & Company.

Gregersen, Erik. 2012. *The Complete History of Wheeled Transportation: From Cars and Trucks to Buses and Bikes*. New York: Britannica Educational Publishing.

Groom, Nigel. 1997. *The Perfume Handbook*. New York: Springer.

Hardart, Marianne, and Lorraine Diel. 2002. *The Automat: The History, Recipes, and Allure of Horn and Hardart's Masterpiece*. New York: Clarkson Potter.

Holtby, Winifred. 2010. *South Riding: An English Landscape*. London: Virago.

Huhtamo, Erkki. 2005. 'Slots of Fun, Slots of Trouble: An Archaeology of Arcade Gaming'. In *Handbook of Computer Game Stories*, edited by Joost Raessans and Jeffrey Goldstein, 3-21. Cambridge: MIT Press.

Joyce, James. 1992. *Ulysses*. Harmondsworth: Penguin.

MacNeice, Louis. 1979. *Collected Poems*. London: Faber & Faber.

Mann, Delbert. *That Touch of Mink*. Universal City, California: Universal Pictures, 2004. DVD.

Marcus, Laura. 2007. *The Tenth Muse: Writing About Cinema in the Modernist Period*.Oxford: Oxford University Press.

Nasaw, David. 1999. *Going Out: The Rise and Fall of Public Amusements*. Cambridge: Harvard University Press.

Orwell, George. 2000a. *Coming Up For Air*. London: Penguin.

Orwell, George. 2000b. *Keep the Aspidistra Flying*. London: Penguin.

Robbe-Grillet, Alain. 1953. *Les Gommes*. Paris: Les Éditions de Minuit.

Rodker, John. 1996. *Poems and Adolphe 1920*. Manchester: Carcanet Press.

Sartre, Jean-Paul. 2000. *Nausea*. Translated by Robert Baldick. London: Penguin.

Steinbeck, John. 2000a. *Cannery Row*. London: Penguin.

Steinbeck, John. 2000b. *The Grapes of Wrath*. London: Penguin.

Trotter, David. 2013. *Literature in the First Media Age: Britain Between the Wars*. Cambridge: Harvard University Press.

Waugh, Evelyn. 2009. *Letters of Evelyn Waugh*. London: Phoenix.

Wells, H. G. 2007. *The Time Machine*. London: Penguin.

Wells, H. G. 2010. *The History of Mr Polly*. London: Weidenfeld & Nicolson.

Williams, Raymond. 1971. *George Orwell*. London: Fontana.

Woolrich, Cornell. 2010. 'Murder at the Automat'. In *A Century of Detection: Twenty Great Mystery Stories, 1841-1940*, edited by John Cullen Gruesser, 323-38. Jefferson: MacFarland & Co.

12

Touch Screen

ESTHER LESLIE

The touch screen is a new familiar, but it has made itself at home in a short period of time. An early version, as a finger-touch device, appeared in the mid-1960s, when E.A. Johnson of the Royal Radar Establishment in Malvern, England, detailed his prototypical work in an article titled 'Touch Display – A Novel Input/Output Device for Computers' (Johnson 1965). This was followed two years later, in 1967, by the more developed 'Touch Displays: A Programmed Man-Machine Interface' (Johnson 1967). This patented proposal was rapidly followed by a different system which was based on pressure and used a stylus rather than a finger to unleash functions. In the 1970s and 1980s, multi-touch systems were developed using infrared sensors and cameras, and, in the next decade, these various technologies were combined to make machines for work, such as Personal Digital Assistants, as well as mobile phones with touch screens. Both usually required stylus inputs and worked with more or less reliable handwriting-recognition systems. From 2000, though, the interest in touch-screen technology emerged in design industries and animation. Large-format touch screens emulated the big boards used by designers to track projects. Where once clay or paper models had sufficed, now there were images, or digital assets, to be conjured up, altered, dismissed, moved around, animated by fingertips. In this same period, Sony developed SmartSkin, a flat surface that could recognise multiple touch points and gestures through sensing elements integrated into the touch-screen surface. Its aim was to let the hand act as it acts habitually in the world, but with its gestures now relating to digital objects. By 2006, a multi-touch device using a biometric concept of 'frustrated total internal reflection' was being lauded for its seemingly interface-free, entirely intuitive responsiveness to human gestures. A repertoire of movements for enlarging, tilting, rotating, and shifting pixelated materials was demonstrated on Ted Talks (see Han 2006). It was followed by other so-called 'Natural User Interfaces', with the technologies involved set up so they might be used intuitively. The word *natural* signified that the operation of the device did not involve an input device, be it stylus or mouse, but simply a hand. The age of hand-operated machinery returned, if perversely. In 2007 the iPhone appeared with one button, no hardware keyboard, and an internet browser. This generation of touch screens had touch points as small as a pixel and virtual software keyboards that appear and disappear just when needed. Screens are responsive, there to be touched. They are to be held, and stroked. Touch-screen technology is incorporated into white goods, black goods, things in the home, the pocket, the office. Touch comes to mean not necessarily physical contact, for near-field communication might be the communication mechanism between human and machine in various smart gadgets that respond to a wave of the arm or hand. But this is an extension of the sense of the interface as natural, as automatic as a shrug of the shoulder, a blink of an eye.

The touch screen appears as a sensitive window onto what Marshall McLuhan described as 'electronic circuitry' through which information flows. In *Understanding Media*, McLuhan observes that electric light is 'pure information', without content – except, he notes, in those cases where it is used to spell out a name or advertisement. If the light is on,

> whether the light is being used for brain surgery or night baseball is a matter of indifference. It could be argued that these activities are in some way the 'content' of the electric light, since they could not exist without the electric light. This fact merely underlines the point that 'the medium is the message' because it is the medium that shapes and controls the scale and form of human association and action. The content or uses of such media are as diverse as they are ineffectual in shaping the form of human association. (McLuhan 1964: 8)

But with the touch screen, information does not just flow past. It can be held up, padded, or swiped into being. In being touched, the screen seems to stop being a screen that obstructs or shuts off. Touching makes the screen act as permeable. However, it also proves to resist permeability, remaining always ever the same glass, the same hard barrier. At this point, intimacy, most often signalled through touch, collapses into distance, be that the inaccessibility of what is beneath the glass, the obscurity of its workings, or its dependence on remote and fragile systems. There may be some people who can 'jailbreak' their devices, such as Kindle e-readers, by installing custom fonts or screensavers, and there might be some who jailbreak their iOS or other operating system, in order to install non-proprietary apps. But for the most part, to customise is to choose from a given selection of screensavers or ringtones or to configure an app the way the user prefers it. To customise is not to compromise the pre-set functions of the machine. It is a machine like any other, pre-programmed, set up to execute predicted operations.

The screen of the touch screen is not a window, but a conduit to the machine's operations. The screen can be fingered, and so it seems as if that which is called up, moved, enlarged, sent, and so on is fingered too. What passes under the fingers or is brought into being by them is varied – tokens of love, work, misery, horror, banality, kitsch – but it all flits through the same system, contained with the dimensions of the small screen. Thomas Hirschhorn's *Touching Reality* (2012), a 4:45-minute video, concentrates on the touch screen as a conduit of brutality. A fixed camera observes a touch-screen device. On it are a series of photographs. These photographs are of carnage and corpses. They are scenes of war and its casualties, victims of bombs, burnings and gunshot, anonymous and in places unknown or unindicated, just as the owner of the fingers is unknown. One hand's fingers pinch and flick across images of mutilated bodies, honing in on details, such as exposed brains or deep gashes, flicking left to move on to the next, right to double-check on a detail, gently tapping to zoom out. The fingers touch the bodies, but do not of course touch them. They touch their image – real finger on mediatized bloody body, missing eye, lost limb. And these fingers touch with such tender gestures, gently avoiding the risk of scratching the screen. Habit sets in, but carelessness does not arise. The finger touch remains poised and gentle. Its caressing operations have been interpreted by Hito Steyerl, who has reflected extensively on our digital condition, as a recognition of the touch screen's traumatic birth, its coming into being through horrendous labour conditions of long hours and poor recompense (Simon 2011). Hirschhorn's title is *Touching Reality*. His screen shows us the reality of war, the brutal images that are censored from the usual media channels, but can be found online (Hirschhorn 2013). The fingers touch this harsher reality (or rather images of it) and, in turn, the reality touches the viewer, or the viewer of the viewer, who observes the artwork on another screen. But of course it can all mean the opposite. There is no touching, just another mediation that can be as casually scanned as any pixelated data, and the touch is only the touch of fingers on cool glass. Reality cannot be touched. Everyone, whoever they are, is already dead anyway.

Walter Benjamin observed a loss of meaning in 1933, which he associated with forms of mediation of stories in the newspaper. The metaphor is one of touch – things 'lose all connection with one another':

> In our writing, opposites that in happier ages fertilized one another have become insoluble antinomies. Thus, science and belle lettres, criticism and literary production, culture and politics, fall apart in disorder and lose all connection with one another. The scene of this literary confusion is the newspaper[.]
> (Benjamin 2005c: 741)

In earlier days, when the newspaper contributed to the formation of bourgeois civil society, it was a vehicle for rethreading the world in reflection, as zones of democratic discussion developed (Habermas 1992: 72). Newspapers make of people a community living through the same time consciously. In the newspaper, the present is experienced as present for the first time (see Müller 2014: 66). But in the modern age, the newspaper echoes only the incoherent babble of modern life, mixing myth and politics, economy and culture, science and art, gossip and misery, all separated out into sections, with little apparent connection to each other. The logic of the internet and what passes on the touch screen exacerbates this. What appears on the screen, commanded by the fingers, loses in particularity, in order to become incoherent, equatable things, a generality, each substitutable by the other. Connection is an electrical question, rather than one of coherence and context. The present that the newspaper brought into being as an experience breaks into illimitable instants, finger taps on myriad pages, in the infinite chain of links.

This body that touch seems to have, the one that responds to fingertips, is our body too. McLuhan describes radio and TV as types of electric technology. This electric technology, he notes further, is connected to our central nervous system (McLuhan 1964: 68). In turn it connects us, brings us in touch with the world, making it impossible to be aloof and dissociated. It produces sense, and when it is off, there is only absence. There is nothing more off than the touch-screen device without power. Its impenetrable darkness is a sign of that. Without it being on, touch and being touched threaten to wane. We are no longer in touch. We fall out of touch. Communications are down. The very capacity to communicate is withdrawn.

What is behind the screen and 'feels' the touch of the finger also withdraws, for it is also only a screen acting as a screen used to do, using its capacity to keep a user out, while transmitting the illusion of an operator reaching through to infinite possible contents. What appears is in permanent movement and that mobility may be more important than the contents or messages. Movements are commanded by users, but functions make sense only as machinic aptitudes that are in communication with other machines, made and operated by humans of course, but nonetheless 'in touch' with a network that may at any moment be devoid of human presence. The machine will command new gestures from the user. It will also retrain experienced fingers that got used to typing on physical keyboards arranged to prevent the tangle of typewriter keys, caused by overly swift typists. The new keyboard may be arrayed alphabetically, and perhaps jabbed with just one finger at a time.

The touch screen is a surface for seeing – a surface on which things are read, images are looked at. It is also a surface on which marks can be made, a place for writing. Handwriting on tablets using a stylus has been, till now, a subsidiary function. Difficulties in getting accurate handwriting-recognition systems have weighed against an extension of this function, and styluses require resistive touch screens for the most part, which are less favoured in the industry. But software keyboards that spring up at the moment they are needed are an integral part of touch screens. The touch screen is also a surface on which the fingers perform a kind of commanding without writing, whereby through the touch of pixels events and actions are unleashed, where once MS-DOS commands had to be written out in newly familiar languages. And as it responds to us, if it is connected to the network of the web, it is also responding to other systems and commands, writing out a trail of our movements, transactions, and communications. The touch screen is a writing machine. New gestures for writing need to be learnt: single-hand or one-finger typing, alphabetic rather than QWERTY keyboard layouts, typing in mid-air with a hand instead of a surface to press against and steady the device. The hand moves as it types and so does the device. Typing with fingers instead of a stylus leads to a motion of the smartphone, especially when this typing takes place as one hand holds the phone. Four factors come into play: the striking force of the finger that types, the resistance force of the hand that holds the phone, the location of the finger as it hits a virtual key, the position of the hand that holds the phone. What seems to be a contingent, intangible set of factors can in fact be mapped from within the machine. The writing that the fingers unleash on the software keyboard might be tracked by those who wish to steal data. Coordinates could be used to rewrite the information, that is to say, to leak it elsewhere, through a malevolent application that has secreted itself on, for example, a smartphone (see Cai and Chen 2011).

As interfaces, touch screens arrange and regulate everyday lives and its activities. Through a touch screen, newspapers are read, moving images watched, radio and music heard. Through it, communications by telephone and other means are made, extending the actuality of touch into the metaphor of being in touch. Every pocket or bag holds a touch screen, a black box, its workings hard to access. It is always there, waiting for activation through a caressing finger. The touch screen has brought the hand into being as a writing tool. The implement is gone. Only the finger jabs to unleash functions, sometimes to write or draw directly. The surface is a responsive sheet, or appears to be so. In actuality it is the top of a sandwich of functions. At the beginning, only one finger could demand responses from the screen. Now the screen is multi-touch and responds to gestures too, reading the body's pinches, spins, flicks, sometimes its specific amount of pressure or tempo of sequential taps. One press and the screen starts up; a few moments delay, if it has been off, and then it responds to the fingertip, to the knuckle, to the tap, the flick, and the swipe. Its surface is smooth and primed to respond. In turn, the fingertips and other parts of the fingers become sensitised in new ways, developing gestures not previously performed, such as the thumb-and-two-finger gesture of expansion. The body's repertoire of movements changes in dialogue with the new machinery. The fingers relate to the smoothness of the screen, but that smoothness which is a surface is also a vector, a new geometry of active surface space, or perhaps what Benjamin termed *Spielraum*, a play space, room for manoeuvre, or wiggle room (Benjamin 2008: 45). Technology is directed to liberate humans from toil; the individual suddenly sees scope for play, a field of action (*Spielraum*), vastly extended. The person does not yet know how to move within or around this space, but still makes demands upon it. *Spielraum* conveys a reorganisation of the self in the world. This space for play – along with other spatialised concepts, such as *Leibraum* and *Bildraum*, body space and image space (see Benjamin 2005b: 217) – is a description of an interpenetration of person and technology, as, for example, in his example, in cinema, where an audience encounters the dynamic film image. For Benjamin, machinery passes through the human being, augmenting the 'sensorium'. A new human is embryonic in the epoch of industrial capitalism, one who connects in altered ways with, in, and through the world, and is learning how to move around the world under different conditions of experience and operativity. This body is mediating and mediated, mutable and adaptable to new experiences of space and time, recomposed endlessly through apparatuses and through images. Its learning to negotiate new circumstances benefits from play. The *Spielraum* is a realm of exploration, of active participation in the new geometries that are invented by technologically produced and distributed forms. *Spielraum* encourages play and flexibility. The touch screen might, however, represent the limit point of *Spielraum*. Benjamin's positively valued concepts of distraction and tactile engagement – whereby things are grasped by the hand, met halfway, consumed as a matter of habit – are pressed into something more akin to permanent commotion and compulsively jabbing fingers. Everything collapses into a relationship between a massive, limitless outside and a delimited fingertip. This finger is bound to the system. Touch-screen technologies permit numerous perceptions of images and texts. They are often annexed to networks, which allow for constant refreshing, seemingly limitless accessibility across space.

The rhetoric of the device insists on touch. Touch makes it work. Touch makes us work. Touch is what the device needs to function in a technical sense. Most touch screens are either analogue, using electrical resistance to sense touches, or digital, using electrical capacitance. A circuit based on capacitance has been most effective to date, with the human working as a conductor. When the finger hits a touch screen, which is composed of a grid of electrodes, a capacitive contact is formed and the AC current of the device elicits from the user a corresponding current – within levels for natural charge conduction in bodies – to complete a circuit. Some other body part – the hand on the back of the phone or the feet on the ground – electrically grounds the device, completing the circuit. We work for the machine in touching it. The touch that touch screens rely on makes of the body an instrument. This aspect of the human whose touch becomes a working function of the apparatus is found in the touch screen's very beginnings. In E.A. Johnson's patent application to the United States Patent Office in 1969, the rationale of the touch-screen interface was speed of input:

> For example, the cathode ray tube may display a list of items and it may be desired to examine one of the items in further detail.

> It is frequently troublesome to indicate to the data processing system which item is the one to be examined. Under these circumstances it should be possible to provide sites on the cathode ray tube which are responsive to touching by the hand of the operator. The effect would be that the operator touches the place on the cathode ray tube screen where the item is displayed and this signals back to the data processing system that that particular item is selected (for further examination, say). (Johnson 1969)

The device exists within the discourse of work and efficiency. It is a rationalised system, a time-motion-aware system, which decreases the possibility of error by restricting inputs to those that are pre-programmed. Indeed, the avoidance of human generated error is a concern of the system, which specifically mentions in the patent the building in of measures generated by the machine to query human actions, tilting the role of overseer away from the human worker to the machine. When the controller uses the touch wire labelled 'ERASE', the computer is programmed to present the words 'CONFIRM ERASURE OF X'. The patent outlines a concept of its functioning as pure medium rather than message, for it was necessary that 'the matter actually displayed on the electronic data display may be varied by the system', depending on job or need. The system produces variance. The operator responds.

> In other words, the display resembles an alpha-numeric keyboard in which the labels attached to the keys are not fixed but can be changed by the system computers in accordance with the required meaning at any time. The effect of this idea is far reaching. Not only does it allow the number of 'keys' to be very limited whilst retaining a large measure of flexibility in their interpretation but it also allows the 'meaning' of a key to be changed as a result of information previously fed to the system. (Johnson 1969)

But touch has other fantasmatic resonances. 'Touching is believing'. So insisted the first Apple iPhone print advertisement in August 2007. In blackness, overwritten to one side by the product name and the strapline, a source of light emanates across a limited range, as a finger brings into being, into life, the touch screen of a phone. It glows blueish white. The finger makes contact with the screen, just as Adam's finger touches God's in Michelangelo's *The Creation of Adam* on the ceiling of the Sistine Chapel. It is not enough to see. But to touch is to know, to make tangible and present, even when what is touched is not, because this touch is like no other. It is not just *The Creation of Adam* that is referenced. The finger on the screen and the strapline evoke Caravaggio's *The Incredulity of Saint Thomas*. Thomas, who doubts that the other disciples have seen a resurrected Jesus, insists: 'Except I shall see in his hands the print of the nails, and put my finger into the print of the nails, and thrust my hand into his side, I will not believe' (John 20: 25). Caravaggio depicts the moment, eight days later, when Jesus appears before Thomas and states 'Reach hither thy finger, and behold my hands; and reach hither thy hand, and thrust it into my side: and be not faithless, but believing' (John 20:27). The finger reaches into the fifth stigma, beneath the burial shroud, while all eyes are trained upon it, and Thomas can no longer disbelieve that the miracle has occurred. It is not enough to see. To touch is truly to know. And what the touch screen lets us know is that it too can perform miracles every day. The Apple advertisement was emulated in an act of Pope Francis in January 2016, when he visited the Paul VI hall at the Vatican (Wyke 2016). His fingers reach out to touch the image of a girl's face on the screen of a mobile phone held up by a worshipper, who wishes for a relative to be blessed. This touch is a miraculous one.

Goethe wrote: 'Seeing with vision that feels, feeling with fingers that see' (Goethe 2005: 69). The line appears in a series of erotic poems titled *Roman Elegies* (1795), and it was occasioned by his reflection on how caressing a woman's skin made him see marble anew. The fingers tapping on the woman's back as he considers the artistic glories of the Renaissance in this new setting reveal to Goethe the commonalities between aesthetic and erotic sensations. Through love and art the body and its senses are reborn. There is a sense in which this lover's look at form and life merges the senses, or confuses the senses, in the quest for knowing a body and exposing oneself to art. The encounter with another and the dislocation, from what seems to him a cold and dull Northern Europe to the South, produce this sensual sensitivity that courses through the fingertips. In what ways might this be captured in a contemporary use of the fingers in close coordination with seeing on the touch screen? Travel and face-to-face, or finger-to-back, contact are replaced in the touch screen by a sense of dislocation and deterritorialisation and by the loss of direct bodily presence. Yet touch is still the sense that is mobilised. But it is touch without feeling, if all that can be felt is the ever same pebble-smooth surface of the screen. Touch is abstracted to a function. There are new resonances to seeing and feeling, when scientific research is pervaded by the tactile vision of the scanning tunnelling microscope, which, in a realm where light does not penetrate, sends out a beam to feel the sample. Touch becomes a means to something else, a visioning, as it does with the touch screen. It is also a vector of touch, in that in a reversal of the operation, researchers use the visual interface to interact at the atomic level with a needle that is able to move individual molecules, producing animations from the invisible realm (see Casavecchia 2012). The touch without touch sensation is not necessarily accepted. There is touch with feeling.

On the Apple watch, physical sensations are sent through the wrist in order to persuade a user that the action performed is continuous with how this action has always been performed before: pressing buttons, scrolling wheels. Technological research pursues 'haptography'. Haptography is a recoding of touch sensations such that they can be recorded and mobilised in equivalent situations. It embeds the message into the medium and its capacity to vibrate and transmit. These recorded touches can be communicated over distance, or so it seems. In fact their local versions are mobilised through the network. Through selecting a 'contact' in the address book, an Apple Watch user can transmit a tap to the wrist of a selected Apple Watch wearer. Heartbeat simulations can be conveyed too. The touch-screen smartphone taps into the wearer's body and extends an abstracted touch to another wearer's body. The touch-screen device touches back. It has a kind of body, or at least borrows our one. This is reinforced to the extent that the touch screens of smartphones develop surfaces that heal themselves, through the use of in-built microspheres that release liquid chemicals that seep into cracks and harden almost imperceptibly. Developers work to render the screen surface more flexible, making it like an organic entity that can grow and shrink. Haptic technology strives to produce touch-screen interfaces that emulate buttons to press or switches to click, vibrations and resistances, as in Immersion's TouchSense® Technology. A physical skeuomorphism is at work. New e-readers have screens textured to feel like paper. Many continue to report a wistful missing of the tactile experience of paper, its sounds, its look. As virtual pages are turned, a vibration is emitted to emulate the feeling of paper sliding over paper. The lack of orientation in an e-reader may change the way in which reading and understanding occurs. E-readers (those who read on screens, rather than the machines) possess no sense of the topography of the text, its context; that is, of where on the page an idea resides, or where in the book one is, except for the numerical indication of percentages or time left to read the whole at an average rate. Studies attempt to establish – and re-establish as expectations change – the extent to which the haptic experience of a book and its pages affects questions of memory, recall, comprehension, and pleasure (see Jabr 2011). Reading with a finger in contact with a surface that is always ever the same whatever the book, whatever the page, may lead to surface – or superficial – reading, assert various studies, without a deep engagement with the text.

The loss of the physicality of the book was imagined before the event of its occurrence. In Stanislaw Lem's *Return From the Stars* (1961) something like a touch-screen e-reader appears on sale in a bookshop that is more like a laboratory:

> No longer was it possible to browse among shelves, to weigh volumes in hand, to feel their heft, the promise of ponderous reading. The bookstore resembled, instead, an electronic laboratory. The books were crystals with recorded contents. They can be read with the aid of an opton, which was similar

to a book but had only one page between the covers. At a touch, successive pages of the text appeared on it. But optons were little used, the sales-robot told me. The public preferred lectons – lectons read out loud, they could be set to any voice, tempo, and modulation. Only scientific publications having a very limited distribution were still printed, on a plastic imitation paper. Thus all my purchases fitted into one pocket, though there must have been almost three hundred titles. My handful of crystal corn – my books. I selected a number of works on history and sociology, a few on statistics and demography, and what the girl from Adapt had recommended on psychology. A couple of the larger mathematical textbooks – larger, of course, in the sense of their content, not of their physical size. The robot that served me was itself an encyclopedia, in that – as it told me – it was linked directly, through electronic catalogs, to templates of every book on earth. As a rule, a bookstore had only single 'copies' of books, and when someone needed a particular book, the contents of the work was recorded in a crystal.

The originals – Crystomatrices – were not to be seen; they were kept behind pale blue enamel the steel plates. So a book was printed, as it were, every time someone needed it. The question of printings, of their quantity, of their running out, had ceased to exist. Actually, a great achievement, and yet I regretted the passing of books. (Lem 1982: 257)

Regrets meet the passing away of the physical book. Reading is redundant and listening becomes the preferred mode of reception. Lem imagines a print-on-demand system. Each book appears only once it is wanted. And mostly they do not appear. They flash up one page at a time from dormant crystals, compressed into silicon.

But, more happily, the touch screen, as it has come to be used in the twenty-first century, provides an opportunity to produce something other than the reading experience facilitated by the book, making the text the site of animations, sound, engagements with scale, non-linear narratives, or all manner of interactive elements. Tactus Technology devotes research to making 'dynamic screens', where buttons 'morph out of the surface of your device' (Tactus Technology 2015). 'Microfluidics', the deployment of tiny quantities of a liquid or gas, plug or make bubbles on a screen, allowing for writing systems such as Braille to disrupt the smooth surface. Touch might be actualised in the bumpy touch screen, but it is also sufficiently abstracted as a capacity that the touch screen may disappear to become pure projection. There is a sense of this in the motion-sensor cameras that can unleash actions in gaming. A wave of the hand throws a dart or strikes a ball. Ultrahaptics is a name given to an extension of this. Ultrasound waves emanating from a computer to a location in the air produce pressure differences that human skin can detect as tactile sensations. As users move their hands around this force field, the air hosts vibrations and pressure points and feedback mechanisms.

Rutted screens and wrinkled air work in a small way against the pervasive image of the touch screen as smooth, without breaks or tears. Byung-Chul Han considers the smartphone with its touch screen to be a main figure, along with Jeff Koons's silver balloon dog and the so-called Brazilian waxing off of pubic hair, in a contemporary aesthetic of smoothness (Han 2015: 9). Han traces in what ways and why this smoothness is the contemporary ideal. Smoothness does not injure. It is emblematic in possessing no resistance. It is shiny and seductive. It demands to be touched. It is a pornographic object which presses in, for touch negates the distance that sight (and worship) demands. This closeness, this to-handness, means that it is not a mystified object. Smoothness for Han is positive and it acts to accelerate the circulation of information, communication, and capital. It augments this circulation by the gadgets' internal dynamic of updates, tweaks, viruses, and ultimately new versions or upgraded forms that insist on adoption. Digital devices bring a new compulsion, a new slavery. These compel us to communicate. Communication is annexed to capital. This speeds up capitalism's circulations. Han points out how the word *digital* is related to the word for finger, which is a counting mechanism. History or stories are, by contrast, accounts, which do not count. Tweets and information are unable to become accounts, being too fragmented and scattergun. They can only count. They are additive and not narrative. Facebook friends are counted too, above all else. This circulation, for Han, though it produces communication between bodies and organisations, engages a circuit only of one. On the smartphone, as on Koons's reflective mirror dogs and the like, one does not encounter the other, only the self. This is emblematised in the reflection of the face on the screen surface when off and, when on, in its camera function, which produces the commentary on a life, exemplified in selfie images and moments of a day uploaded to networks. It is not multitude but solitude that forms (Han 2013: 50-51).

The touch screen is ready to hand, or ready to finger. What is the touch screen as a reader? There are idiosyncratic ways of touching the screen, but are these themselves legible? Individuality is for it a forensic issue only, in those cases where fingerprints provide access. The fingerprint that one leaves on the screen is a marker of each person's uniqueness, and yet that print's uniqueness is not currently important to the function of bridging the gap in the electrical circuit. Everything is caught up in the screen's capacity. Flexibility has become less a recognition of specific modes of interacting and producing on the machine and more, in recent technical developments, a desired property of the screen itself, a bendy surface, a wearable surface that develops new proximities to the body. It seeks inputs only.

As the screen is used, it deteriorates. Its ideal form is to be wholly reflective, unblemished. In its use it is constantly smeared, despite the coatings of oleophobic materials, repelling the grease of body parts. Fingerprints leave their mark. In time, the screen gets scratched or broken. The touch screen is destroyed by its own functioning. It loses something of itself from the very first moment of use. It wears and tears, stripping from itself constantly its exchange value, as the cerium oxide dulls. But exchange value depletes anyway, as it is so tightly enmeshed in the logic of improved capability, rapid upgrades, new models, new functions and features. With each moment, it heads towards worthlessness. The screen itself as something touched comes into vision, as it does when it is broken. It passes into history, as something dying or superseded. Isaac Asimov's *Foundation* (1951) described something like a tablet, and even in imagining it before its appearance, Asimov imagined too that nothing, human or technological, exists without wear and tear:

> Seldon removed his calculator pad from the pouch at his belt. Men said he kept one beneath his pillow for use in moments of wakefulness. Its gray, glossy finish was slightly worn by use. Seldon's nimble fingers, spotted now with age, played along the files and rows of buttons that filled its surface. Red symbols glowed out from the upper tier. (Asimov 1951: 17)

Technologies emerge from science and dreams. They emerge concretely out of other technologies and even from their dead ends. The touch screen is a hybrid of typewriter and TV. Both these were imagined as other to themselves, and that other that they left behind became the touch screen. In *One Way Street*, a brochure from 1925 on urban experience, Benjamin wondered about the impact of the typewriter and its consequences for the writing hand. He imagined the typewriter otherwise to itself. He was interested in projecting forwards from this writing-machine start and speculated on the possibility of future modes of notating thought mechanically. This derives from a discontent with the typewriter, for he suspects that the mechanical writing action of the typewriter will be chosen over handwriting only once flexibility in typeface choice is obtainable:

> The typewriter will alienate the hand of the literary writer from the pen only when the precision of typographic forms has directly entered the conception of his books. One might suspect that new systems with more variable typefaces would then be needed. They will replace the pliancy of the hand with the innervation of the commanding fingers. (Benjamin 2005a: 457)

Such flexibility is a necessity because only then can all the nuances of thought and of expression be captured by and for the writer, whose writing down is dependent on his or her physical connection to the words, the paper, the pen. One single standardising typeface could not provide this, he argues. Once versatility is achieved the writer might happily compose directly on the machine, rather than with pen in hand - this would of course affect the resultant composition, and books would be composed according to the capabilities of the machine. Commanding fingers hitting keys are said to bring new types of text, composed differently into the world, with varied typefaces that orient meaning.

The touch screen has to date usurped many of the functions of the television, not least because it is the place for watching moving-image material. When McLuhan conceptualised TV in *Understanding Media*, he made the argument that 'TV will not work as background'. TV was a cool medium: 'It engages you. You have to be with it' (McLuhan 1964: 332). Curiously this had found a form in the 1950s in a hugely popular programme for children that used TV otherwise to how it settled into the home. Each TV screen as an interactive surface. *Winky Dink and You*, which aired from 1953 to 1957 on the CBS network, was presented by Jack Barry and his hapless friend Mr Bungle, who introduced clips of the character Winky Dink involved in situations in which viewers were asked to participate. They did this by covering their TV screen with a 'magic drawing screen', a piece of vinyl plastic, which they had purchased. This was rubbed before being applied to the screen, in order to generate the static electricity that would hold it in place. With Winky Dink crayons viewers could take part in a 'join the dots' game, completion of which was designed to help the story continue – a bridge might be drawn across a river that needed crossing, a ladder to reach a height, a cage to trap a lion. The screen could be used for decoding messages and to outline characters. Without the screen and its drawings parts of the programme became redundant. TV was imagined as an interactive medium, if in a limited sense. It moved towards what McLuhan proposed as native to it.

The touch screen is based on interactivity, if only in the very minimal sense that it is based on touch. There is a banalised form of interactivity as a property of touch. The discourse of marketing and business psychology promotes touch as a vector to sales. A slide presentation directed at branders and advertisers in the retail sector by PHD Media Worldwide and researchers specializing in business psychology at University College London emphasises how touch impacts emotions. It uses this knowledge to build an argument about emotional affect and consumer desire. It observes how in Apple stores the low 'kitchen-like' tables invite consumers to touch and try the products, on the assumption that to make a connection with the device encourages purchase. Furthermore, the gadgets may have been shifted off-centre or to the edge of a table by sales staff, as this appeals to the potential buyer to make that initial contact, nudging the device back to the middle of the table, nudging the self towards possession. The presentation details a series of experiments with print and touch-screen-based advertising, devising situations in which people were invited to touch advertising images with their fingers or with a mouse. Those who touched the images on the screen were found subsequently to remember many more of the products. Tactile-tablet advertisements had a much higher '[s]pontaneous awareness' than non-touch PC versions ('Touching is Believing' 2015).

Touch is an emotional vector, and it appears it can be – and will be – mobilised for purposes of affect in the realm of consumption. This is a limited version of interactivity, one that is captured easily for the logic of accumulation, though, of course, the same conclusions can be used for other ends: memory, work, play, education. What is proper to the touch-screen device? Embedded animations, clips, text that reformulates over time, art catalogues where the text changes but the image discussed remains the same in the same place, new forms of narrative that draw the hand and fingers in: these are smaller signals of a touch-screen-specific culture of writing. A broader touch-screen aesthetic has been articulated, culminating in a flurry of activity around 2012. Designers began to think their outputs in relation to the mode of interaction with the touch screen. One example is the branding for the telecommunications company Ollo. As the designers at Bibliothèque phrase it:

> The logo is the first to exploit the new multi-touch hardware of smart phones and tablets. Custom software allows for interactive manipulation of the logo to become a creative tool in building the visual language. Playing with the interactive logo allows the designer to create an infinite number of brand-orientated digital assets that can be integrated into the brand. (Bibliothèque)

The logo is a swirl of loops in bright colours spelling 'Ollo'. It can be easily made by one finger sweeping over a screen, but it can be pulled about at will, unravelled, and twisted, using all the panoply of multi-touch gestures, until it careers across the screen like a wriggling snake. The logo is touchable, and in touching it the consumer makes it act. In this way, affection is sought. This logo was another contribution to what has been defined as a New Aesthetic which takes its lead from how touch-screen swipes are represented in instruction manuals (see Streitz and Stephanidis 2013). An example is again from a communications brand, Telefonica's TU, whose logo, launched in 2012, was a slightly crude set of lines making up the letters, with overlaps of the strokes signalled by differing colours. In 2012, too, the logo for the first device to be called Microsoft Surface (later renamed Pixelsense) was a pink swirl that looked as if it emerged from a free touch-screen gesture. The concept of the 'New Aesthetic' was broached by James Bridle in 2011 at a South By South West conference on music, films, and emerging technologies. Bridle observed how unprecedented digital forms were appearing in the visual world – for example, pixels in fashion, splinter camouflage, glitsch sound and visual effects (see Bridle 2011). The concept was publicised further by Bruce Sterling, who located it as a typical avant-garde movement (Sterling 2012). Bridle drew attention to a series of paintings by Evan Roth from 2012. Titled *Multi-Touch Paintings*, these large-scale canvases derived from the performance of routine tasks on multi-touch hand-held computing devices. Fingerprint smears or dots jump around in red and back. Vastly enlarged, they make the gesture – the new gesture – the object, and they return finger painting, a primitive child's gesture, as a high-technology feat (Roth 2012). This brings the gesture into a new visibility, one that has also been documented by the artist Meggan Gould. From 2012, Gould made artworks by scanning the smeared and sticky screens of her family's iPads (Gould). Each screen's content was then removed and all that can be seen remaining are the trails of grease and dust and dirt, as touch accumulates and takes on some sort of form, an insistently material one, on the touch screen. The touch screen contributed to aesthetic vocabularies in 2012. Perhaps the gestures and surfaces by now so well integrated with our senses and minds nowadays tend towards invisibility.

Works Cited

Asimov, Isaac. 1951. *The Foundation Trilogy*. New York: Doubleday.

Benjamin, Walter. 2005a. *Selected Writings, Volume 1, 1913-1926*. Edited by Marcus Bullock and Michael W. Jennings. Cambridge: Harvard University Press.

Benjamin, Walter. 2005b. *Selected Writings, Volume 2, Part 1, 1927-1930*. Edited by Michael W. Jennings, Howard Eiland, and Gary Smith. Translated by Rodney Livingstone and Others. Cambridge: Harvard University Press.

Benjamin, Walter. 2005c. *Selected Writings, Volume 2, Part 2, 1931-1934*. Edited by Michael W. Jennings, Howard Eiland, and Gary Smith. Translated by Rodney Livingstone and Others. Cambridge: Harvard University Press.

Benjamin, Walter. 2008. *The Work of Art in the Age of Its Technological Reproducibility and Other Writings on Media*. Edited by Michael W. Jennings, Bridget Doherty, and Thomas Levin. Translated by Michael W. Jennings. Cambridge: Harvard University Press.

Bibliothèque. 'Ollo'. http://www.bibliothequedesign.com/projects/branding/ollo/.

Bridle, James. 2011. 'Waving at the Machines'. http://www.webdirections.org/resources/james-bridle-waving-at-the-machines/.

Cai, Liang, and Hao Chen. 2011. 'Touchlogger: Inferring Keystrokes on Touch Screen from Smartphone Motion'. *HotSec'11 Proceedings of the 6th USENIX conference on Hot topics in security*.

Casavecchia, Nico. 2012. *A Boy and his Atom*. California: IBM Research. http://www.research.ibm.com/articles/files/a-boy-and-his-atom.mp4.

Goethe, Johann Wolfgang von. 2005. *Selected Poetry*. Translated by David Luke. London: Penguin.

Gould, Megan. 'Megan Gould'. http://www.meggangould.net/.

Habermas, Jürgen. 1992. *The Structural Transformation of the Public Sphere: An Inquiry into a Category of Bourgeois Society*. Cambridge: Polity.

Han, Byung Chul. 2013. *Im Schwarm, Ansichten des Digitalen*. Berlin: Matthes and Seitz.

Han, Byung-Chul. 2015. *Die Errettung des Schönen*. Frankfurt am Main: S. Fischer.

Han, Jeff. 2006. 'The Radical Promise of the Multi-touch Interface'. TED Talk, February. https://www.ted.com/talks/jeff_han_demos_his_breakthrough_touchscreen?language=en.

Hirschhorn, Thomas. 2013. 'Why is it Important – Today – to Show and Look at Images of Destroyed Human Bodies?' In *Critical Laboratory: The Writings of Thomas Hirschhorn*, edited by Lisa Lee and Hal Foster, 99-104. Cambridge: MIT Press.

Jabr, Ferris. 2013. 'The Reading Brain in the Digital Age: The Science of Paper versus Screens'. *Scientific American*, April 11. http://www.scientificamerican.com/article/reading-paper-screens/.

Johnson, Eric Arthur. 1965. 'Touch Display – A Novel Input/Output Device for Computers'. *Electronics Letters* 1: 219-20.

Johnson, Eric Arthur. 1967. 'Touch Displays: A Programmed Man-Machine Interface'. *Ergonomics* 10: 271-7.

Johnson, Eric Arthur. 1969. Touch displays. US Patent 3,482,241 A, filed August 2, 1966, and issued December 2, 1969.

Lem, Stanislav. 1982. *Tales of Pirx the Pilot; Return from the Stars; The Invincible*. Penguin, Harmondsworth.

McLuhan, Marshall. 1964. *Understanding Media: The Extensions of Man*. London: McGraw-Routledge & Kegan Paul.

Müller, Lothar. 2014. *White Magic: The Age of Paper*. Cambridge: Polity.

Roth, Evan. 2012. 'Multi-Touch Paintings'. http://www.evan-roth.com/work/multi-touch-finger-paintings/.

Simon, Joshua. 2011. 'Neo-Materialism, Part Three: The Language of Commodities'. *E-Flux* 28. http://www.e-flux.com/journal/neo-materialism-part-three-the-language-of-commodities/.

Sterling, Bruce. 2012. 'An Essay on the New Aesthetic'. *Wired*. http://www.wired.com/2012/04/an-essay-on-the-new-aesthetic/.

Streitz, Norbert, and Constantine Stephanidis, eds. 2013. *Distributed, Ambient, and Pervasive Interactions: First International Conference, DAPI 2013, held as part of HCI International 2013, Las Vegas, NV, USA, July 21-26, 2013, Proceedings.* Heidelberg: Springer.

Tactus Technology. 2015. 'Tactus Technology'. http://tactustechnology.com/.

'Touching is Believing: Newsworks, UCL, and PHD Research'. 2015. http://www.newsworks.org.uk/Platforms/Touching-is-believing/75580.

Wyke, Tom. 2016. 'The Hand of God: The Touching Moment Pope Francis Blesses a Photograph of a Young Child on a Woman's Mobile Phone'. *Daily Mail*, January 17. http://www.dailymail.co.uk/news/article-3402562/Pope-Francis-takes-time-busy-schedule-bless-lady-s-photograph-young-child-phone.html.

13
Poetry in the Medium of Life: Text, Code, Organism

JULIAN MURPHET

In what follows, we follow a strange but nonetheless determinate path from Shakespeare to the 'extremophile' bacterium *Deinococcus radiodurans*. Informing this curious trajectory is a certain conception of inscription, and with it a certain inscription of conception; which is to say a *technography of the organism* as such, a writing machine hell-bent on replication, exact and iterable mimesis, the infinitely faithful copying of itself, with just enough mutation and variation to keep things interesting – and therefore indistinguishable, at an abstract level, from a literary genre. The hypothesis is that we misunderstand technography if we do not grasp the extent to which we are, all of us, at least since Watson and Crick, implicated in a logic of inscription that has seized hold of our organisms from the very moment of our conception. We are, under the hegemony of DNA, constantly in the process of being written, in the prodigious factory of mechanical and biochemical productivity that is our 'genetic code', which is anything but an inert blueprint of our natures. Rather, it is an immensely energetic and generative engine of chemical performativity, working through substitutions and leaps of mediation to promote the perpetuity of a 'selfish gene' without which life would not live. But what if this very model, the thriving 'poetics of DNA' as Judith Roof has characterized it – 'the various analogies, metaphors, and other figurations of DNA that have taken nucleic acid from its sets of complementary components to the answer to all question' (Roof 2007: 2) – is a belated echo of the extraordinary figural play of *The Sonnets* themselves? *The Sonnets*, I wish outrageously to aver, furnished a technography that prepared, over hundreds of years, for the legibility and salience of 'genetics' as a science. What is more, the great scientists and engineers have known this perfectly well and, as we shall see, have occasionally returned the favour.

Resembling Tautology

The argument of Shakespeare's *Sonnets*, at least until we reach the Dark Lady, is double, and concerns the preservation of the 'true image' or 'sweet semblance' of the beautiful youth, alarmingly subject as it is to the ravages of time. First, there is a powerful insistence, in the early 'breeding cycle,' on sexual reproduction as the surest and most expedient path: 'Die single, and thine image dies with thee' (Shakespeare 1999: 78); but 'till' an 'uneared womb' with 'thy husbandry' (78), 'Make thee another self' (81), 'get a son' (80), and lo, you will find yourself 'living in posterity' (79).

> [For] nothing 'gainst time's scythe can make defence
> Save breed to brave him when he takes thee hence. (82)

Second, however, and with increasing emphasis, the Sonnets themselves surreptitiously claim the reproductive rights here allotted to Nature. Alongside heterosexual reproduction, there arises an ostensibly contradictory means to the immortality of the glorious image – homosexual poetics. 'As [Time] takes from you I engraft you new' (84), we read, the supplement of poetry resisting decay and age; despite being rather 'barren' (84) when compared to reproduction, nevertheless 'My love shall in my verse ever live young' (86). Deixis clinches that claim:

> So long as men can breathe or eyes can see,
> So long lives this, and this gives life to thee. (85)

The pronoun shifter dramatically performs its own argument: our eyes, here and now, make true the outrageous hyperbole of the prediction.

And yet, what looks like a tension or contradiction between sex and poetics is no such thing. Rather, both strands of the argument figurally reinforce one another. On the one hand, the sonneteer can hardly resist sexual metaphors in construing his own art: 'How can my Muse want subject to invent, / While thou dost breathe, that pour'st into my verse / Thine own sweet argument […]?' (95). The feminized poet cannot prevent a fertilization taking place whose faithful issue is spontaneously recorded in his 'verse' – he is a womb in which the 'sweet [fecundating] argument' of the youth is daily, hourly, 'poured'. On the other hand, what is sexual reproduction but a kind of technography? '[Nature] carved thee for her seal, and meant thereby / Thou shouldst print more, not let that copy die' (82). The rival poets who emerge later in the sequence are given one powerful piece of advice: 'Let him but copy what in you is writ' (118); as if to say, poetry merely extends the originary writing that makes the image in the first place, and which automatically (or mystically) gets rewritten in the act of breeding.

So, writing is breeding, and breeding is writing. The apparent tension is revealed as a tautology:

> But were some child of yours alive that time,
> You should live twice: in it, and in my rhyme. (85)

'In reproduction,' John Kerrigan tells us, 'Shakespeare found a resemblance resembling tautology' (27). And such was, precisely, what he wanted his sonnets to be: perfect copies, tautological offprints, of the mortal semblance, which was itself already a fair copy ('Thou art thy mother's glass,' 78) of an image for which there was no ultimate original. His argument against flattery and the excesses of encomium found in Nature's printing press a perfect ethical exemplar for the poet's proper craft. For what print, or literature, does is to make an image immortal – both as a line of descendants in which it is preserved, and as poetry that will not cease to be read.

> Not marble, nor the gilded monuments
> Of princes, shall outlive this powerful rhyme;
> But you shall shine more bright in these contents
> Than unswept stone, besmear'd with sluttish time.
> When wasteful war shall statues overturn,
> And broils root out the work of masonry,
> Nor Mars his sword, nor war's quick fire shall burn
> The living record of your memory.
> 'Gainst death, and all oblivious enmity
> Shall you pace forth; your praise shall still find room
> Even in the eyes of all posterity
> That wear this world out to the ending doom.
>   So, till the judgment that yourself arise,
>   You live in this, and dwell in lovers' eyes. (104)

At this point in the sequence, the homage to Horace and Ovid suggests the mutual implication of at least four kinds of 'rhyme' – the rhyme of Renaissance English culture with Classical Rome, the rhyme of Nature's script with the poet's, the rhyme between father and son, and that between line-endings in a poem. Moreover, the sonnet knows well that its script is a mere 'tomb' (85) without the living eyes and breath of future lovers, of unborn young people motivated to read and make love to its accompaniment. Without sexual procreation, literary labour is a dead letter. Still further, the *Sonnets* know that literature has a vital role to play in all posterity: it has become the very incentive for sexual coupling in the first place. Literature supplies the erotics that the beautiful narcissistic youths lack, the suasion that mere biology can no longer be counted on to supply. Precisely in its excess over function and need, modern sexuality cannot exist without the supplement of this immortal letter that 'dwells in lovers' eyes'. 'Cut a letter into small pieces', writes Lacan, 'and it remains the letter that it is'. Sustained by desire, the letter is an indestructible medium of posterity. Žižek describes this as the 'immanent materiality of the ideal order itself' (Žižek 2014: 56). And the stubborn persistence of this 'weird ideal materiality' in the republic of letters is expressed nowhere better than in Humanism's supreme statement of the ethics of good copy.

The Sonnets are thus a model of what I will call the technographic double-helix of humanist modernity. They forge a coordinating chiasmic figure – of print as sexual and of sex as a kind of printing – whose underpinning logic is that of the modern nation itself: a complex machinery of mutual inscription, of bodies upon bodies, bodies upon texts, texts upon bodies, and texts upon texts. Nations (geographies of the *natio*) exist in time only because sexuality is mediated by print technology, and vice versa; their 'imagined communities' are inextricable from both the print technologies that promulgate their ideologies and the birth-rates vouchsafed by that mediation. The effect of this sustained homology between sexual and literary reproduction is to present *inscription* as the shifting ground of all human futurity. What the sonneteer is doing, and showing that he is doing throughout the sequence, is effectively what the body does during reproductive sex: namely, writing what is writ in the parents into the newborn. Just as Shakespeare is writing anew the code provided by Daniel's *Delia*, Sidney's *Astrophil and Stella*, and Watson's *Hekatompathia*, in order to vie for literary immortality, he urges his subject to yield to the biological demand to re-write his image in a son's face, and again in this sequence's generic portraiture.

This is not to argue that Shakespeare knew anything about modern genetics; it is to suggest that our understanding of genetic inscription owes much to Shakespeare's inspired double-metaphor. DNA is an idea *The Sonnets* seem to engender in the heat of their figural amphibology. In them, the sonnet form is presented as a kind of selfish gene. The 'image' it contains is perfectly generic, empty, non-specific. You cannot call its picture to mind: 'my pupil pen / Neither in inward worth nor outward fair / Can make you live yourself in eyes of men' (Shakespeare 1999: 84). What matters is that it goes on writing itself, warding off competition and holding fast to its theme with adaptive ingenuity. So it is with DNA: the medium is the message. It doesn't matter what the exact 'image' is that it writes in the foetus; what matters is that it gets written, and that it provides the wherewithal for writing itself again, indefinitely. That is its beauty: not that it satisfies any aesthetic criteria in the realm of appearance, but that it works the way these sonnets do, battening on other sequences to make their own sequence better, stronger, more resilient. Their beauty is informational rather than representational, though one consequence of Shakespeare's argument is that representation is exposed as an effect of information. Who is this youth? What is his name? What does he look like? Who can say? By the end of the *Sonnets* we have absorbed only a didactics of technography, performing itself virtuously out of the metaphorical heat generated between sexual and literary posterity. The image dissolves into the rhetoric of its propagation.

To the Ending Doom

But what future have we written in the Anthropocene? The double-helix of modernity may well be defunct, and one sure way of testing its exhaustion is by looking carefully at the strange destiny of *The Sonnets*. In mid-2012, George Church and Sri Kosuri managed to store 5.5 petabytes of data – around 700 terabytes – in a single gram of DNA. In our computers, binary data is usually encoded as magnetic regions on a hard-drive platter; but in the groundbreaking experiment of Church and Kosuri, strands of DNA that store 96 bits were synthesized, with each of the bases (TGAC) made to represent a given binary value (T and G = 1; A and C = 0). Once it was stored, the information could then be accessed by sequencing it, converting the TGAC bases back into a binary sequence intelligible to a computer.

Taking the letters 'ferential DN' as a sample sequence, we can see how the alphabetical letters are first transcoded into binary strings – f = 01100110, e = 01100101, etc. – then encoded as combinations of nucleic acid bases – 01100110 = aTGaaTTc, 01100101 = aTTcaTaT, etc. – which are next synthesized into actual DNA strands using a gene synthesizer; these strands can then be de-coded into the original binary strings by a standard gene sequencer. There is almost no error in this method of storage, and its implications are momentous, not least for matters of data storage space and capacity, and the increasingly important issue of power. The primary advantages of the technique are twofold: first, it is incredibly dense – one gram of DNA can store the equivalent of what 450 kilograms' worth of hard drives will now hold. As George Church puts it in his book *Regenesis*, which he printed 40 billions times in DNA in advance of the standard book version, 'this printing method is inexpensive and 100 million times more compact than Blu-ray disc data' (Church and Regis 2012: 280). This means that, in a hypothetical future where biological storage has become the norm, there will be no further need to do what we now routinely do to most data: namely, erase it to create more room. And second, it is incomparably stable and durable – where other still precarious bleeding-edge storage mediums need to be kept in sub-zero vacuums, DNA can survive hundreds of thousands of years in a box in a garage (Anthony 2012: n.p.).

Barely 6 months later in early 2013 scientists at the European Bioinformatics Institute (EBI – part of the European Molecular Biology Lab) announced a staggering improvement upon the Harvard experiment – achieving three times the density of storage, or 2.2 petabytes per gram of DNA. And what text did the team at the EBI think to encode on their first major trial? Nothing other than Shakespeare's *Sonnets*, of course, which have already proven to be the most durable hymn to human data storage in history. Along with an MP3 of parts of Martin Luther King, Jr.'s 'dream' speech, a PDF of the Watson/Crick paper on the structure of DNA, and a JPG image of the EBI grounds, a TXT file of the Sonnets was synthesized into thousands of pieces of DNA and then sequenced in order to read them back again – the sonnet sequence re-sequenced, after a detour through biological matter. This experiment has squared the circle kept open by *The Sonnets*; namely, between the storage capacities of text and the storage capacity of cellular matter. The EBI's synthesized DNA hosts an image that will now (thanks to the longevity of the molecular form) last at least 10,000 years, if not quite to the 'ending doom' itself. Although on this point, the chief engineer has something quite provocative to say: 'Goldman adds that DNA storage should be apocalypse-proof. After a hypothetical global disaster, future generations might eventually find the stores and be able to read them. "They'd quickly notice that this isn't DNA like anything they've seen," says Goldman. "There are no repeats, and everything is the same length. It's obviously not from a bacterium or a human. Maybe it's worth investigating"' (Yong 2013: n.p.). And there, on the far side of the end of days, it will rise again: the immortal image of Shakespeare's beautiful youth.

Thus are the *Sonnets* conscripted, once again, to a cause whose not-so-secret ambition is to outwit Time itself, bypass decay, dissolution, the ephemerality of the precarious human 'face drawn in sand at the edge of the sea' (Foucault 1973: 387), by way of storage media that resist the Apocalypse and allow the Humanist self-image to perpetuate itself for the wonder of 'future generations'. And once again, the message is the medium itself: for if Derrida was right that the paper archive was marked by the 'nuclear event' in the manner of an impending (albeit hypothetical or hyperstitional) 'irreversible destruction, leaving no traces [...] – that is, total destruction of the basis of literature' (Derrida 1984: 26), then here literature's reconfigured 'basis' in strings of deoxyribonucleic acid accomplishes an end that will have been been the subject of speculative fantasy for the whole of Humanism's life-span. Organic matter, much as the *Sonnets* had envisaged, is after all the proper vessel for the human image; only this organic matter is not our own. The remarkable technography of biology itself outstrips the faith in inorganic compounds that has characterized the typical science-fictions of Humanism's missives to posterity: from the printed sonnet form itself, through the fable recounted by Marcello Mastroianni in Theo Angelopoulos' *Suspended Step of the Stork* (1991) about a kite released from the dying earth to fly aloft, bearing upon it the inscribed repository of all the world's poems, through the gold-adonized aluminium plaques affixed to the Pioneer spacecrafts, etched with images of a naked man and woman (Figure 1), and the gold-plated copper phonograph records carried by the Voyager spacecrafts containing recordings of Beethoven and birdsong (Figure 2) down to the fable told by Jean-François Lyotard in *The Inhuman* and *Postmodern Fables*, about an artificial human intelligence downloaded into inorganic matter and slung-shot on board a spacecraft into the depths of space – we have tended to turn to non-organic media as our technographies of choice when contemplating the inscription of our image in the post-human wilderness. But Shakespeare had intuited, and

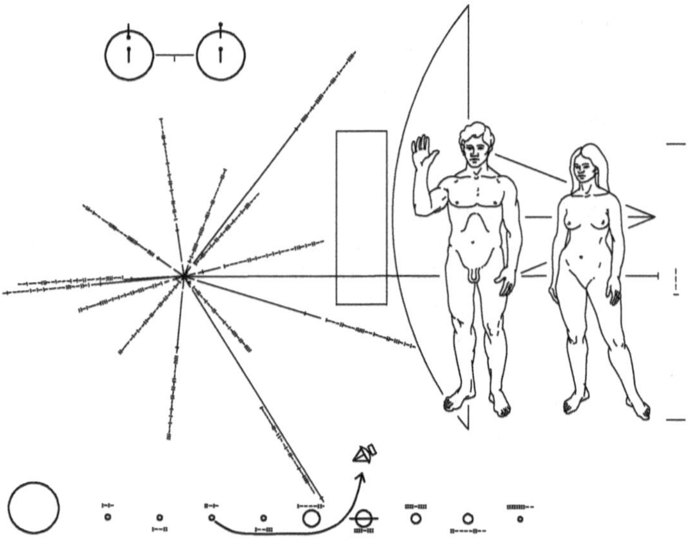

Fig. 1. Linda Salzman Sagan. 1972. *Pioneer Plaque*. NASA.
https://commons.wikimedia.org/wiki/File:Pioneer_plaque_%28transparent%29.svg

Church, Kosuri, and Goldman have confirmed, that life is the medium of choice for the beautiful and ageless image of 'Man': 'His beauty shall in these black lines be seen, / And they shall live, and he in them still green' (108).

Technographies of Life

Only, 'lives' is not quite the right word here. The DNA used in these experiments, is not located in any living organism: it is synthesized from what is called 'naked' DNA in dead cells. And this affects the manner in which we relate to such technography; as Drew Endy of Stanford University puts it, this research 'should develop into a new option for archival data storage, wherein DNA is not thought of as a biological molecule, but as a straightforward non-living data storage tape' (Richards 2013: n.p.). Withdrawn from the reproductive cycles of organic life, DNA ceases to engage the double-valence of its own status as a literally *living* language. But what happens when, in the true spirit of the *Sonnets*, we move to living cells? Bacteria are generally considered to be the optimal hosts for implanted data because they replicate quickly, generating multiple copies of the data in the process. But live DNA has a few associated problems. First, of course, the logic of reproduction is also a logic of variation: fast rates of replication invariably degrade the initial 'information' through mutation. And second, there is a real risk that the inserted DNA could interfere with the host bacteria's normal cellular processes, destabilizing the bacterial genome. Add to this the obvious fact that, without a culture, any individual bacterium has an unpredictable lifespan, and it is

Poetry in the Medium of Life: Text, Code, Organism   215

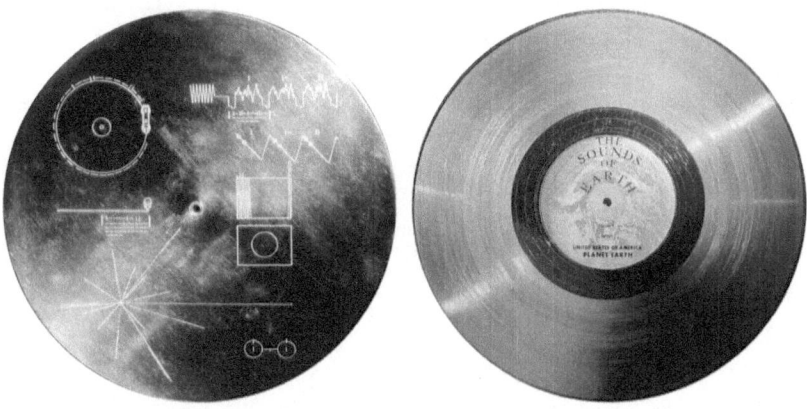

Fig. 2. *Voyager Golden Record*. 1977. NASA.
Source: https://en.wikipedia.org/wiki/Voyager_Golden_Record

clear why the push has been away from live DNA storage. But this may not long be the case. Drew Endy's celebrated course at MIT in 2003, in which *E. coli* bacteria were made periodically to 'emit a dim luminescence, flashing on and off like a stoplight', only not within the lifespan of the constituent bacteria but in oscillatory 'periods longer than the cell division cycle of the bacterium itself' (Church and Regis 2012: 188), opened the door to a staggering range of experimental possibilities for the conversion of living matter into informational processes. At the iGEM jamboree in 2004, the 'stars were the Texans [from the University of Texas at Austin], who added photoreceptor genes to *E. coli*, created a thin film of the light-sensitive bacteria, and got it to display the phrase "Hello World" in the form of deposited pigments' (191).

This organic technography, in which living matter is programmed at the genetic level to write messages fit for human eyes, is different in form and method to the loading of strings of data into an endlessly self-replicating genetic vessel, but it illustrates the potential of bacterial cells as carriers of information: smart matter other than brain cells. The true informational breakthrough was left to the Chinese University of Hong Kong iGEM contestants in 2010, whose

> goal was to convert *E. coli* bacteria into information storage devices, something on the order of microbial flash drives – or as they called them, bio-hard discs. The group titled its abstract 'Bio-cryptography: Information En/Decryption and Storage in *E. cryptor*,' *E. cryptor* being the team's name for its designer *E. coli* microbe, which members also referred to as 'a living data storage system'. They presented a scheme by which all 8,074 characters of the US Declaration of Independence could be encoded,

> encrypted, and stored in engineered *E. coli*, and then decrypted, decoded, and retrieved back as text. (195)

Claes Gustafsson had already described a novelty give-away by his company DNA2.0 over the 2005 Christmas season, of free synthetic DNA

> encoding the first verse of the poem *Tomten* by Viktor Rydberg (50 words, or 800 base pairs). The verse was rewritten using the single-letter amino-acid code where O (no amino acid) was replaced by Q (glutamic acid) and spaces omitted. The protein sequence was backtranslated to DNA using the codon bias of reindeer (*Rangifer tarandus*). The gene was synthesized and cloned behind an *Escherichia coli* promoter in a pUC-derived vector. The construct was then lyophilized on filter paper and sent out as a Christmas card (see http://tinyurl.com/cxhy9a). The nucleotide and protein sequence of *Tomten* is available in GenBank, accession number EU600200. To our knowledge, this is the first example of an organism that 'recites' poetry. (Gustafsson 2009: n.p.)

Citing Christian Bök as his inspiration, Gustafsson claimed that 'the emergence of *de novo* gene-synthesis technology now makes the tools available to build poetry directly into coding genes' (n.p.). But before we turn to Bök, the final destination of this paper, I want to look briefly to some recent efforts in what is called bio-art, to give an idea of how contemporary aesthetics are latching on to living matter as an appropriate medium for artistic expression.

Probably the best-known bio-artist is Eduardo Kac, a Brazilian performance artist who migrated into the field of what he calls 'transgenic' art. In 1999, with a work called 'Genesis,' he pioneered the creation of an 'artist's gene.'

> The Genesis DNA is a synthetic gene that was created by Kac by translating a sentence from the biblical book of Genesis into Morse Code and converting the Morse Code into DNA base pairs according to a conversion principle specially developed by the artist for this work. The gene was then incorporated into an *E. coli*. bacterium. Using the Internet (and a computer station in the gallery), visitors can switch on an ultraviolet light that triggers mutations in the bacterium. Little by little, the quote from the Bible is also mutated. ('Genesis' 1999)

Kac also genetically engineered, in 2000, the world's first fluorescent green rabbit, Alba, who is part of a larger artwork called 'GFP (green fluorescent protein) Bunny'. Another of his works is entitled 'Natural History of the Enigma,' and consists of a genetically engineered hybrid of a petunia and his own DNA. One of Kac's genes is expressed in each and every cell of the red veins, where it produces a unique protein.

Meanwhile, the Critical Art Ensemble is a collective of five American tactical media practitioners – including Steve Kurtz and Beverly Schlee. Their works have included 'Intelligent Sperm' (1998), about the new eugenics, 'Molecular Invasion' (2002-2004), which involved attempts at reverse-engineering genetically modified food products, and 'Target Deception' (2007), which replicated germ warfare experiments by the US government in the 1950s. The group became infamous when, in 2004 under augmented counter-terrorism laws, Steve Kurtz was arrested without charge by the FBI under suspicion of bioterrorism. After an emergency call to 911 to report the sudden death by natural causes of his wife, Kurtz's home was discovered to be full of materials associated with his artistic practice: petri dishes, biological specimens, and laboratory equipment. This anecdote then served as the point of departure for Richard Powers's latest novel, *Orfeo* (2014), about which it will be worthwhile to say a few words.

The narrative of *Orfeo* concerns a retired avant-garde composer who attempts, at home, in a wholly amateurish fashion, to upload music files into living cells, in this case the bacterium *Serratia marcesens* – a discovery of Pythagoras, who also did the original maths on harmonics. He never achieves his goals, as his place is raided by federal agents before any real results have been conclusively produced. But in the novel's finale we are treated to the creation of a *virtual* bio-art event, as, on the run from the authorities and embracing an imminent death, Peter Els lays claim to his terrorist rap-sheet and tweets its concept in 140-character doses to the world. 'My piece might be all around you,' reads one tweet, 'and you'll never know. Cellular songs everywhere, by the hundreds of millions' (Powers 2014: 273). Before long, carried by the short bursts of words, the unwritten, non-existent musical composition 'turns lethal. Music to panic a whole country. A thing of silence and nothingness. Required listening. [...] *An epidemic of invisible music*' (345-6). The Keatsian paradox of the sweetness of unheard melodies allows Powers to close out his novel on a gust of the sublime: 'Once you hear the music of the spheres, the stuff you earthlings make is a bore' (347). And we are tantalised by the post-human promise of a genetic message in a bottle – 'I left the piece for dead, like the rest of us. Or for an alien race to find, a billion years after we go extinct' (359). The whole thing is conceived of as a fitting culmination of 'a hundred years of uncompromising experiment' (361), of the avant-garde, of modernism; albeit played out under the postmodern banner of the virtual.

But this aesthetic affinity, felt so keenly by the central character, is scarcely something one would suspect of Powers himself, or his novel, which is written yet again in perfectly conventional novelese and without taking a single high-stakes risk at the level of form. Powers is a plodding artist, but a good 'ideas man', a prosaic bellwether for symptomatic currents and tendencies that run deeper, aesthetically, than he is capable of going. And despite beginning as something like a roman-à-clef of the Kurtz affair, it is not to Kurtz, finally, that the novel points, but to the Canadian poet and artist, Christian Bök.

A Poet in the Medium of Life

Standing at the crossroads of contemporary science and bio-artistic practice, and drawing on a century of avant-garde poetics, Bök has enthusiastically embraced

> the degree to which the biochemistry of living things has become a potential substrate for inscription. Not simply a 'code' that governs both the development of an organism and the maintenance of its function, the genome can now become a 'vector' for heretofore unimagined modes of artistic innovation and cultural expression. 'In the future,' he speculates, 'genetics might lend a possible, literary dimension to biology, granting every geneticist the power to become a poet in the medium of life. (Voyce 2007: n.p.).

His 'xenotext' experiment, however, entirely bypasses the sexually reproductive and so dialectical template of Shakespearean 'poetry in the medium of life', and sides instead with the inhuman, bacteriological pattern of organic replication – bacteria store their DNA only in the cytoplasm, and not in membrane-bound organelles the way we sexual beings do; they reproduce by way of regular mitosis. The experiment thus seeks to make good on William Burroughs's diagnosis that 'the word is now a virus': to identify words with bacteria in a literal sense, the way Els hypothetically had with music in Powers's book. Bök's goal over the ten or more years of this experiment has been to 'manufactur[e] a "xenotext" – a beautiful, anomalous poem, whose "alien words" might subsist, like a harmless parasite, inside the cell of another life-form' (Bök 2008: n.p.).

He has chosen a bacterium that shares something of its hue with *Serratia*, but sounds, in character, very much like Ridley Scott's alien: *Deinococcus radiodurans*. This organism has been classified as the 'most DNA damage-tolerant ever identified' (Battista 1997: 203), and has unsurpassed survival rates in the most inhospitable conditions, withstanding extremely low temperatures, water deprivation, partial vacuum, and 1000-times the dose of gamma radiation fatal to human beings. Whatever this impervious organism carries within its DNA is very unlikely to degrade or alter over time. Bök's idea is that, in such an extremophile carrier, the xenotext 'might persist long after terrestrial civilization has gone extinct, persisting like a secret message in a bottle flung at random into a giant ocean' (Bök 2008: n.p.). After all, his ambition is to write a book 'that is quite literally immortal,' not just in the limited, humanistic sense of Shakespeare's *Sonnets*, which still require human breath, eyes, and mouths (that is, the sexual reproduction of *Homo sapiens sapiens*) to make their images live, but in an implacable inhumanist sense – for this book will go on re-writing itself forever for no-one at all, only itself, perhaps the ultimate autotelic aesthetic artefact.

But the really ingenious thing about using this robust little bacterium as a book is that, because it is alive, its nucleotides do not just passively accept new DNA strings inserted into its genome – rather, they actively respond to genetic manipulation with spontaneous syntheses. Here, we are at the crucial point of transfer between DNA and RNA, between deoxyribonucleic acid and ribonucleic acid. DNA is structured as a paired double-strand (the double helix) and is composed out of the nitrogenous bases G (guanine), A (adenine), T (thymine), and C (cytosine); while RNA is mostly structured as a single strand folded on itself, and is written with the nitrogenous bases G (guanine), A (adenine), U (uracil), and C (cytosine). It can take two forms: messenger RNA and transfer RNA. The sequence of DNA nucleobases along the backbone of the double helix is the genetic 'script' for the organism: the full code of its biological information. But that information has to be decoded, which is where RNA comes in. Using the DNA strands as templates in a process called *transcription*, mRNA strands are created as ciphers of the DNA. The transcoding is simple: adenine in the DNA becomes uracil in the RNA; cytosine becomes guanine; guanine becomes cytosine; and thymine becomes adenine. Under the overarching genetic code, these RNA strands *translate* the DNA sequence into the exact sequence of amino acids that will be added during protein synthesis. That is, very simply, how genetic information gets 'actioned' within the organism, and in this process of transcription and synthesis, Bök has seized on an opportunity.

After modifying a string of the bacterium's DNA, he introduces it into the cell's cytoplasm where, thanks to the genetic code, the cell's mRNA will run a transcription of it into its own bases. And this is where the poetry takes place. Bök has engineered the DNA to bear an encryption of a one-line poem: 'Any style of life is prim' (Figure 3). Each of these basal clusters is then transcribed by the mRNA into its corresponding cipher clusters, and these become strings of protein during synthesis: the organism produces its own coded chain of signifiers. Calling his introduced DNA the 'Orpheus' string, and the reactive RNA strings 'Eurydice', Bök has thereby cajoled the participation of an unwilling unicellular organism in the production of a mythically superintended two-line poem, in call-and-response manner. When Orpheus speaks 'Any style of life is prim', Eurydice responds automatically 'The faery is rosy of glow'. The inner life of these modified *Deinococcus radiodurans* bacteria will become one ceaseless chorale of genetic euphony, at the level of the script of life itself – provided we (a) accept the arbitrary code that Bök has implemented in his passage between nucleotide bases and the alphabet, and (b) continue to 'employ the metaphor of DNA's nucleic acid letters making up genetic words and sentences rather than think of it as a landscape or gear,

220 Julian Murphet

Text	DNA code	mRNA transcription	Xenotext
A	AGG	UCC	T
N	CCT	GGA	H
Y	GAG	CUC	E
	GCA	CGU	
S	CTA	GAU	F
T	CTC	GAG	A
Y	GAG	CUC	E
L	CCC	GGG	R
E	ATG	UAC	Y
	GCA	CGU	
O	CGA	GCU	I
F	ATT	UAA	S
	GCA	CGU	
L	CCC	GGG	R
I	CAG	GUC	O
F	ATT	UAA	S
E	ATG	UAC	Y
	GCA	CGU	
I	CAG	GUC	O
S	CTA	GAU	F
	CGA	GCU	
P	CGC	GCG	G
R	CGT	GCA	L
I	CAG	GUC	O
M	CCG	GGC	W

Fig 3. DNA-RNA Transcriptions in Bök's 'Xenotext' experiment.

both equally (if not more) accurate models' (Roof 2007: 15). Within those determinate limits, which indicate inevitable ironies implicit in the post-Humanist initiative, the *Xenotext* maps out the same kind of undecidability as that explored in the *Sonnets*: namely, the helpless complication of genetics with inscription, of living matter with text; 'the nucleotide is already a poem, with endless permutations' (Majzles 2013: n.p.). Living matter is a technography, only in this case, we are projected entirely beyond the domain of desire and publication, text and sexuality, the double-helix of nationality and Humanism. Bök's experiment is instead the post-Humanist 'rhyme' to Shakespeare's exuberant Humanist double-helix.

And yet it is perfectly susceptible to a close reading, and thus to a re-inscription within the very Humanist architectonic that Bök has gone so far out of his way to avoid. 'Any style of life is prim' is a line in very strict trochaic tetrameter, composed of four monosyllables and a bisyllable, whose inner dynamism concerns a play on the various 'i' and 'y' vowel sounds (three short, two long) embedded within a matrix of privileged consonants: two l's, two s's (one soft, one hard), two f's (one soft, one hard). The phrase 'style of life' is a translation of a well-known psychiatric term coined by Alfred Adler – *Lebensstil* – to denote a person's unique, if unconscious, repetitive way of responding to the stimuli and functions of civilization; a kind of psychic automatism. It morphed into the verbal cliché 'lifestyle'. If it is 'prim' here, then that is because the silent, spontaneous disapproval it feels for what is not regulated, non-normative, is precisely what defines it as a 'style of life', what holds it reactively in place: fear of the outside, the deregulated, the excessive. Just as the line holds its tensions compact within a rigid metre and set of sonic constraints, and forges a strong feeling of unity out of its components, so the 'thought' or 'sense' made possible by its sounds expresses a preference for the propriety of customary form. In other words, the 'text' imported into the DNA molecule of Bök's *Deinococcus radiodunans* bacterium is a performatively conservative one, making a conspicuous virtue of the extremely economic means whereby it slides so fitly into the network of coding, recoding, transcoding, and decoding that will be its molecular fate.

The 'xenotext', meanwhile – 'The faery is rosy of glow' – which is automatically transcribed by the Eurydice of mRNA processes, is a three-stress line built metrically out of an anacrusis, two dactyls, and a final stressed syllable. Two strong bisyllables are packaged in between unstressed monosyllables, and followed by that concluding stressed monosyllable, and in this once again strongly constrained metric three shorter 'i' and 'y' vowel sounds recur, one at the end of each of the two bisyllables. The 'f' of 'faery' gathers up the two 'f's of the previous line and splices it with what is now another major consonant, the 'r', which has sounded in 'prim', and will repeat again in 'rosy'; the glissade of two close 's' sounds in 'is rosy' establishes a pattern of sonic repetition now building to a conclusion. 'Of' is repeated in both lines (one of only two repeated words) and firmly establishes the darker 'o' vowel, already sounded in 'rosy', on which the poem will close – this shift from the lighter 'i' sounds to the rounder and darker 'o' is definitive of the poem's tonal movement; 'glow' repeats the pattern of a concluding monosyllabic word beginning with a complex consonantal cluster. Thematically, 'Rosy Glow' is a trademarked Dior blush tone, a Teleflora bouquet name, and part of a well-established verbal cliché about nostalgia. But the 'faery' is of course translatable as the aesthetic, *Schein*, the spirit of artworks, as Adorno might put it; in contradistinction to the primness of a settled bourgeois style of life, it is what exceeds and defies practical necessity. In this case it is the 'harmless parasite' (shades of Serres) lodged inside a host body without any further consequence beyond some uncontrollable, rubicund facial reflux. For Adorno, the blush is what breaks through the prim, as a deathless remnant of the moral law carried within each of us, no matter how modern and cynical, how 'free' from ethical constraints: the blush is a helpless affective attunement to the Categorical Imperative that we have done our best to forget. It leaves us 'rosy of glow', flushed with the palpable evidence of something in us more than us: a code put there by God. The 'xenotext', then, answers Bök's text with a sly reminder about the aesthetic as a delightful 'purposiveness without a purpose', without having fully circumvented the residual claims of the moral law itself. Its progressive opening toward the 'o' vowel sounds loosens the strictures of the short 'i' sounds of primness, but tacitly resounds with corporate trademarks and clichés, as if to undermine its own naïve belief in 'faery'.

But what is still more, the whole sequence, call and response, text and xenotext, DNA and RNA, settles into what is English poetry's most stubbornly and traditionally popular poetic metre, the ballad or hymn metre of the fourteener: 7 stresses broken 4:3 over two lines, gathering mass in the second with the extra unstressed syllables vouchsafed by two back-to-back dactyls. So it is that Bök's exemplary avant-gardist and post-Humanist poetic gesture – leaping the traces of paper, of linearity, and even of letters in their manifest form – rejoins the very wellsprings of poetic utterance in English, the humus out of which Shakespeare was to have cultivated his genius, as if to say the forced passage of verse through the genetic code of bacterial microbes must be made at the formal cost of a conventionality seen nowhere else in Bök's oeuvre: poems made of LEGO bricks, using exclusively single vowels, or modelled on the molecular structures of crystals. Whether or not such adherence to convention is to be read ironically, the poem at the very least performs the inner ideological torsions of the post-human as a species of discourse, no more capable of sublating the human being as a locus of meaning-making than Shakespeare's *Sonnets* are of seeing the 'ending doom' through anything other than 'lovers' eyes'. Text, code, organism: it is only the archaic figures and forms, the originary metaphors out of which the human was built to begin with, that make such automatisms legible and valuable in the first place. The truest extremophile is our own dauntless belief that we can engineer a technography that exceeds our limits.

Works Cited

Anthony, Sebastian. 2012. 'Harvard Cracks DNA Storage, Crams 700 Terabytes of Data Onto a Single Gram'. *ExtremeTech*. August 17. http://www.extremetech.com/extreme/134672-harvard-cracks-dna-storage-crams-700-terabytes-of-data-into-a-single-gram.

Battista, J.R. 1997. 'Against All Odds: The Survival Strategies of *Deinococcus radiodurans*'. *Annual Review of Microbiology* 51: 203-224.

Bök, Christian. 2008. 'The Xenotext Experiment'. *SCRIPTed* 5. http://www.law.ed.ac.uk/ahrc/script-ed/vol5-2/editorial.asp.

Church, George, and Ed Regis. 2012. *Regenesis: How Synthetic Biology Will Reinvent Nature and Ourselves*. New York: Basic Books.

Derrida, Jacques. 1984. 'No Apocalypse, Not Now (Full Speed Ahead, Seven Missiles, Seven Missives)'. Translated by Catherine Porter and Philip Lewis. *Diacritics* 14: 20-31.

Foucault, Michel. 1973. *The Order of Things: An Archaeology of the Human Sciences*. New York: Vintage.

'Genesis'. 1999. http://www.ekac.org/geninfo2.html.

Gustafsson, Claes. 2009. 'For Anyone Who Ever Said There's No Such Thing as a Poetic Gene'. *Nature*, April 8. http://www.nature.com/nature/journal/v458/n7239/full/458703a.html.

Majzels, Robert. 2013. 'The Xenotext Experiment and the Gift of Death'. *Jacket 2*. Special issue, *North of Invention*, edited by Sarah Dowling. March 29. http://jacket2.org/article/xenotext-experiment-and-gift-death.

Powers, Richard. 2014. *Orfeo*. London: Atlantic Books.

Richards, Sabrina. 2013. 'DNA-based Data Storage Here to Stay'. *Scientist*, January 13. http://www.the-scientist.com/?articles.view/articleNo/34109/title/DNA-based-Data-Storage-Here-to-Stay/.

Roof, Judith. 2007. *The Poetics of DNA*. Minneapolis: University of Minnesota Press.

Shakespeare, William. 1999. *The Sonnets and A Lover's Complaint*. Edited by John Kerrigan. London: Penguin.

Voyce, Stephen. 2007. 'The Xenotext Experiment: An Interview with Christian Bök'. *Postmodern Culture* 17. http://literature.proquest.com.wwwproxy0.library.unsw.edu.au/searchFulltext.do?id=R04985497&divLevel=0&queryId=2834804935549&trailId=14969467CBF&area=criticism&forward=critref_ft.

Yong, Ed. 2013. 'Synthetic Double-Helix Faithfully Stores Shakespeare's Sonnets'. *Nature News*. January 23. http://www.nature.com/news/synthetic-double-helix-faithfully-stores-shakespeare-s-sonnets-1.12279.

Žižek, Slavoj. 2014. *Absolute Recoil: Towards a New Foundation of Dialectical Materialism*. London: Verso.

www.ingramcontent.com/pod-product-compliance
Lightning Source LLC
Chambersburg PA
CBHW030107170426
43198CB00009B/533